DANIGO!

FRENCH GRAMMAR REORGANISED

a textbook and workbook

Ian H. Magedera

DANIGO!

FRENCH GRAMMAR REORGANISED

a textbook and workbook

Les Presses de l'Université Laval

Les Presses de l'Université Laval reçoivent chaque année du Conseil des Arts du Canada et de la Société d'aide au développement des entreprises culturelles du Québec une aide financière pour l'ensemble de leur programme de publication.

Nous reconnaissons l'aide financière du gouvernement du Canada par l'entremise de son Programme d'aide au développement de l'industrie de l'édition (PADIÉ) pour nos activités d'édition.

Mise en pages : Diane Trottier

Maquette de couverture : Diane Trottier

ISBN 2-7637-8101-2

Distribution de livres Univers
845, rue Marie-Victorin
Saint-Nicolas (Québec)
Canada G7A 3S8
Tél. (418) 831-7474 ou 1 800 859-7474
Téléc. (418) 831-4021
http://www.ulaval.ca/pul

ACKNOWLEDGEMENTS

Most recent French language textbooks have been written by teams of authors, but having battled on my own over the last six years to turn the ideas for this book into reality, I now may enjoy the singular privilege of expressing my personal thanks to those who witnessed it at various stages of its development. I profited from their reactions, and made this a better book because of them. Thank you Marie-Anne Hintze, Erika Hannevold, Pat Häusler, Carol Chapman, Kate Marsh, Claire Bruyère, Matthew Mirow and Penny Williams! A person called Hanna Hofhansl automated the contents in 2001, but this did not accelerate the progress of the book; she has been called Hanna Magedera for over a year now and it is only just finished. This may prove that French grammar offers no impediment to courtship and marriage; but let no one say that they were a distraction. And, now, finally, I can pay a tribute to the generosity of my friend Guy Danigo, by using his dynamic Breton name in the title.

Liverpool and Vienna, September 2003

STUDENTS' INTRODUCTION

You can use this book as either a quiz-based grammar textbook and workbook or a grammar terminology buster. The bulleted paragraphs below (•) will give you specific guidelines on how to use *Danigo!* in these ways.

This book aims to teach you how to remember the core of French grammar; you can use it either in class or by yourself at home. It has a different structure from grammar books of the past because its anchor is everyday English, rather than the systems and terminology handed down to your tutors by the grammarians of Ancient Greece and Rome. To use *Danigo!* profitably, you will have already learned the basics of French grammar (by whatever method), but now want to review and practise your knowledge, building on it to internalise the core of French grammar. In this book you learn by doing and don't get patronised.

Danigo! is organised in a new way: its **Tables of Contents** group the main points of French grammar according to the thirteen ways in which they differ from English. Here is a summary; you can see that French is more complicated than English in Chapters 1 to 6 because there are more ways of saying something in French than in English. However, in Chapters 11 to 13 the reverse applies and English is more complicated than French. Chapter 7 is right in the middle contains those grammar points which are the exact opposites of each other in French and English. Chapters 9 and 10 contain nuances, where English and French use a form of words more frequently than the other language. It is only Chapter 8 which contains those grammar points in French which have no parallel in English. Most other grammar books assume that the whole of French is like Chapter 8.

Chapter 1	Chapter 2	Chapter 3	Chapter 4	Chapter 5	Chapter 6	Chapter 7
There are **two** ways of saying something in French, where there is only **one** in English	There are **three** ways of saying something in French, where there is only **one** in English	There are **four** ways of saying something in French, where there is only **one** in English	There are **five** ways of saying something in French, where there is only **one** in English	There are **seven** ways of saying something in French, where there is only **one** in English	There are **eight** ways of saying something in French, where there is only **one** in English	French is the **exact opposite** of English

Chapter 8	Chapter 9	Chapter 10	Chapter 11	Chapter 12	Chapter 13
French has **unique structures** which are not found in English	**French** uses this form **frequently**, where English hardly uses it at all	**English** uses this form **frequently**, where French uses it hardly at all	There are **two** ways of saying something in English, where there is only **one** in French	There are **three** ways of saying some thing in English, where there is only **one** in French	There are **five** ways of saying something in English, where there is only **one** in French

PART ONE – THE GRAMMAR QUIZ TEXTBOOK

After reorganising French grammar into these thirteen types of difference between French and English, each chapter then presents individual grammar points in sections (1.1, 1.2 and 1.3. and so on), which are ordered to help you remember the contents and to provide variety. Each grammar point is presented as a question (quiz-style), followed by examples which illustrate it. The examples consist of an English sentence followed by its French translation. In this way you can always understand the examples and it will usually be possible for you to work out the answer for yourself. In any case, you can make sure that your understanding was right because the answer is given in a full and clear form at the end of the quiz on each grammar point.

Danigo! aims to teach you the French used in normal conversation by educated adult speakers. Examples which are more suited to written French are followed by the style label 'FORMAL' and those used by younger or less linguistically sophisticated speakers are labelled: 'INFORMAL'.

PART TWO – THE GRAMMAR WORKBOOK

To internalise it and to be able to use it in the future, it's not enough just to read a grammar point; you need to put that point into practice. And that is exactly what the second part of the book aims to help you to do. First there are **Questions** consisting of gap-filling and translation exercises. Then come the **Explanations** which give you a hint for each question (if you need it). This means that you don't have to look at the answers straightaway and can go back and try to answer the question again. Finally, there are the **Answers** for checking your work.

- If you want to use *Danigo!* as **a quiz-based grammar textbook and workbook**, then you can either work through it from cover to cover, or use it selectively. In either case the extra practice will help you to perform better in your end-of-unit or end-of-year French tests.

  - If you work through the book from cover to cover, you will find that you will remember more of the grammar points if you do a little *Danigo!* on a regular basis: that is to say, up to four grammar points per week. It's fine to work with the book alongside more traditional grammar course books because it is beneficial to approach the same material from different directions. When you come to the end of the first six chapters, which deal with types of difference where 'French has more ways of saying something than English', you can then perhaps look at the last three chapters, which present grammar points where 'English has more ways of saying something than in French'.

  - If using the book selectively, the **Index and Grammar Terminology Buster** at the back of *Danigo!* and the **Tables of Contents** at the front, will help you to isolate the areas of grammar which are most difficult for you. By using the book in this selective way, you are making solid anchor points on the rock face of French grammar from which you can then move sideways, exploring related sections within the chapter. To use the book more efficiently, look at some of your corrected work to see where you make the most mistakes; the vast majority of errors tend to be core grammar points. Eliminating these basic errors is the first step towards better grades. After that, you will be helped to build on this core knowledge by teaching you more complicated points and exceptions.

- If you want to use this book as **a terminology buster** to understand grammatical terms mentioned by your tutors either in class or in corrections of your written work, you will find them all listed at the back of *Danigo!* in both English and French. The entries in the terminology buster will help you to locate both the quiz-style presentation of the point in the textbook (**Part One**) and the gap-filling and translation exercises on it in the workbook (**Part Two**). First try to understand the grammar point in terms of the type of difference between English and French. In this way you can make sense of the point using a more logical and simpler understanding of grammar.

TUTORS' INTRODUCTION

THIS BOOK CAN BE USED AS:

- the <u>basis of a language course</u> for intermediate and advanced students of French.

- a tutors' <u>source book</u> of gap-filling and translation exercises to supplement grammar textbooks from beginners to advanced level.

- a comprehensive <u>self-study workbook</u> on grammar for intermediate and advanced students of French.

Please refer to the bulleted paragraphs below for specific instructions on how to use *Danigo!* in these ways.

REORGANISATION AS AN AID TO REMEMBERING FRENCH GRAMMAR

As specialists in French language, we can justly take professional pride in the way that we have been able to internalise a good part of the system of French grammar. However, as pedagogues, many of us have come to question whether the terminology and structure of that system as it is currently constituted, are contributing positively to our students' learning. It is often the case that this metalanguage of grammar resembles a second foreign language and forms a barrier that our students have to tackle at precisely the same time that they are coming to grips with the complexities of a language such as French. This is illustrated by the fact that many of today's grammar workbooks contain glossaries of grammatical terms. The second language barrier can lead to the demotivation of students; something which must be avoided at all costs in the context of the recent decline in numbers of English-speaking students learning French at college and university level.

FRENCH GRAMMAR IN THIRTEEN CATEGORIES

This book has reorganised grammar according to the differences between English and French and it only includes indispensable grammatical terms. As far as a theory of language acquisition is concerned, *Danigo!* simply takes literally Saussure's comment regarding language as a system of differences and applies it to two languages ('[a] linguistic system is a series of differences of sounds combined with a series of differences of ideas', translated from: *Cours de linguistique générale*, Paris, Editions Payot, 1972, p. 166). This produces the following thirteen types of difference and the lower box indicates the number of grammar points in each chapter (full details of individual points are given in the **Tables of Contents** below).

Chapter 1	Chapter 2	Chapter 3	Chapter 4	Chapter 5	Chapter 6	Chapter 7
There are **two** ways of saying something in French, where there is only **one** in English	There are **three** ways of saying something in French, where there is only **one** in English	There are **four** ways of saying something in French, where there is only **one** in English	There are **five** ways of saying something in French, where there is only **one** in English	There are **seven** ways of saying something in French, where there is only **one** in English	There are **eight** ways of saying something in French, where there is only **one** in English	French is the **exact opposite** of English
thirty five grammar points	eighteen grammar points	nine grammar points	one grammar point	one grammar point	one grammar point	fifteen grammar points

Chapter 8	Chapter 9	Chapter 10	Chapter 11	Chapter 12	Chapter 13
French has **unique structures** which are not found in English	**French** uses this form **frequently**, where English hardly uses it at all	**English** uses this form **frequently**, where French uses it hardly at all:	There are **two** ways of saying something in English, where there is only **one** in French	There are **three** ways of saying some thing in English, where there is only **one** in French	There are **five** ways of saying something in English, where there is only **one** in French
twelve grammar points	five grammar points	two grammar points	eighteen grammar points	three grammar points	two grammar points

This method has a stronger pedagogical rationale than traditional grammars and grammar workbooks because a point is taught by means of a comparison with what is familiar to students – English language usage. This is the first grammar textbook and workbook to make practical use of the ease with which the differences between French and English can be systematised. This means that this book is free of a large part of the usual complicated terminology of grammars, while covering the same ground as conventional grammar textbooks at intermediate level. *Danigo!* has rationalised and simplified the framework in which French grammar is delivered.

The book includes those points which, following the collation of data from error surveys of British university students, were shown to present particular difficulty to Anglophone learners of French. In 1997-8 and 1999-2000 second-year students at the Universities of Leeds and Liverpool were asked survey corrected examples of their own work from a two-year period and compile a personal checklist of the ten most frequent types of grammatical errors in French. Students then used the results to develop a systematic method of checking written assignments (see Rod Hares and Geneviève Elliot, *Compo*, London, Hodder and Stoughton, 1982, p. 14).

PART ONE – THE GRAMMAR QUIZ TEXTBOOK

Once they have been ordered within the framework of differences between English and French, individual grammar points are introduced as questions. They are followed by short example-sentences in French, each of which is preceded by an English translation (this is so that any individual gaps in a student's vocabulary will not hinder the understanding of the example). These sentences allow students to attempt to distinguish the grammar point for themselves, if they are able to. They are memorable because they are concise and are taken from the domains of relationships (personal and family), sport and current affairs. Sentences are given the style markers 'INFORMAL' and 'FORMAL' when they depart from the register that educated adult native speakers might use in non-specialised conversation. After the example-sentences, there follows a comprehensive but jargon-free answer to the original question, which constitutes the grammar rule.

PART TWO – THE GRAMMAR WORKBOOK

The **Grammar Workbook** is efficient and easy to use because it does not separate the exercises from the answers, something which necessitates a great deal of distracting flicking back and forth in other grammar books. *Danigo!* has a unique intermediate **Explanations** stage (between the **Questions** and the **Answers**), which consolidates the understanding of the student who is still unsure, before the answers are presented. The answers are in exactly the same format as the questions and explanations and all are presented on a single page, so they can be located immediately without searching from one part of the book to another. All this means that the student's concentration is not dissipated at a critical stage in the learning process.

The book has also been designed to be used by students who have learned traditional grammatical terminology (either in English or in French); they can navigate around the book by means of the **Index and Grammar Terminology Buster**. This is also useful for students who may be unsure of the point of grammar referred to in class or in the corrections of their assignments. They will be directed from the index to examples and exercises on the point of grammar in question.

GUIDELINES FOR USING THIS BOOK AS:

- the <u>basis of a language course </u>(cover to cover use)

This book is intended to be the grammatical textbook and workbook at the centre of an ever-changing palette of authentic written material which teaches and reviews French grammar, concentrating on writing and reading skills.

The internet is still underused in language instruction. However, it does provide an enormous and ever-increasing bank of good quality texts (and some audio and video clips) written by native speakers of French which can be exploited for language teaching, without the need to wait for the day when every student has reliable and simultaneous access to the internet during class time. Tutors can acquire suitable texts by means of a keyword search on the Internet. Search Engines such as Google (www.google.com) or AltaVista (www.altavista.com) allow more advanced searches, where it is possible to specify language and also use Boolean expressions as in the following example: 'chaque AND chacun' which will yield the web addresses of documents with both determiners. It is possible to add a thematic dimension to your search by the addition of 'AND jazz'. Once the web addresses have been generated and the page has been called up, either the 'find in page' or the 'Find (on This Page)' commands of the browser can be used to locate specific points.

The prime criterion for the inductive use of texts in a language course based on *Danigo!*, is not their overall grammatical content, but their interest to the students <u>and</u> to you. These texts should be selected on the basis of their individual style. The range of texts available online means that it is possible to locate this type of material for learners from a basic intermediate to a final advanced level (by the use of individual homepages – some of them written by francophone adolescents – and *contes* for example). It is precisely this sort of material which makes current language text-books, so voluminous, expensive and so quickly outdated. Which tutor can continue to communicate enthusiasm about the French language with non-literary texts used year after year? Downloading and copying texts from the Internet (with the appropriate acknowledgement of sources; see: Janice Walker and Todd Taylor, *The Columbia Guide to Online Style*, New York, Columbia University Press, 1998 and http://www.columbia.edu/cu/cup/cgos/) is a means of ensuring the primacy of enjoyment for both students and the tutor. If students have first enjoyed a text they can better be encouraged to read it again for grammar using this book.

This can be done in two different ways. After asking students to look through one of the types of difference between French and English at home, in class the tutor can work through the text with students, asking them to isolate the specific examples of that type. One could begin with the types of difference in Chapters 1 and 11 for example because they only involve one language being twice as complicated as the other. After this, students could do the practice sentences on the grammar point in the **Grammar Workbook**. Finally, as an assignment, students could be asked to find and comment on their own examples. Alternatively, the tutor can draw students' attention to the grammatical points (and the categories of differences to which they belong) as they arise in the reading of the text. Following this and a review of vocabulary and/or oral comprehension questions, the tutor can ask students to look up and study the entries in the **Grammar Quiz Textbook (Part One)** and the **Grammar Workbook (Part Two)** which relate to a selection of the points from the text that they read in class.

- a source book of practice exercises (selective use)

Tutors frequently need a source of practice sentences to prepare students for the tests at the end of the academic year or for the contextualised texts corresponding to the theme of a particular lesson. *Danigo!* provides an exercise of between five and twenty-five questions on each point of grammar, according to how difficult it is. The **Index and Grammar Terminology Buster** allows tutors to easily locate exercises on the point of grammar that they want to assess.

- a comprehensive <u>self-study workbook</u> (selective use)

Learning grammar and in part remedying a student's frequent errors requires a high degree of individualisation. *Danigo!* meets this need by enabling individual students to practise in their own time those aspects of grammar that they find the most difficult. This can take place as part of a directed process of self-analysis, with students looking through past examples of their corrected work with the aim of drawing up a list of the mistakes that they tend to make as individuals. This list can then be used in conjunction with the both the **Tables of Contents** and the **Index and Terminology Buster**, depending on whether formal terminology is used or not, to provide targeted remedial practice on the student's areas of difficulty. The two parts of *Danigo!* provide two different ways of approaching the same material. The **Grammar Quiz Textbook (Part One)** tells and shows. Whereas the **Grammar Workbook (Part Two)** encourages the practice and consolidation of the individual points.

EASY-TO-READ CONTENTS IN TABLES

1. **There are two ways of saying something in French, where there is only one in English.**

	FRENCH	ENGLISH
1.14	How do I translate and use *quelque chose*?	meaning 'something'
1.15	*avec laquelle* and *avec qui* to translate 'who...with' you always have a choice except with *parmi lequel* and *entre lequel*	'who...with', 'amongst which' and 'between which'
1.16	Do I use *en* or *dans* with a duration of time?	'in'
1.17	*jour* or *journée* and *soir* or *soirée*, *an* or *année* and *matin* or *matinée*?	'day', 'evening', 'year', 'morning'
1.18	*il a été* or *il fut* or *il était*?	past tense
1.19	*voici* or *voilà*?	'here'
1.20	*celui-ci* or *celui-là*?	'this one' 'that one'
1.21	*celle-ci* or *celle-là*?	'this one' 'that one'
1.22	*il* or *ce*?	'it' in phrases like 'it is difficult to...'
1.23	*dans le* or *en*?	'in' with départements and counties
1.24	*dans le* or *en*?	'to' with, départements and counties
1.25	*dans le* or *en*?	'in' with US states, Canadian provinces
1.26	*dans le* or *en*?	'to' with US states and Canadian provinces
1.27	*aux* or *dans les*?	'in' with countries and regions which have plural names like the 'The Netherlands'
1.28	*aux* or *dans les*?	'to' with countries and regions which have plural names like 'The Netherlands'
1.29	*en plus* or *de plus*?	the specific translation depends on context, is related to 'more'
1.30	*se rappeler* or *se souvenir de*?	'to remember'
1.31	*rendre visite à* or *visiter*?	'to visit'
1.32	*offrir* or *donner*?	'to give'
1.33	*dépenser* or *passer*?	'to spend'
1.34	*la langue* or *le langage*?	'language'
1.35	*tu* or *vous*?	'you'

2. There are three ways of saying something in French, where there is only one in English.

		FRENCH	ENGLISH
2.1		*avant, avant de* or *avant que?*	'before'
2.2		*que, jusque* or *jusqu'à ce que?*	'until'
2.3		*il y a, voilà* or *voici?*	'ago'
2.4		*être de long, faire deux mètres de long* or *avoir une longueur?*	measurements
2.5		With a doing word do I say *tout, toute,* or *toutes?*	'completely'
2.6		*ce, cette* or *cet?*	'this'
2.7		*demander, demander à* or *demander de?*	'ask'
2.8		*depuis, pendant* or *pour?*	'for'
2.9		How do I say when referring to towns and cities?	'to'
2.10		After doing words, do I have *à* or *de* or nothing at all?	English does not usually have anything in these cases
2.11		*penser* on its own, then *penser à* or *penser de?*	'to think'
2.12		*manquer* on its own, then *manquer à* or *manquer de?*	'to miss' (and 'to lack')
2.13		*décider* on its own, *se décider à* or *décider de?*	'to decide'
2.14		*jouer* on its own, *jouer à* or *jouer de?*	'to play'
2.15		*pire, plus mauvais* or *plus mal?*	'worse'
2.16		*le pire, le plus mauvais* or *le plus mal?*	'the worst'
2.17		*il allait chaque matin à la piscine, voulez-vous m'aider* or *j'aimerais vous aider*	'would'
2.18		*nombre, numéro* or *chiffre?*	'number'

3. There are four ways of saying something in French, where there is only one in English

		FRENCH	ENGLISH
3.1		*une fois, une époque, l'heure* or *le temps?*	'time'
3.2		*faire, rendre, fabriquer, confectionner?*	'to make'
3.3		*vieux, vieil, vieille* or *vieilles?*	'old'
3.4		*tout, toute, toutes,* or *tous?*	'all'
3.5		*de, d', du* or *des* when speaking about towns and cities?	'from'
3.6		*à, au, aux* or *dans* when speaking about towns and cities?	'in'
3.7		*Il s'est lavé,* the base form of *se laver* in the 'have' tense (the perfect), frequently changes, adding 'o', 's' or 'es', but when?	he washed
3.8		*de la, du, de l'* or *des?*	'some'
3.9		Usually words like *joué, fini* and *rendu* (and other simple past participles) don't change, but sometimes they take 'e' 's' or 'es'? When?	'played', 'finished', 'gave'

4. There are five ways of saying something in French, where there is only one in English

	FRENCH	ENGLISH
4.1	*mou, mol, molle, mous* or *molles? nouveau, nouvel, nouvelle, nouveaux* or *nouvelles? fou, fol, folle, fous* or *folles? beau, bel, belle, beaux* or *belles?*	'soft', 'new', 'mad', 'beautiful'

5. There are seven ways of saying something in French, where there is only one in English

	FRENCH	ENGLISH
5.1	*ce qui, ce que, que, dont, quel, quoi* or *comment?*	'what'

6. There are eight ways of saying something in French, where there is only one in English

	FRENCH	ENGLISH
6.1	*la moitié, à moitié, mi, un demi-, un demi, une demie, et demi* or *et demie?*	'half'

7. French is the exact opposite of English

	FRENCH	ENGLISH
7.1	*janvier*	January
7.2	*mardi*	Tuesday
7.3	*le grec*	Greek
7.4	*parisien*	Parisian
7.5	*la physique*	physics
7.6	*connaissances*	knowledge
7.7	*les Dupont*	the Duponts
7.8	*le capitaine Cook*	captain Cook
7.9	*le Canada*	Canada
7.10	Must I repeat *à, de* and *en* in lists?	no repetition in English
7.11	Do I use *le, la* and *l'*, when writing general, non-specific statements?	English just uses the naming word
7.12	*Elle est gendarme*	She is a gendarme
7.13	*Elle est bouddhiste*	She is a Buddhist
7.14	*Louis XIV*	Louis the Fourteenth
7.15	*les années soixante*	'the sixties'

8.   French has unique forms which are not found in English

	FRENCH	ENGLISH
8.1	le mardi	'on Tuesdays'
8.2	How is it possible to say whether some words take *la* or *le*?	'the' is the only word which performs this function in English
8.3	Which naming words take -aux in the plural?	's' is the usual plural in English
8.4	What are the two ways to say and write words beginning with a letter 'h' in French?	no similar form in English
8.5	When is there an *é* at the start of a word and when not?	no accents in English
8.6	What is the unique pattern of describing words with *gens*?	no genders with 'people' in English
8.7	On occasions the *vous* and *tu* form are mixed, in a form which is neutral.	no similar form in English
8.8	Which French doing words have 'ç', an extra 'e', an 'è', a double letter, or a change from 'y' to 'i' and when?	no similar form in English
8.9	Which tenses which follow *venir de*?	no similar form in English
8.10	Which tenses which follow *depuis* and *depuis que*?	no similar form in English
8.11	Which tenses accompany both parts of sentences with *si* meaning 'if'?	no similar form in English
8.12	When is *aurait dit* not translated by 'would have said'?	no similar form in English

9.   French uses this form frequently, where English hardly uses it at all.

	FRENCH	ENGLISH
9.1	What is the subjunctive in French and how do I use it?	'may', 'long live the King!'
9.1.1	After which type of expressions of feeling and emotion do I have to use the subjunctive?	no similar form in English
9.1.2	After which type of expressions of argumentation do I have to use the subjunctive?	no similar form in English
9.1.3	Which other expressions of emotion and argument also take the subjunctive?	no similar form in English
9.2	What is the 'historic present' and when do I use it?	limited use of this tense to make a story come alive
9.3	What are the frequent differences in word order between French and English?	English has more regular word order than French
9.4	How are simple naming words in French used to translate rarer English doing words?	English has a rich range of expressions with doing words. For example: 'to rise to one's feet'

10. English uses this form frequently, where French uses it hardly at all

	FRENCH	ENGLISH
10.1	French tends to avoid the passive	English uses the passive frequently
10.2	French tends to avoid doing words ending in '-ant'	English often uses doing words ending in '-ing'?
10.3	Do the colours in French change to follow *le*, *la* and *les*, when I add *clair* and *sombre*, the words for 'light' and 'dark'?	There is no change in English

11. There are two words, or ways of saying something in English, where there is only one in French

	FRENCH	ENGLISH
11.1	*y*	'it' or 'them' with doing words with *à*
11.2	*en*	'it' or 'them' with doing words with *de*
11.3	*même*	'same' or 'even'?
11.4	*son*	'his' or 'her'?
11.5	*sa*	'his' or 'her'?
11.6	*aussi*	'also' or 'therefore'?
11.7	How does a change in position affect the words *ancien*, *anciens*, *ancienne* and *anciennes*?	'ancient' or 'former'?
11.8	*faire*	'make/do' or 'have something done'?
11.9	*ce que je dis*	'What I say' or 'What I am saying'
11.10	*merci*	'thank you' or 'no thank you'?
11.11	*cher*	'expensive' for someone or 'dear' to a person?
11.12	*pauvre*	'poor, pitiable' or 'poor, with no money'?
11.13	*propre*	'clean' or 'own'?
11.14	*regarder*	'look at'
11.15	*payer*	'pay for'
11.16	*attendre*	'wait for'
11.17	*écouter*	'listen to'
11.18	*demander*	'ask for'

12 There are three ways of saying something in English, where there is only one in French

	FRENCH	ENGLISH
12.1	How do I translate *il y a*?	'ago', 'there is', or 'there are'
12.2	How do I translate *lui*?	'him' in three different circumstances
12.3	When do I use *leur* (and *leurs*)?	'their' in three different circumstances

13 There are five ways of saying something in English, where there is only one in French

	FRENCH	ENGLISH
13.1	*on*	'you', 'one', 'we', 'it' or 'they'?
13.2	*zéro*	'zero', 'nought', 'nil', 'o', or 'love'?

FULL CONTENTS

PART ONE – THE GRAMMAR QUIZ TEXTBOOK

12. There are three ways of saying something in English, where there is only one in French 185

13. There are five ways of saying something in English, where there is only one in French 189

PART TWO – THE GRAMMAR WORKBOOK

1. There are two ways of saying something in French, where there is only one in English 195

2   There are three ways of saying something in French,
     where there is only one in English 215

PART ONE

THE GRAMMAR QUIZ TEXTBOOK

1

There are two ways of saying something in French, where there is only one in English

1.1 When do I say *si* and when *oui*, meaning 'yes'?

In French there are two ways of saying 'yes'; but when do we use *si*, the second form of 'yes'? Look at these fragments of conversation and try to see how the first two set up a different meaning of 'yes' from the last two. You will find the answer below!

GROUP A.

Samuel:	Are we going to see each other again?
Janine:	Yes, certainly, but when?
Samuel:	*Est-ce que nous allons nous revoir?*
Janine:	*Oui, je veux bien, mais quand?*
Max:	Is your brother a star?
Natalie:	Yes of course he is!
Max:	*Votre frère, c'est une vedette?*
Nathalie:	*Oui bien sûr!*

GROUP B.

Jacques:	Come on! You're not going to go out with her, are you?
Antoine:	Yes, and that's none of your business!
Jacques:	*Allez! Tu ne vas quand même pas sortir avec elle!*

Antoine:	*Si, et cela ne te regarde pas!*
Mme Ali:	I don't think that the boss would have said that…
Mme Ducrop:	Yes, since I say so!
Mme. Ali:	*Je ne crois pas que le patron ait dit cela.*
Mme Ducrop:	*Si, puisque je te le dis!*

ANSWER

In Group b the second form of 'yes' *si* is used when you are disagreeing with another person. What they say will be in the negative; but you can then counter what they have said with a clear and firm *si*. Always imagine *si* being said in a clear and firm way.

1.2   How do I say 'to know': *savoir* or *connaître*?

Take a look at these examples and try to work out how the type of knowledge in the first group of examples is different from the second. You will find the answer below.

GROUP A

I know where he has hidden his money!
Je sais où il a caché son argent!

Of course I know that Azzédine is Franco-Algerian.
Bien entendu je sais qu' Azzédine est franco-algérien.

I know who she would like to go out with. (INFORMAL)
Je sais avec qui elle aimerait sortir. (INFORMAL)

You speak terrible English and yet I know that you have made several trips to Britain.
Tu parles un anglais horrible et pourtant je sais que tu as fait plusieurs séjours en Grande-Bretagne.

Do you know where the Golden Boar restaurant is?
Sais-tu où se trouve le restaurant 'Au Sanglier d'or'?

GROUP B

Yes of course, I know it and they say it is a very good restaurant.
Oui, bien sûr, je le connais et on dit que c'est un très bon restaurant.

Miriam? Yes, I know her quite well.
Myriam? Oui, je la connais assez bien.

Depression in the Autumn, oh yes, I know that very well.
La déprime d'automne, oh oui, je connais très bien cela.

Johnny knew Vanessa for five years before marrying her.
Johnny a connu Vanessa pendant cinq ans avant de l'épouser.

The new police chief doesn't know much about our region.
Le nouveau commissaire de police ne connaît pas grand chose à propos de notre région.

That lad, he doesn't know his own strength.
Ce gars-là, il ne connaît pas sa force.

ANSWER

Basically, *savoir* is 'hard' and *connaître* is 'softer than *savoir*.' You can test and apply the type of facts and knowledge of *savoir*. Whereas *connaître* is always used for people and for knowing in the sense of having a **feeling about** something or a **sense for** something. This is a type of knowledge that comes from experience that we have gained and amassed inside ourselves. If we have it, we are connoisseurs (*connaisseurs* in French) and that contrasts with the hard *savoir*-type knowledge which is more often the result of rational information processing.

1.3   Do I say *sans* or *sans que*?

Have a look at the sentences in groups a and b. This time, you are looking for two types of difference in what follows *sans* and *sans que*.

GROUP A
That goes without saying.
Cela va sans dire.

You have to go and see her without me.
Il faut que tu ailles la voir sans moi.

You think you can go out like that, without asking?
Tu crois que tu peux sortir comme ça, sans demander?

The old man went out in the storm without anything on his head.
Le vieillard est sorti pendant la tempête sans rien sur la tête.

Without your collaboration we would be lost.
Sans votre collaboration, nous serions perdus.

GROUP B

The burglar was able to get into the house without my knowing.
Le cambrioleur a pu pénétrer dans la maison sans que je m'en aperçoive.

Yes, Captain, Bond was able to escape without our agents seeing him.
Oui, mon capitaine, Bond a pu s'échapper sans que nos agents le voient.

Alas, the meeting took place without my being able to attend it. (FORMAL)
Hélas! la réunion a eu lieu sans que j'aie pu y assister.(FORMAL)

But did all that happen without the prefect noticing anything?
Mais tout cela s'est-il déroulé sans que le surveillant ne remarque rien?

ANSWER

Looking at group b first, the phrase that follows *sans que* is mostly much longer than what follows the single word *sans* in group a. Also the phrases which follows *sans que* in group b resemble complete sentences in their own right, with a person or thing which does an action. This is usually not the case with the shorter one-word *sans* phrases in group a. You probably also noted that the doing word following *sans que* is in the subjunctive. So, when you need to continue with a sentence-like phrase, use *sans que*.

1.4   Do I say *pour* or *pour que*?

What differences in form and meaning can you detect between the sentences in groups a and b?

GROUP A

Whether it's for your child, or for yourself, you have to stop smoking.
Que ce soit pour ton enfant, ou pour toi-même, il faut que tu arrêtes de fumer.

Yesterday I saw the film on rap for the second time.
Hier j'ai vu le film sur le rap pour la deuxième fois.

Jeanne, do you understand? You don't have to do everything for your boss.
Jeanne, comprends-moi? Tu n'es pas obligée de tout faire pour ton patron.

The walk that you are thinking about doing is too long for me.
La randonnée que tu envisages de faire est trop longue pour moi.

I fear that this exercise is too easy for me.
Je crains que cet exercice ne soit trop facile pour moi.

GROUP B

You have to revise all the lecture notes, so that you can manage to pass the exam.
Il te faut revoir toutes les notes des cours magistraux, pour que tu réussisses l'examen.

I have really done everything in order to make Giles successfully complete his studies.
J'ai vraiment tout fait pour que Gilles mène à bien ses études.

They wanted to improve the facilities so that their team might succeed.
Ils ont voulu améliorer les locaux pour que leur équipe réussisse!

I wonder what I have to do so that he understands our situation.
Je me demande ce que je dois faire pour qu'il comprenne notre situation.

What measures have been taken so that they can tell the truth?
Quelles mesures ont été prises pour qu'ils puissent dire la vérité?

ANSWER

Looking at group b first, the phrase that follows *pour que* is most much longer than what follows the single word *pour* in group a. Also the phrases which follows *pour que* in group b resemble complete sentences in their own right, with a person or thing which does an action. The meaning of the sentences in group b are also stronger: they mean 'in order for' or 'in order that' and not just 'for' as in group a. So you use *pour que* when you have a phrase that is more like a sentence.

1.5   Do I say *plus de* or *plus que*?

Look at the sentences in the groups a and b below and see if you can work out for yourself the difference between what follows *plus de* and what follows *plus que*. Remember, you are looking for differences meaning between the word or phrase in group a and group b which immediately follows *plus que* and *plus de*.

GROUP A

It is now more than three times that he has fallen without hurting himself.
Ça fait maintenant plus de trois fois qu'il est tombé sans se faire de mal.

I can't manage to do it, although I have made more than twenty attempts.
Je n'y arrive pas, bien que j'aie fait plus de vingt tentatives.

Do you really think that Barbara is more than sixty years old?
Est-ce que tu crois vraiment que Barbara a plus de soixante ans?

More than one sailor felt seasick during the naval exercise.
Plus d'un matelot a eu le mal de mer pendant les manœuvres navales.

GROUP B

I found his words more than hurtful. I am very disappointed.
J'ai trouvé ses propos plus que blessants. Je suis très déçu.

More than the colour, it's the size of the dress which bothers me.
Plus que la couleur, c'est la taille de la robe qui me gêne.

Frankly, I see more than a simple mistake there.
Franchement je vois là plus qu'une simple erreur.

The others felt the cold more than me.
Les autres ont senti le froid plus que moi.

ANSWER

In the sentences with *plus de* in group a you always have naming words; they are independent and specific; however, the most important thing is that they are countable. They are things or points in time. For instance, in the last sentence in the group, the singular form of the doing word is used because the whole group is seen as an individual.

Group b concerns non-countable things on their own. This means that the word 'more' relates to qualities and things that a person cannot touch. In addition, *plus que* is used before naming words (e.g. *erreur*) which are accompanied by a describing word (e.g. *simple*).

1.6   Normally doing words use *avoir*, but how can I remember which ones use *être*?

Look at the list of doing words below and in group b see if you can make a phrase, using the first letter of each one. You may have to rearrange the letters a little because some of them appear twice.

GROUP A

Oh no! I have put salt into my coffee!
Oh, c'est pas vrai! J'ai mis du sel dans mon café! (*mettre*)

Have you heard the news? Barbara is expecting.
Avez-vous entendu la nouvelle? Barbara attend un enfant. (*entendre*)

He had thought of sending Ebony some roses for her birthday.
Il avait pensé à envoyer des roses à Ebony pour son anniversaire. (*penser*)

Will he have reached the summit before sunset?
Est-ce qu'il aura atteint le sommet avant le coucher du soleil? (*atteindre*)

Would the ambassador have been aware of the spy's activities?
L'ambassadeur aurait-il été au courant des activités de l'espion? (*être*)

GROUP B

Has Marie already come down?
Est-ce que Marie est déjà descendue? (*descendre*)

On hearing the news I immediately returned to the country.
En entendant la nouvelle je suis retourné tout de suite à la campagne. (*retourner*)

Yes, we had arrived on time.
Oui, nous étions arrivés à l'heure (*arriver*)

We left on holiday.
Nous sommes partis en vacances. (*partir*)

They came into the building.
Ils sont entrés dans le bâtiment. (*entrer*)

Who did you go home with?
Tu es rentrée avec qui? (*rentrer*)

Yes, he remained alone all of his life.
Oui, il est resté seul toute sa vie. (*rester*)

I went out without my umbrella.
Je suis sorti sans mon parapluie. (*sortir*)

Francis and Francine have come to France.
Francis et Francine sont venus en France. (*venir*)

Oh yes Jonathan! And what became of him?
Ah oui, Jonathan! Et qu'est-ce qu'il est devenu? (*devenir*)

Where did you go yesterday?
Où es-tu allé hier? (*aller*)

He was born on the twenty fifth of December.
Il est né le vingt-cinq décembre.   *(naître)*

My grandmother died the day before yesterday.
Ma grand-mère est morte avant-hier.   *(mourir)*

ANSWER

The words D-R-A-P-E-R-S' V-A-N will help you to remember which doing words use *être*.

> D *descendre*
>
> R *retourner*
>
> A *arriver*
>
> P *partir*
>
> E *entrer (rentrer)*
>
> R *rester*
>
> S' *sortir*
>
> V *venir, devenir, revenir and survenir*
>
> A *aller*
>
> N *naître/mourir*

Add this threesome to the D-R-A-P-E-R-S' V-A-N; two doing words for 'UP' *monter/remonter* and one meaning 'DOWN' *tomber*.

Sandrine went upstairs to look for her gloves.
Sandrine est montée chercher ses gants.   *(monter)*

The mountaineer went back up to the summit to save his comrade.
L'alpiniste est remonté au sommet pour porter secours à son camarade.   *(remonter)*

Gerard blacked out. (INFORMAL)
Gérard est tombé dans les pommes. (INFORMAL)   *(tomber)*

IMPORTANT NOTE:

The following doing words can be used to carry out an action on an object or on a person: *sortir, resortir, descendre, redescendre, monter* and *remonter*. When they are used in that way they become 'normal' group a doing words and are written as follows:

My father took down the bins.
Mon père a descendu les poubelles.

Did you take the tractor out this afternoon?
Est-ce que tu as sorti le tracteur cet après-midi?

I have brought up the suitcases so that you can settle up in this room.
J'ai monté les valises pour que tu puisses t'installer dans cette chambre.

Yesterday I went back up the slope from bottom to top.
Hier j'ai remonté la pente de bas en haut.

1.7   What is the right word order if I start a phrase with *peut-être*?

Have a look at the two groups of sentences below; what are the differences?

GROUP A

Perhaps that footballer is going to go out with my sister, but I am not sure.
Peut-être que ce footballeur va sortir avec ma sœur, mais je n'en suis pas sûr.

I didn't see him at the party yesterday, perhaps he has left on holiday.
Je ne l'ai pas vu à la fête hier, peut-être qu'il est parti en vacances.

Perhaps we will have good weather tomorrow.
Peut-être que nous aurons du beau temps demain.

GROUP B

Perhaps they have already left for town.
Peut-être sont-ils déjà partis en ville?

Perhaps they will get married in the town where Vanessa was born?
Peut-être se marieront-ils dans la ville natale de Vanessa?

Perhaps he gets a salary of more than two thousand euros per month?
Peut-être touche-t-il un salaire de plus de deux mille euros par mois?

ANSWER

Here there is absolutely no difference in meaning between the two groups; but did you spot the differences in word order? In group a *peut-être* is followed by *que* and you keep the word order as normal. In group b, the word order is reversed, putting the doing word before the person or thing who/which does the action. Perhaps you also noticed that the sentences in group b which begin with *peut-être* all end with a question mark?

1.8   How do I say 'good': *bon* or *bien?*

Have an look at the groups of examples below and try to distinguish from the meaning of the sentences, which word to use to say 'good'?

GROUP A
Yes, I think he is a good boss.
Oui, je trouve qu'il est bien comme patron.

All things considered, it would be good if we could warn him.
En fin de compte ce serait bien si on pouvait le prévenir.

GROUP B
This is a good car.
Ça c'est une bonne voiture.

Germany has a good road system.
L'Allemagne possède un bon réseau routier.

Ah, grilled salmon tastes good!
Ah, le saumon grillé, c'est bon!

Oh Ghislaine you smell good, what perfume are you using?
Ah, Ghislaine tu sens bon, quel parfum utilises-tu?

ANSWER

The sentences in group a using *bien* concern judgements. This is different from the first two sentences in group b which present **judgements** as if they were **facts**. The final two sentences in group b refer to smelling and tasting food with *sentir* or *être*.

1.9   How do I say 'better': *mieux* or *meilleur?*

Have a look at the groups of examples below and try to distinguish, from the meaning of the sentences, which word to use to say 'better'?

GROUP A

Nobody does it better than George.
Personne ne le fait mieux que Georges.

It's better that way.
C'est mieux comme ça.

GROUP B

This nightclub is better than that one.
Cette boîte est meilleure que celle-là.

My racket is better than yours.
Ma raquette est meilleure que la tienne.

ANSWER

1.   When it refers to a doing word like *faire* 'better' is *mieux* (no agreement).

2.   'better' is *meilleur* when it refers to a naming word, it agrees with that person or thing.

1.10   How do I say 'best': *le mieux* or *le meilleur?*

Have a look at the groups of examples below and try to distinguish from the meaning of the sentences, which word to use to say 'best'?

GROUP A

I beg you, sir, to accept the expression of my best feelings (a literal translation of the set phrase found at the end of letters).
Je vous prie d'agréer, Monsieur, l'expression de mes meilleurs sentiments OR Je vous prie d'agréer, Monsieur, l'expression de mes sentiments les meilleurs.

GROUP B

Here is the chorister who sings the best.
Voilà le choriste qui chante le mieux.

We have done our best.
Nous avons fait de notre mieux.

Without doubt, it's Estelle who reads the best.
Sans aucun doute c'est Estelle qui lit le mieux

ANSWER

1. When it refers to a naming word, 'best' is *le meilleur* and it agrees with the person/thing.

2. 'best' is *le mieux* when it refers to a doing word (it is always *le* even if it refers to a woman).

In a few cases when 'best' refers to **quantity** then it can be translated by *plus* in French:

Which of the cakes do you like the best?
Lequel des gâteaux te plaît le plus?

You use *plus* in this case because something pleases you more or less and not better, worse or best. The final example above is therefore different from the rest of the sentences here which all relate to quality; this one concerns quantity.

1.11   How do I say 'whatever': *quel... que* or *quoi...que*?

If you look at the groups below, you will perhaps be able to see a difference between group a and group b in the type of word which follows the French words for 'whatever'.

GROUP A

Whatever the problem, your friends will support you.
Quel que soit le problème, tes amis te soutiendront.

Whatever the problem between two regions in the world, the UN must attempt to resolve it.
Quel que soit le problème entre deux régions du monde, l'ONU doit essayer de le résoudre.

GROUP B

Whatever she eats, she never gets fat.
Quoi qu'elle mange, elle ne grossit jamais.

Whatever I say, she never listens to me.
Quoi que je dise, elle ne m'écoute jamais (FORMAL).

ANSWER

———————————————————————————————————

Use this test. You have two choices. If 'whatever' appears with a naming word, use *quel que* (always written in two words) and its relations (*quelle que*, *quels que* and *quelles que*). Or, if 'whatever' appears with a doing word, use *quoi que* and the subjunctive. *Quoi que* does not change for masculine, feminine or plural.

Remember that both *quel que* and *quoi que* take the subjunctive.

———————————————————————————————————

1.12   How do I say 'each': *chaque* or *chacun(e)*?

Contrast both groups of French examples and their translations below and see if you can discover the difference between the type of words in front of which *chaque* or *chacun* are placed.

GROUP A

Each time you say goodbye, I cry.
Chaque fois que tu me dis 'au revoir', je pleure.

Each person should know his or her limits.
Chaque personne devrait connaître ses limites.

GROUP B

Each (one) will get a bonus of one thousand euros.
Chacun(e) touchera une prime de mille euros.

In democracy each person is free to express his or her opinions.
En démocratie chacun est libre d'exprimer ses opinions.

Each person to his or her own taste.
À chacun son goût.

ANSWER

You can use this test to find out whether to use *chaque* or *chacun(e)*.

EITHER 'each' is a describing word (i.e. it describes a naming word, a person/thing); if it is, use *chaque*, which never changes according to masculine and feminine words.

OR 'each' is working like a *je*, *tu*, *il*, *elle*, *nous*, *vous*, *ils*, *elles*; if it is, use *chac+un* or *chac+une* written as one word. Think about it as each+one. The *chac* bit does not change, but *un* and *une* change according to masculine and feminine words. The final sentence in Group b is a set phrase.

1.13   How do I use negatives in French?

1.13.1   Do negatives like *ne...pas* always have two parts in French?

Take a look at the examples of sentences with negatives below. After identifying the two parts of the negative, can you work out where they come in the word order of the sentence?

GROUP A

I am not going to repeat it.
Je ne vais pas le répéter.

Karima hasn't seen this film.
Karima n'a pas vu ce film.

I am only nineteen years old.
Je n'ai que dix-neuf ans.

The poor little boy did not have a chance.
Le pauvre petit n'avait aucune chance.

Going round the world in a balloon is hardly possible.
Le tour du monde en ballon n'est guère possible.

I didn't want to buy anything in that designer boutique.
Je ne voulais rien acheter dans cette boutique de haute couture.

ANSWER

Most negatives of doing words have two parts and in simple sentences they go either side of the main doing word, or either side of past tenses with *être* and *avoir* (the 'have', the 'had' and the 'would have' tenses, i.e. perfect, pluperfect and conditional perfect). They enclose the main doing word, boxing it in from the front and from behind. This does not apply when the sentence contains words like *lui*, 'him', 'her', *leur* 'them', *le*, 'it' and *y*, 'there' these words come and take the place of *ne* immediately before the doing word. When the sentence is a question with reversed word order, fragments, such as '*-t-il*'. In addition, when the 'to' form of a doing word is negated, the two parts of the negative stick together and come before it.

Don't show it to him!
Ne le lui montre pas!

Isn't he breathing?
Ne respire-t-il pas?

Julian hopes to never come here again.
Julien espère ne jamais revenir ici.

1.13.2   What negatives take a different position and when?

'Who wants to come with me into the basement?' asked Jack. No one answered.
'Qui veut m'accompagner au sous-sol?' demanda Jacques. Personne ne répondit.

Who is the murderer? Nobody knows.
Qui est l'assassin? Nul ne le sait.

Not one customer wanted to buy Dario's paintings.

Aucun amateur ne voulait acheter les tableaux de Dario.

I had heard nobody.
Je n'avais entendu personne.

ANSWER

These negatives all negate the presence of people and are translated as 'no one', 'nobody', 'not one' (person). Sometimes they can be quite sad sentences! In the case of those which start a sentence, both parts of the negative come before the main doing word. In the final example, *ne...personne* doesn't start the sentence, in this case it encloses both parts of the doing word.

1.13.3   How do I say 'neither...nor'?

We are neither going to tell you nor even give you a clue.
Nous n'allons ni te le dire ni même t'en donner un indice.

Neither I nor my girlfriend have been to that club.
Ni moi ni ma petite amie ne sommes allés dans cette boîte-là.

Neither Pierre, Paul, nor Patricia are fit enough to play polo.
Ni Pierre, ni Paul, ni Patricia ne sont pas assez en forme pour jouer au polo.

ANSWER

Again, French has one more element than the English negative. You put *ni* before each person/thing and only *ne* before the doing word.

1.13.4   How do I negate a person or thing?

I think that is a Victorian tea cosy, not a Tibetan hat!
Je pense que cela est un couvre-théière de l'époque victorienne, et non pas un chapeau tibétain!

You must turn here and not there.
Il faut tourner ici, et non là-bas.

ANSWER

In these cases negate with *non pas* (following the guideline that French has two elements where English only has one) or even *non* by itself and especially in conversation, *pas* can be used instead of *et non*).

1.13.5   How do I negate a describing word?

The neighbours' children are rather mature, not childish.
Les enfants des voisins sont plutôt mûrs, et non puérils.

ANSWER

In this case you negate with *non* by itself.

1.13.6   How is the negation of *pouvoir, oser, cesser de* and *savoir* different?

When making the following doing words negative in formal language, you only need the first part of the negative enclosure. These doing words can be made negative from the front.

That's right. We cannot establish the facts in this case. (FORMAL)
C'est exact. Nous ne pouvons établir les faits dans cette affaire-ci. (FORMAL)   *(pouvoir)*

I am sorry Madam, our team will not attempt such a surgical
procedure. (FORMAL)
Je suis désolé, madame notre équipe n'osera tenter une telle technique   *(oser)*
chirurgicale. (FORMAL)

The witness didn't dare to tell the truth before the court. (FORMAL)
Le témoin n'a osé dire la vérité devant la cour. (FORMAL)   *(oser)*

The judge has not stopped wondering why the accident happened.
(FORMAL)
Le juge n'a cessé de se demander pourquoi l'accident s'est produit.   *(cesser de)*
(FORMAL)

We do not know how to make Brussels pâté. (FORMAL)
Nous ne savons comment préparer le pâté de Bruxelles. (FORMAL)   *(savoir)*

Even the gastronomy specialist did not know which wine to choose
with this dish. (FORMAL)
Même le gastronome ne savait quel vin choisir avec ce plat. (FORMAL)   *(savoir)*

Politicians in this country do not know how to finish their speeches.
(FORMAL)
Les hommes politiques dans ce pays ne savent comment terminer leurs discours.   *(savoir)*
(FORMAL)

ANSWER

Pouvoir, oser and *cesser de* only take *ne*. So does *savoir* when followed by question words such as: 'who', 'what', 'where', 'why', 'how' and 'which'. In INFORMAL spoken French, people negate these words with *ne* and *pas*. For example:

I do not know how he was able to enter in to the strongroom of this bank.
Je ne sais pas comment il a pu entrer dans la salle des coffres de cette banque.

1.13.7   How is it possible to negate in very informal contexts?

I am not going to repeat it.
Je vais pas le répéter.

Karima hasn't seen this film.
Karima a pas vu ce film.

ANSWER

It is possible to negate with *pas* alone in very informal contexts.

1.13.8   How is it possible to make combinations of negatives?

He stood there without saying anything to anybody.
Il se tenait là sans rien dire à personne.

Nobody said anything; then he left.
Personne n'a rien dit; ensuite il est parti.

ANSWER

When combined with other negatives *ne...personne* loses its *ne* and is placed at the beginning or at the end of the sentence.

1.14   How do I translate and use *quelque chose,* meaning 'something'?

This time you get the answer in the sentences below! However, what is the obvious difference between *quelque chose* and 'something', apart from the fact that one is French and the other is English?

Darling, I think that there is something under the wardrobe.
Chéri, je crois qu'il y a quelque chose sous l'armoire.

Yves you are silent. Say something!
Yves, tu ne dis rien. Dis quelque chose!

ANSWER ONE:

Translate 'something' in TWO words in French.

Here's a supplementary question: what is surprising about that follows *quelque chose* in the following sentences?

Are you going to give me something good?
Vas-tu m'offrir quelque chose de bon?

If you notice something suspicious, let us know immediately.
Si vous remarquez quelque chose de suspect, prévenez-nous immédiatement.

Is there something interesting on television this evening?
Est-ce qu'il y a quelque chose d'intéressant à la télé ce soir?

ANSWER TWO:

Quelque chose takes both *de* and the masculine. This is rather unusual because you say *la chose*. So, there you have some things, well, only really <u>two</u> things to remember about the form and use of 'something' in French!

How do I translate and use *quelque chose*, meaning 'something'?

1.15 How do I translate 'who...to', 'who...about', 'who...around' and 'who...with'?

Do you know that you have a choice of two possibilities in French?

The woman who he was speaking with is my aunt (The woman to whom he was speaking is my aunt: FORMAL).
La femme avec laquelle il parlait est ma tante.
OR La femme avec qui il parlait est ma tante.

This is the child who the report was written about (This is the child about whom the report was written).
Voici l'enfant sur lequel on a fait le rapport.
OR Voici l'enfant sur qui on a fait le rapport.

The star who the youths gathered around (The star around whom the youths gathered).
La star autour de laquelle tout le monde s'est pressé, s'est évanouie.
La star autour de qui tout le monde s'est pressé, s'est évanouie.

You're the man who I want to live with.
Tu es l'homme avec lequel je veux vivre.
OR Tu es l'homme avec qui je veux vivre.

There are people for whom Manchester United has acquired a sacred reputation (WRITTEN).
Il y a des gens pour lesquels l'United de Manchester a acquis une réputation sacrée.
Il y a des gens pour qui l'United de Manchester a acquis une réputation sacrée.

ANSWER

You can use the position words (such as 'around', 'for' and 'with') followed by both *qui* and *lequel* or its relations (*laquelle*, *lesquelles* and *lesquels*). All these examples refer to people and you have a choice **only** when the example refers to people.

Translating 'amongst which', 'amongst whom', 'between which' and 'between whom' is different because with *parmi* and *entre* **only** *lequel* and its relatives (*laquelle*, *lesquels* and *lesquelles*) can be used:

What did the sculptures look like, amongst which the artist scattered petals?
À quoi ressemblaient les sculptures parmi lesquelles l'artiste a éparpillé des pétales?

The fans amongst whom Karim could be found on Saturdays, were very young.
Les supporters, parmi lesquels on pouvait trouver Karim le samedi, étaient très jeunes.

The people between whom he was fidgeting in the queue, were ignoring him.
Les gens entre lesquels il s'agitait dans la queue, ne lui prêtaient aucune attention.

The two fat rugby players, between whom I was stuck on the plane, were snoring.
Les deux gros rugbymen entre lesquels j'étais coincé dans l'avion ronflaient.

1.16   Do I use *en* or *dans* to mean 'in' when taking about a duration of time?

Look at the sentences below, what is the difference in how each group refers to the period of time?

GROUP A

In eight days he has been able to learn five hundred words of Chinese.
En huit jours, il a pu apprendre cinq cents mots de chinois.

In two months I see no change at all in his state.
En deux mois je ne vois pas le moindre changement dans son état.

GROUP B

I will finish this book in ten days.
Je terminerai ce livre dans dix jours.

ANSWER

The sentences in group a refer to a period of time as a duration; they refer to the whole span of the time. The sentences in group b are different they point to the end of the period of time, as is indicated by the doing words used: *terminerai* and *sera de retour*.

In phrases such 'a week next Sunday' *en* is used. It is as if French speakers want to signal a whole span or block of time between today and the same day in seven day's time.

Your father will be back from California a week next Sunday.
Dimanche en huit votre père sera revenu de Californie.

Note also that you can also refer to the end of the period of time with *d'ici* followed by the time period.

Within two days you will have prepared everything.
D'ici deux jours vous aurez tout préparé.

1.17   When do I say *jour* and when is it right to say *journée* and *soir/soirée*, *an/année* and *matin/matinée*?

Which two words for 'evening', 'morning', 'year' and 'day' do I use in French? Try to discover a difference between the way of looking at the time period referred to in the words in the two groups.

GROUP A

We spent the whole evening drinking and playing the guitar.
Nous avons passé toute la soirée à boire et à jouer de la guitare.

This rail workers' strike took up our morning.
Cette grève des cheminots nous a fait perdre notre matinée.

The next day, Jean and Jeanne had a lie in.
Le lendemain, Jean et Jeanne ont fait la grasse matinée.

I think that I have made a lot of progress during this academic year.
Je pense avoir fait beaucoup de progrès pendant cette année universitaire.

I had a terrible day at the office.
J'ai passé une journée épouvantable au bureau.

Sandrine wished me a happy new year and good health.
Sandrine m'a souhaité une bonne année et une bonne santé.

1995 is a very good year for claret.
1995 est une très bonne année pour les vins de Bordeaux

Last year I attended a performance of *Tosca* in Milan
L'année dernière j'ai assisté à une représentation de La Tosca à Milan.

GROUP B

Which date is Armistice Day?
C'est quelle date le Jour de l'Armistice?

Normally my parents stay at home on New Year's Day.
D'habitude mes parents restent à la maison le jour de l'an.

We do not know the future of the earth in 4000.
On ne sait pas l'avenir de la terre en l'an 4000.

The Olympic Games took place in Seoul last year.
Les Jeux Olympiques ont eu lieu à Séoul l'an dernier

The lucky man, he gets up at eleven every morning.
Le veinard, il se lève à onze heures tous les matins.

Most of the M.P.s are more than forty years old.
La plupart des députés ont plus de quarante ans.

Mum, how many more days to Christmas?
Maman, il reste encore combien de jours avant Noël?

ANSWER

The longer forms in group a: *soirée, matinée, année* and *journée* refer to specific years in the near future or past, a duration of time, or, as in the final example to some time within that duration that the speaker is not highlighting. The short forms in group b: *soir, matin, an* and *jour* are used for references to named days, pinpointing them in the calendar and counting them with numbers, as well as to specific years in the distant future or past.[1] This is particularly applicable to years in round figures, such as 2000, 3000 etc.

Bonsoir, bonjour is a greeting you say and share with the other person and it is experienced by you and the person directly as a shared moment together. *Bonsoir* can also be used when taking your leave of somebody. However, *bonne soirée* and *bonne journée* go beyond the moment and refer to the wish that you make for a person for the rest of the day or evening to come when you may not be together. Therefore, *bonjour* is momentary and *bonne soirée* refers to a duration in the period of the time. When you meet some one you don't know for the first time, people simply say *Monsieur, Madame* or *Mademoiselle*. This is also a momentary greeting.

1.18 Which past tense should I use in French, and when?

Have a look at the sentences below, it's quite a challenge to work out the difference between the groups according to the way in which the past is being expressed. The difference between a dot and a long line may help you.

GROUP A

This is an example of a completed action which has no direct effect on the present.

England won the football World Cup in 1966.
L'Angleterre a gagné la Coupe du Monde en 1966.
OR L'Angleterre gagna la Coupe du Monde en 1966. (FORMAL).

---

1. See Jean-Paul Tremblay, *Grammaire comparative du français et de l'anglais à l'usage des anglophones*, Sainte-Foy (Québec) : Les Presses de l'Université Laval, 1971; pp. 208-9.

These are events in a story which follow one after the other; one has to finish before the next one begins.

They looked at each other, they began to smile and they became friends.
Ils se sont regardés, ils se sont mis à sourire, et ils sont devenus amis.
OR Ils se regardèrent, ils se mirent à sourire et ils devinrent amis.

This period has an end, even though, the period is very long.

Before I met you I never washed my feet, except in the bath.
Avant de te rencontrer je ne me suis jamais lavé les pieds, sauf dans le bain.
OR Avant de te rencontrer je ne me lavai jamais les pieds sauf dans le bain.

GROUP B

This is a description of a continuous state or state of mind.

Her/his business was very successful.
Son entreprise marchait très bien.

He didn't know what it was like to work nights.
Il ne savait pas ce que c'était que de travailler la nuit.

A continuous event where the beginning and end are not clear.

While the others danced, he drank.
Pendant que les autres dansaient, lui, il buvait.

This is a habitual action. If 'used to' fits the idea, then it's habit.

You used to say you loved me…but I didn't care.
Tu disais que tu m'aimais… mais cela m'était égal.

ANSWER

In group a, you can see that there are actually two tenses: the 'have' tense (the perfect) and the past historic. The 'have' tense will always be fine in the type of examples above, but don't use the past historic if you are speaking or writing a letter.

So the short answer to the question about the difference between groups a and b is: if you can see a beginning or an endpoint in the idea, use the 'have' tense/past historic, if not then it's the 'was' tense. Habitual actions will perhaps seem to better belong in group b if you imagine the individual actions sticking together in habit to form a line, which is as long as the person lives in that place and does that particular thing on a regular basis.

1.19   When do I say *voici* and when *voilà,* meaning 'here'?

Look at the two groups of sentences below, can you work out when you use *voici* and when you use *voilà* in French?

GROUP A

Here is the biscuit that you started, I am giving it back to you because you have had your meal.
Voici le biscuit que tu as entamé, je te le rends puisque tu as pris ton repas.

Look closely, here is the postman who is opening the garden gate.
Regardez bien, voici le facteur qui ouvre la porte du jardin.

GROUP B

Here are my paintings; now I remember that I hid them at the back of the cellar.
Voilà mes peintures, je me rappelle maintenant que je les ai cachées au fond de la cave.

Be careful, here is the ticket collector coming from the other carriage.
Fais attention, voilà le contrôleur qui arrive de l'autre wagon.

ANSWER

Voici is usually used for things closer to the speaker, remember that this closeness is indicated by the word *ici* within *voici*. *Voilà* is used in a different way which indicates that the object or the person is further away from the speaker. Remember that it contains *là* within it, the word for 'there'. *Voici* and *voilà* are not always in used in opposition to each other. They can also be used interchangeably.

1.20   When do I say *celui-ci* and when *celui-là*?

GROUP A

Which of the loaves do you want? I think I am going to have this one, the wholemeal loaf.

Lequel des pains veux-tu? Je pense que je vais prendre celui-ci, le pain complet.

GROUP B

Which of the puppies do you like best? I like that one, yes, the one right at the back of the cage.

Lequel des chiots vous plaît le plus? J'aime celui-là, oui, celui tout au fond de la cage.

ANSWER

Celui is only used for masculine people or things. When they are found in one sentence, one after the other, *celui-ci* and *celui-là* mean, the former and the latter. *Celui-ci* is used to refer to things and people which are near the speaker; remember that *ici* means 'here', near the speaker. *Celui-là* is used to refer to things and people which are further away from the speaker; remember that *là* means 'there', 'over there.'

1.21   When do I say *celle-ci* and when *celle-là*?

GROUP A

Choose another non-alcoholic drink, since this one has such a high alcohol content.

Choisissez une autre boisson non-alcoolisée, puisque celle-ci a un taux d'alcool si élevé.

GROUP B

What is the best dress in this shop? I recommend that one to you without hesitation.

Quelle est la meilleure robe dans ce magasin? Je vous recommande celle-là sans aucune hésitation.

ANSWER

Celle is only used for feminine people or things. When they are found in one sentence, one after the other, *celle-ci* and *celle-là* mean, the former and the latter. *Celle-ci* is used to refer to things and people which are near the speaker; remember that *ici* means 'here', near the speaker. *Celle-là* is used to refer to things and people which are further away from the speaker; remember that *là* means 'there', 'over there.'

1.22 How do I say 'it' in phrases like 'it is difficult to…', with *il* or *ce*?

See if you can spot the difference in word order which determines whether you use *il* or *ce* in group a and group b below.

GROUP A

It is easy to reach such conclusions.
Il est facile d'arriver à de telles conclusions.

It is impossible to estimate the turnover of M. Lejeune's company at the moment.
Il est impossible d'évaluer le chiffre d'affaires de l'entreprise de M. Lejeune en ce moment.

GROUP B

If you can, avoid crossing this region, it is too dangerous.
Si vous le pouvez, évitez de traverser cette région, c'est trop dangereux.

Rudeness, that's really a thing that I find it very difficult to bear.
L'impolitesse, ça c'est vraiment une chose que j'ai beaucoup de mal à supporter.

Did the CAC-40 (index) of the Paris Stock Exchange really go up 0.23 percent yesterday? Yes it's true.
Le CAC-40 (say: "kak-quarante") de la Bourse de Paris a-t-il vraiment gagné 0,23 pour cent hier? Oui, c'est vrai.

ANSWER

Il refers forward, whereas *ce* refers back. You will see sentences where that order is reversed particularly in INFORMAL spoken French, but it will never be wrong to follow the guidelines of *il* as forward and *ce* as back. You could think of it as the curled letters 'c' and 'e' also pointing back.

The same pattern works, when you mention for the second time, people to whom you have already referred:

Here's Malik, he is a good goalkeeper.
Voici Malik, c'est un bon gardien de but.

Look at the Bokker brothers, they were little savages when they were very young.
Regarde les frères Bokker, c'étaient de petits sauvages quand ils étaient tout petits.

1.23   Do I say *dans le* or *en* when I mean 'in' with *départements* and counties?

As you will see, British counties are easy to remember and all of them take *dans* and are found in group a. However, what is the difference between the form of the word for the French *départements* in group a, contrasted with group b?

GROUP A

I was born in Yorkshire, whereas my brother came into the world in Hertfordshire.
Moi, je suis né dans le Yorkshire, alors que mon frère est venu au monde dans le Hertfordshire.

The town of Exeter is in Devon.
La ville d'Exeter se trouve dans le Devon.

Jacques told me that in the Haut-Rhin there are lively towns like Colmar.
Jacques m'a dit que dans le Haut-Rhin il y a des villes animées comme Colmar.

There are fewer people in Corrèze than in Gironde with the Bordeaux conurbation.
Il y a moins de gens dans la Corrèze que dans la Gironde avec l'agglomération de Bordeaux.

GROUP B

The town of Chartres, where my cousin Michelle lives, is in Eure-et-Loir.
La ville de Chartres, où habite Michelle, ma cousine, se trouve en Eure-et-Loir.

In Ille-et-Vilaine, Rennes is the prefecture town of the département.
En Ille-et-Vilaine, le chef-lieu du département est Rennes.

There are many vineyards in Saône-et-Loire.
Il y a beaucoup de vignobles en Saône-et-Loire.

ANSWER

As we said British counties are easy, for them, you always use *dans le*. With French *départements*, the pattern becomes clear when you look at how many words the name of the *département* has. So, it's *en* for all the ones which are two words, joined by an *et* and *dans* for all those which just have one word. However, there are some exceptions, for example: *en Corrèze* and you can say both *dans le* and *en* for Maine-et-Loire.

1.24 Do I say *dans le* or *en*, when I mean 'to' with, *départements* and counties?

You are looking to reidentifiy a type of difference between the groups that you already know.

GROUP A

You told me that we were going to the Indre-et-Loire *département* and, yet, it's not true at all.
Tu m'avais dit qu'on allait en Indre-et-Loire et pourtant, ce n'est pas vrai du tout.

When I go from Paris to Chartres, it must not be forgotten that I am also going to Eure-et-Loir.
Quand je vais de Paris à Chartres, il ne faut pas oublier que je vais également en Eure-et-Loir.

GROUP B

This woman climber always wants to go to the Jura to climb.
Cette alpiniste veut toujours aller dans le Jura pour faire de l'escalade.

Do you want to come to Warwickshire this weekend to see our farm?
Veux-tu venir dans le Warwickshire ce week-end pour voir notre ferme?

ANSWER

The pattern here is exactly the same as with *dans* and *en* meaning 'in'. That is *en* used when the name is doubled with an *et* (*en* and *et* look similar).

1.25 Do I say *dans le* or *en*, when I mean 'in' with US states, Canadian provinces and geographical regions?

Have a look at these two groups of examples; what is it about the word for the state or province which determines whether *dans* or *en* is used?

GROUP A

In the middle of the countryside in Texas you can see the storms coming in from afar.
En pleine campagne dans le Texas on peut voir les orages arriver de très loin.

I prefer to spend the summer in Colorado and the winter in Arizona.
Je préfère passer l'été dans le Colorado et l'hiver dans l'Arizona.

Many of the cultural projects in New York State are funded by private benefactors.
Beaucoup des projets culturels dans l'État de New York sont subventionnés par des mécènes.

A great deal of wheat is grown in Saskatchewan, a province of Canada.
On cultive beaucoup de blé dans le Saskatchewan, province du Canada.

That's nothing! I met my girlfriend on a camping site in the Limousin.(INFORMAL)
Ça, c'est rien! J'ai fait la connaissance de ma petite amie dans un camping dans le Limousin.
(INFORMAL)

Most of the tourists who stay in Périgord enjoy the food there.
La plupart des touristes qui séjournent dans le Périgord y apprécient la cuisine.

Group b

In the film, there were amazing sequences which were shot in Louisiana.
Dans le film, il y avait des séquences étonnantes qui ont été tournées en Louisiane.

In this film, the car race began in Florida and finished in California.
Dans ce film, la course automobile a commencé en Floride pour se terminer en Californie.

The city of Seattle isn't very far from Vancouver, which is in British Columbia.
La ville importante de Seattle n'est pas très loin de Vancouver qui se trouve en Colombie-Britannique.

You remember Ursula? Well, she was the one who taught German in Nova Scotia.
Tu te souviens d'Ursula? Eh bien, c'est elle qui a enseigné l'allemand en Nouvelle-Écosse.

There's that song about the roads of… where was it? Somewhere in Virginia.
Il y a cette chanson, non? Qui parle des chemin de… où c'était déjà? Quelque part en Virginie.

Sorry that was the wrong answer. The town of Yakutsk is in Siberia.
Désolé, c'était la mauvaise réponse. La ville de Iakutsk se trouve en Sibérie.

Sambroni is a Corsican who would have liked to spend all his life in Corsica.
Sambroni, c'est un Corse qui aurait voulu passer toute sa vie en Corse.

ANSWER

Group a states and provinces do not modify the English name when they are written in French (if an English form of the name exists); they are all masculine and take *dans le* or *dans l'État de*.

The states, provinces and regions in group b take *en*. They are all modify the English name are feminine and end in 'e'.

1.26   Do I say *dans le* or *en*, when I mean 'to' with US states, Canadian provinces and geographical regions?

Do you remember the pattern here?

GROUP A

At school, no one understood why I wanted to go to Alberta to see the wild countryside there.
À l'école, personne ne comprenait pourquoi je voulais aller dans l'Alberta pour y voir la campagne sauvage.

Since they wanted to do something different after their A levels, Charles and Tina went to Alabama.
Puisqu'ils voulaient faire quelque chose de différent après leur bac, Charles et Tina sont partis dans l'Alabama.

If you go to the North of Europe in winter, you will perhaps see the Northern Lights.
Si vous vous rendez dans le Nord de l'Europe en hiver, vous pourrez peut-être voir une aurore boréale

Do you really want to go to Saskatchewan?
Veux-tu vraiment aller dans le Saskatchewan?

GROUP B

Do you realise that the first American colonists left the East coast in wagons to go to California?
Est-ce que tu te rends compte que les premiers colons américains sont partis en chariots de la côte est pour aller en Californie?

If you want to visit Disneyworld, you have to go to Florida.
Si vous voulez visiter Disneyworld il faut aller en Floride.

The daughter of the ex-president came to Europe to continue her studies.
La fille de l'ancien président est venue en Europe poursuivre ses études.

Each year my father goes to Normandy to spend his Summer holidays.
Chaque année mon père va en Normandie pour passer ses grandes vacances.

You can drink some excellent rosé wines, if you go to Anjou.
On peut boire des rosés excellents, si on va en Anjou.

I really want to go to Ontario.
Je veux vraiment aller en Ontario.

ANSWER

Group a. The US states and Canadian provinces written in French in group a do not modify the English name, are masculine and take *dans le* or *dans l'État de*. The points of the compass are all masculine and therefore if you refer to a part of a region with one of them, you put it first and the region (or even the country) becomes masculine. Thus *le Nord de l'Angleterre* is correct and ~~dans l'Angleterre du Nord~~ is wrong.

In group b the US states which take *en* all modify the English name, are feminine; they and the French regions end in 'ie'. French regions and Canadian provinces which take *le* and begin with 'a', 'e', 'i', 'o' or 'u' such as Anjou, Ardèche, Auvergne and Ontario all take *en*.

1.27 Do I say *aux* or *dans les,* when I mean 'in' with countries and regions which have plural names like the 'The Netherlands'?

The pattern that you are looking for here is related to the geographical shape of the country or region in the individual groups! This is a very unusual distinction.

GROUP A

My uncle owns a holiday home in the Maldives.
Mon oncle possède une maison de vacances aux Maldives.

In the period when Margaret Thatcher was the British Prime Minister there was a armed conflict in the Falklands.
À l'époque où Margaret Thatcher était premier ministre britannique, il y eut un conflit armé aux Malouines.

In relation to the South East of England there are very few people in the Hebrides in Scotland.
Par rapport au Sud-est de l'Angleterre il y a très peu de gens aux Hébrides en Écosse.

GROUP B

The novel *Wuthering Heights* takes place in the Yorkshire moors.
Le roman « Les Hauts de Hurlevent » se passe dans les landes de Yorkshire.

During the First World War there was terrible fighting in Flanders.
Pendant la Première Guerre mondiale, de terribles combats se sont déroulés dans les Flandres.

My uncle is an officer and at present he is in the Balkans.
Mon oncle est officier et il se trouve actuellement dans les Balkans.

ANSWER

So, all the countries and regions in both groups have in common the fact that they are in the plural. Those in group a, taking *aux*, are independent countries *or* groups of islands. Those in group b are continental geographical regions which are not countries.

1.28 Do I say *aux* or *dans les*, when I mean 'to' with countries and regions which have plural names like 'The Netherlands'?

The pattern that you are looking for here is related to the geographical shape of the country or region in each group.

GROUP A

In the past French seafarers used to go to the Cormoros to look for spices.
Autrefois les navigateurs français allaient aux Comores pour chercher des épices.

And other sailors went as far as the Philippines to look for exotic wood from tropical forests.
Et d'autres navigateurs allaient jusqu'aux Philippines pour en ramener des bois exotiques des forêts tropicales.

GROUP B

If you want to go to France's southwest frontier, you have to go to the Pyrenees.
Si on veut aller à la frontière sud-ouest de la France, il faut se rendre dans les Pyrénées.

After her trial, *Thérèse Desqueyroux,* in Mauriac's novel, must go back to the Landes.
Après son procès, « Thérèse Desqueyroux », dans le roman de Mauriac, doit retourner dans les Landes.

ANSWER

This was the really unusual pattern where those in group a, taking *aux*, are independent countries *or* groups of islands. Those in group b are continental geographical regions, which are not independent countries.

1.29   What is difference between *en plus* and *de plus*?

Can you see any differences in usage between the use of *en plus* and *de plus* in the sentences below?

GROUP A

Jean: mum, I forgot to tell you that I also lost my glasses in the pond.
Mum: and that on top of everything!
Jean: maman, j'ai oublié de te dire que j'ai aussi perdu mes lunettes dans l'étang.
Maman: et ça en plus!

On top of her studies in engineering, she works twenty hours a week in a city-centre bar.
En plus de ses études d'ingénieur, elle travaille vingt heures par semaine dans un bar du centre-ville.

We were charged two euros fifty extra for an envelope of that size
On nous a demandé deux euros cinquante en plus pour une enveloppe de cette taille.

GROUP B

Adèle is only eleven months older than her brother Jeremy.
Adèle n'a que onze mois de plus que son frère Jeremy.

Come on, you have already eaten two hamburgers, I am not going to by you another one.
Allez, tu as déjà mangé deux hamburgers, je ne t'achèterai pas un de plus.

Furthermore, I think that the second part of this concert was unbearable.
De plus, je trouve que la deuxième partie de ce concert était insupportable.

ANSWER

In group a, the sense of *en plus* is excess and a step too far. In group b, the examples have an element of comparison with a number or a quantity which came before. The final example in group b is a set phrase.

1.30   How do I say 'to remember': *se rappeler* or *se souvenir de*?

Look at the two groups of examples below and see if the doing word is being used in different types of situations.

GROUP A

Mum, do you remember your first boyfriend?
Maman, est-ce que tu te souviens de ton premier petit ami?

Yes, now I remember who you are talking about now.
Oui, maintenant je me souviens de qui tu parles.

I only vaguely remember my grandmother.
Je ne me souviens que vaguement de ma grand-mère.

GROUP B

Remind me of your name please.
Rappelez-moi votre nom, s'il vous plaît.

They will always remember that their father left them.
Ils se rappelleront toujours que leur père les a quittés.

Do you remember Vanessa Paradis's first hit?
Vous rappelez-vous le premier tube de Vanessa Paradis?

ANSWER

Se souvenir de is mainly used for persons. Whereas *se rappeler* stands on its own without *à* or *de* and is used for things, events and times.

1.31   What is the difference between *rendre visite à* and *visiter*?

Have a look at the examples in group a and b below. Here there is a difference in the meaning between the type of 'visiting' in French?

GROUP A

As soon as we arrive in a new town in France, my grandfather wants to visit all the museums.
Dès que nous arrivons dans une nouvelle ville en France, mon grand-père veut visiter tous les musées.

Living in Oxford you have probably been able to visit London on several occasions.
Habitant Oxford vous avez pu sans doute visiter Londres à plusieurs reprises? (FORMAL)

GROUP B

Guy, when I move into a larger house, you will be able to visit me, ok?
Guy, quand j'emménagerai dans une maison plus grande, tu pourras me rendre visite, d'accord?

In view of his state of health, you have to visit him at least twice a week.
Vu son état de santé, il faut que tu lui rendes visite au moins deux fois par semaine.

ANSWER

So here it depends if you are visiting people or places. In group a *visiter* is used with places and *rendre visite à* is used with people.

1.32 When to I use *offrir* and when *donner*, meaning to 'give'?

Take a look at the sentences in the groups below and see if you can distinguish a difference in the meaning of 'to give' between group a and group b?

GROUP A

Give me a glass of red, please. (INFORMAL)
Donne-moi un verre de rouge, s'il te plaît. (INFORMAL)

He gave him the money in his pocket.
Il lui a donné l'argent dans sa poche.

GROUP B

My colleagues gave me a holiday in Greece for my fiftieth birthday.
Mes collègues m'ont offert un voyage en Grèce pour mes cinquante ans.

To mark your departure from our company, allow me to give you a small gift.
À l'occasion de votre départ de notre entreprise, permettez-moi de vous offrir un petit cadeau.

ANSWER

Group a has sentences with a generalised use of 'give'; whereas the sentences in group b relate to a special type of giving, that of presents. So, as soon as there is a mention of a gift, get ready to use *offrir*, instead of *donner*.

1.33 When do I use *dépenser* and when *passer*, meaning 'to spend'?

The French words for 'to spend' in the groups are clearly different from each other; how?

GROUP A
I spent too much money during the Christmas holidays!
J'ai dépensé trop d'argent pendant les vacances de Noël!

How much money do you spend each week to buy clothes?
Combien d'argent dépenses-tu chaque semaine pour acheter des vêtements?

GROUP B
'Will you be coming to spend the Christmas holidays with us?' mum asked me.
"Est-ce que tu viendras passer les vacances de Noël avec nous?" me demanda maman.

Yesterday, I spent four hours on the trot at the local bar.
Hier, j'ai passé quatre heures de suite au bar du coin.

ANSWER

This is quite a simple one. Group a with *dépenser* refers to spending money and group b with *passer* concerns spending time.

1.34   What is the difference between *la langue* and *le langage*?

Can you discern the differences in meaning between the examples in group a and group b below?

GROUP A

I find it brilliant that you speak three languages fluently.
Je trouve ça génial que tu parles trois langues couramment.

Oh, French, I have been studying this language for six years and I still make grammatical mistakes.
Ah, le français, voilà six ans que j'étudie cette langue et je fais encore des fautes de grammaire.

GROUP B

During my year in France, I had to familiarise myself with administrative language.
Pendant mon année en France j'ai dû me familiariser avec le langage administratif.

The new professor is constantly taking in journalistic language.
Le nouveau professeur parle sans cesse dans un langage journalistique.

ANSWER

Group a refers to the whole of a national language in the sense of a national tongue belonging to a particular people; they are language blocks. In group b you see smaller subdivisions of language in which the speaker does not need to refer to nation. These groups concerns particular professions and spheres of life. So, *la langue* is wider, larger and more diverse than the more specialised and narrow *langage*. However, because we are dealing with language and not mathematics, there are a few exceptions which have to be learned as fixed expressions. They are subdivisions of language, so you would expect *langage* to be use, but, in fact, they are written with *langue*. They are: 'mother tongue' = *langue maternelle*, '(the) French (language)' = *la langue de Molière* and 'the same old phrases' = *langue de bois*.

1.35 What is the difference between *tu* and *vous*, meaning 'you'?

Can you sketch out hints for usage after looking at the use of *tu* and *vous* in the sentences in groups a and b below.

GROUP A

Come, come here my little kitty, you are <u>my</u> little cat. Oh you are a beautiful cat!
Viens, viens ici mon petit minou, tu es mon petit chat à moi. Oh, comme tu es un beau chat!

Ok, shall we use the *tu*-word to each other? Yes by all means James. So, are you coming into town with me this evening?
Bon, on se tutoie..? Oui, volontiers James. Alors tu viens en ville avec moi se soir?

Take great care about what you say to me Claire, I am the older sister.
Fais très attention à ce que tu me dis Claire, je suis l'aînée.

GROUP B

Jack, let me introduce you to M. Jolin who is the new accountant.
Jacques, je vous présente M. Jolin qui est le nouvel agent comptable.

But you are going to leave now. Who is going to leave, mum? You and your father, my sweet.
Mais vous allez partir maintenant. Qui va partir, maman? Toi et ton père, mon chou.

Welcome to our company Mr. Legendre and allow me to have you shown around the premises.
Soyez le bienvenu dans notre entreprise Monsieur Legendre et permettez-moi de vous faire faire le tour des locaux.

ANSWER

Tu is used for family, friends and animals and *vous* for every one else. So much for the distinction between *tu* and *vous,* when speaking to individuals; however, it is important to remember that when speaking to more than one person, you use *vous,* even if you call them *tu* when addressing them alone. So, if you are in the world of work, you will use *vous* with most of the people with whom you speak. And if someone is introduced to you with their job title, this is a signal that you will continue your conversation using *vous.* This is different from student life, where everyone is considered part of a group and so, generally speaking, the older you are, the fewer people you will call *tu.*

2

There are three ways of saying something in French, where there is only one in English

2.1 How do I say 'before': *avant, avant de* or *avant que*?

How do I say 'before' in French? In each of the three groups below, can you see any difference in what follows the word 'before'?

GROUP A

I congratulate you. You came before me.
Je te félicite. Tu es arrivée avant moi.

Do you think that anybody has visited this place before us?
Croyez-vous que quelqu'un ait visité cet endroit avant nous?

We definitely have to sort out this business before you leave.
Il faut absolument qu'on règle cette affaire avant ton départ.

GROUP B

You have to train on the beach before going windsurfing in the sea.
Il faut s'entraîner sur la plage avant de faire de la planche à voile en mer.

That's strange. You have to pay for your drinks before sitting down. (INFORMAL)
Voilà quelque chose de bizarre! Il faut payer ses boissons avant de s'asseoir. (INFORMAL)

GROUP C

Please tell him that before he leaves.
Dites-le lui, s'il vous plaît, avant qu'il ne parte.

The prime ministers are going to have discussions before a crisis breaks out between both countries. (FORMAL)
Les premiers ministres vont s'entretenir avant qu'une crise n'éclate entre les deux pays. (FORMAL)

ANSWER

GROUP A

So, *avant* by itself is the most common and shortest way of saying 'before'. The portion of the sentence which follows it is frequently short, sometimes only a word or two long.

GROUP B

This second way of saying 'before' *avant de* is followed by the form of the French doing word that is found first in dictionaries (the infinitive); for example often followed by a phrase with a naming and a doing word.

GROUP C

This way of saying 'before' *avant que* plus subjunctive is followed by more details than the second. For example: a distinguishable person or idea performing an action. This way of saying 'before' is also much more formal and so is found more frequently in written rather than spoken French; it is useful if you want to give your French a touch of class. The main doing word is followed by a single *ne*. This is not a negative, but points to the state that the speaker wants to maintain <u>before</u> it is too late.

2.2   Do I use *que, jusque* or *jusqu'à ce que*, meaning 'until'?

How do we say 'until' in French? How do differences in the doing words in the sentences influence the translation of 'until'?

GROUP A

We are going to wait for her to tell us the truth.
Nous allons attendre qu'elle nous dise la vérité.

He waited until his children had grown up before going to work abroad.
Il a attendu que ses enfants soient adultes avant d'aller travailler à l'étranger.

Do you think that Paul is going to wait until we are back?
Tu crois que Paul va attendre que nous soyons de retour?

GROUP B

He continued to refuse our help until the last moment.
Il a continué à refuser notre aide jusqu'au dernier moment.

We danced until the early hours.
Nous avons dansé jusqu'à l'aube.

Until now my teacher hasn't made any objection…
Jusqu'à maintenant mon professeur n'a rien trouvé à redire…

GROUP C

We are going to stay here until you have finished this task.
Nous allons rester ici jusqu'à ce que tu aies terminé cette tâche.

He struck the door until it gave way. (FORMAL)
Il a donné de violents coups sur la porte jusqu'à ce qu'elle cédât. (FORMAL)

ANSWER

GROUP A

The most important thing to remember is that 'to wait until' is just *attendre que* plus subjunctive. This shortest form probably came about because we say 'wait until' so often and longer forms would simply be too clumsy.

GROUPS B AND C

The other two ways of saying 'until' are longer – they have more letters! The second way is *jusque* which is followed by a naming word. If you look at group c, the longest (and most complicated) way of saying until (*jusqu'à ce que* plus subjunctive) you will find that that is followed by whole phrases (with a naming and a doing word). Those phrases, just like the examples in group one are invited by the free-standing *que*.

So you can also think about 'until' in terms of a flow chart. Here's what you do if you have an English sentence with 'until' to translate into French:

- Is 'until' followed by a whole phrase (with a doing <u>and</u> a naming word)?

- If yes, then the phrase following 'until' will be in the subjunctive.

- If no, the answer is *jusque.*

- Is the doing word in question 'to wait until'?

- If yes, the answer is *attendre que?*

- If no, the answer is *jusqu'à ce que* plus the subjunctive.

2.3   How do I say 'ago': *il y a, voilà* or *voici*?

There is no difference of meaning between the three groups here and the three ways of saying 'ago' are used in the same contexts. However, remember to be on the look out for sentences like those in group b and c as they are rarer.

GROUP A

Jacques Miller won his first international competition ten years ago.
Jacques Miller a gagné son premier concours international il y a dix ans.

Two years ago my family were still living in Tunis.
Il y a deux ans ma famille habitait encore Tunis.

How long ago did you start your German course?
Vous avez commencé votre cours d'allemand, il y a combien de temps?

GROUP B

He began to learn how to ski two and a half years ago.
Il a commencé à apprendre à faire du ski voilà deux ans et demi.

I broke my leg two months ago and I am still limping a little bit.
Je me suis cassé la jambe voilà deux mois et je boîte encore un tout petit peu.

GROUP C

Audrey's grandfather passed away two years ago, but she misses him a lot.
Le grand-père d'Audrey est décédé voici deux ans mais il lui manque beaucoup.

The Saragongs invaded this country two centuries ago.
Les Saragongs ont envahi ce pays voici deux siècles.

Also try to use the types of sentences in groups b and c as an alternative to *il y a* when it might cause confusion.

2.4   How do I express measurements in French?

How do you express measurements in French? For instance, what are the possible ways of saying: 'the swimming pool is twenty five metres long?'

GROUP A
Listen, I know that the swimming pool is twenty five metres long.
Écoutez, je sais que la piscine est longue de vingt-cinq mètres.

On Saturdays the queue in front of the club is two hundred metres long. (INFORMAL)
Le samedi la file d'attente devant la boîte est longue de deux cent mètres. (INFORMAL)

In our garden we have trees which are more than six metres tall.
Dans notre jardin nous avons des arbres qui sont hauts de six mètres.

The ribbon is three centimetres wide.
Le ruban est épais de trois centimètres.

GROUP B
Simon says that the swimming pool is twenty five metres long.
Simon dit que la piscine fait vingt-cinq mètres de long.

Margaret's boyfriend is more than two and a half metres tall.
Le petit ami de Marguerite fait plus de deux mètres et demi.

The river is almost one kilometre wide.
Le fleuve fait presque un kilomètre de large.

GROUP C
The swimming pool is twenty five metres long, isn't it?

La piscine a vingt-cinq mètres de long, n'est-ce pas?

Are you sure that the Eiffel Tower is over five hundred metres high?
Es-tu sûr que la Tour Eiffel a plus de cinq cents mètres de hauteur?

At the port of Liverpool the river Mersey is more than five metres deep.
Dans port de Liverpool la Mersey a une profondeur de plus de cinq mètres.

ANSWER

It's a case of three alternatives which mean the same here and it was the doing word which varies in each of the groups. The way to express measurements which is closest to English is by using *être* – the examples in group a, but if you do it in that way you have to make the describing word agree with the thing which is being measured: *longue* agrees with *piscine*.

In group b *faire* is used with *de* and there is no need to change the describing word to match the naming word if it is feminine or plural or both.

The most complicated way is in group b where *avoir* is used in three related ways (perhaps you could use one of the other ways instead). The first sentence in that group has a similar form to those in group b, but you have to bear in mind that you cannot use the describing words *profond* and *épais* in this way with *avoir*. Instead, the naming words used in the second and third sentences in group c are *hauteur* and *profondeur*. The second sentence put the numerical measurement before the naming word and the third sentence puts it afterwards with *de*.

— —

2.5   With a doing word do I say *tout, toute,* or *toutes?*

In both English and French words which describe doing words don't usually change at all. For example: 'he definitely does not sing quietly', *doucement*. Or 'Get a move on Claude; you have to walk quickly' *vite*. However, there are three ways of using the word *tout* in French which correspond to the word 'completely' in English. Look at the groups of examples below and see if you can puzzle out why *tout* stays the same (in Group a) and why it adds an 'e' (in the Group b) or 'es' (in Group c).

GROUP A
That evening Hugh was completely nervous.
Ce soir-là Hugh était tout nerveux.

This little girl is completely impertinent.
Cette petite fille est tout impertinente.

Estelle is entirely happy about it.
Estelle en est tout heureuse.

Even the soldiers were completely moved by the film.
Même les soldats étaient tout émus par le film.

GROUP B
On learning the news Patricia was completely joyful.
En apprenant la nouvelle Patricia était toute joyeuse.

Look, Sandra is completely pale.
Regardez, Sandra est toute pâle.

GROUP C

Why are these women completely naked in front of the camera?
Pourquoi ces femmes sont-elles toutes nues devant la caméra?

Ginette and Marie were completely disappointed this time.
Ginette et Marie étaient toutes déçues cette fois.

ANSWER

Imagine the options as if they were a flow chart. First check whether the French word for 'completely' comes before a describing word starting with 'a', 'e', 'i', 'o', 'u' and some words starting with 'h' (see 8.4). If that is the case, then there is no agreement, there is no change. That is the usual case for words which describe doing words in French and in English and applies to the examples in Group a where you have *tout* with masculine singulars, masculine plurals, feminine singular and feminine plurals. The fun starts when you have not a vowel, but a consonant (all letters in the alphabet <u>except</u> 'a', 'i', 'e', 'o', 'u' and 'h' in French). If the *tout* comes before a consonant which is also masculine there is no change, just like in the first example in Group a.

However, if it comes before a consonant in a sentence which is centred around a female singular *tout* adds an 'e' to become *toute* (as in all the examples in Group b above). This means that the resulting *toute* is agreeing with the feminine person or thing acting in the sentence.

Also, if it comes before a consonant in a sentence which is centred around a female plural *tout* adds 'es' to become *toutes* (as in the examples in Group c above) This means that the resulting *toutes* is agreeing with the feminine plural people or things in the sentence.

2.6   Do I use *ce, cette* or *cet,* meaning 'this'?

See if you can work out what determines the choice of word in French.

GROUP A
This CD is brilliant! (INFORMAL)
Ce CD est génial! (INFORMAL)

This guy dances well. (INFORMAL)
Ce type danse bien. (INFORMAL)

GROUP B
Do you know this song?
Est-ce que tu connais cette chanson?

There is an unbearable smell in this bedroom!
Il y a une odeur insupportable dans cette chambre!

This introduction is worth absolutely nothing.
Cette introduction ne vaut absolument rien.

GROUP C
This example confirms my suspicions.
Cet exemple confirme mes soupçons.

This man is annoying me.
Cet homme m'agace.

May I stop this interview now? (FORMAL)
Puis-je arrêter cet entretien maintenant? (FORMAL)

ANSWER

There are three options:

Group a: *ce* is used for words which take *le* and begin with consonants (all other letters apart from a, e, i, o u).

Group b: *cette* is used for all words which take *la*.

Group c *cet* is used for words which both take *le* and which begin with "a', 'e', 'i', 'o', or 'u'.

Words beginning with the letter 'h' are a special case (see point 8.4); those which take *la* belong to Group b and there is nothing surprising about that (for example:

cette haine and *cette hache* and *cette honte*). However, there are two possibilities for those which are masculine; *cet* is used for most of them, for example *l'homme* becomes *cet homme* because 'h' is partly considered as a vowel and so they belong in group c. However, but there is also a group beginning with 'h' which is written with the full *le*, making them belong to group a. In this case *le haschisch* becomes *ce haschisch*, *le hasard* become *ce hasard*. Other masculine words which belong to this category are: *le hibou* (the owl), *le hautbois* (the oboe), *le hamac* and *le havre* (the harbour).

2.7   When do I use *demander* on its own, then *demander à* or *demander de*?

In the sentences in the groups below, it is what the words following *demander* refer to which determines what (if anything) follows it.

GROUP A

Go on, ask for another bowl of soup.
Vas-y, demande encore un bol de soupe.

In this situation most reasonable people only ask for peace.
Dans cette situation la plupart des gens raisonnables ne demandent que la paix.

Driving for long periods on motorways requires a lot of concentration.
Conduire longtemps sur les autoroutes demande beaucoup de concentration.

GROUP B

Janine is always asking to go out.
Janine demande à sortir tout le temps.

During the karaoké evening David didn't ask to sing.
Pendant la soirée karaoké David n'a pas demandé à chanter.

I only ask to glimpse my favourite singer.
Je ne demande qu'à entrevoir mon chanteur préféré.

GROUP C

Madeleine asked them to come and see her.
Madeleine leur a demandé de venir la voir.

I asked Jacques to bring a winebox to the party this evening.
J'ai demandé à Jacques d'apporter un cubitainer à la fête ce soir.

It's not worth asking your boss to be able to bring your dog into work.
Ce n'est pas la peine de demander à ton chef de pouvoir amener ton chien au travail.

ANSWER

In group a *demander* is followed by a direct reference to a thing; in group b *demander* is followed by and refers to a doing word. In group c *demander* refers to a person first (the person comes after it) and then to a doing word.

2.8   When saying 'for' in relation to time in French, do I use *depuis, pendant* or *pour*?

Have a look at the sentences below and compare the different types of time period in order to try to work out which word for 'for' to use.

GROUP A
I have been working here for seven years.
Je travaille ici depuis sept ans.

I have been living in a hall of residence for three years. I have had enough of it.
J'habite dans une résidence universitaire depuis trois ans. Et j'en ai assez.

GROUP B
For two years she tried to save her marriage.
Elle a essayé pendant deux années de sauver son mariage.

The firefighters battled against the flames for nearly twenty four hours.
Les pompiers ont lutté contre les flammes pendant presque vingt-quatre heures.

We will be on holiday for a week in total.
Nous serons en vacances pendant une semaine en tout.

GROUP C
What? You are going to go to France for ten months!
Quoi? Vous allez partir en France pour dix mois!

ANSWER

The different types of time relate to continuity and to whether the time period was 'sealed' with an expression of time, or whether there was a projection into the future. In group a there is continuity for an indefinite time period because you use *depuis* when the state of affairs described in the sentence is still going on. In group b the time period is clearly marked by an expression of time and the sentences emphasise the full duration of the time period. In group c, there is a projection into the future; these sentences refer to people's intentions for blocks of future time.

2.9   How do I say 'to' when referring to towns and cities?

How do we translate 'to' when referring to towns and cities in French?

GROUP A

Once I went from Dover to Canterbury on foot.
Une fois je suis allé de Douvres à Cantobéry à pied.

Have you ever been to La Rochelle, Madam?
Avez-vous eu l'occasion d'aller à La Rochelle, Madame?

His/her lawyers would have had to go to The Hague.
Ses avocats auraient dû aller à La Haye.

You want to go to Vera Cruz? (INFORMAL).
Tu veux aller à la Vera Cruz? (INFORMAL).

Lenin never went to Havana.
Lénine n'est jamais allé à La Havane.

We are going to Amsterdam this weekend.
On va à Amsterdam ce week-end.

His/her parents moved from New York to Seattle.
Ses parents ont déménagé de New York à Seattle.

There is a famous rally which goes from Paris to Dakar.
Il existe un célèbre rallye qui va de Paris à Dakar.

GROUP B

This ship is definitely going to Cairo.
Ce bateau va certainement au Caire.

Can I take the boat from Portsmouth to Le Havre?
Est-ce que je peux prendre le bateau pour aller de Portsmouth au Havre?

Gerard had to enquire to find out if there was a flight to Cape Town that afternoon.
Gérard devait se renseigner pour savoir s'il y avait un vol pour Le Cap cet après-midi.

GROUP C
The Chamberlain family go to Les Andelys every summer.
La famille Chamberlain va aux Andelys tous les étés.

Our mother goes to Les Arcs every year to see her female cousin.
Notre mère va aux Arcs tous les ans pour voir sa cousine.

ANSWER

GROUP A
In the vast majority of cases it is just *à*, followed by the name of the town or city, this also applies when the name of the town begins with *la* as in the case of *La Rochelle*.

GROUP B
There are a few towns and cities whose names begin with *le* in French, such as *Le Caire* (Cairo). In these cases, *au*, the usual combination of *à* and *le* is used. When the city is just mentioned by itself, without a reference to 'to', a capital letter is used: *Le Caire*.

GROUP C
There are even fewer towns and cities whose names are preceded by *les* in French. As you would expect the combination *aux* is used to translate 'to' in these cases.

Did you know that...? So that passengers in French railway stations do not confuse the short words *à* and *de* (and to maintain a level of formality), trains going to a specific place are frequently referred to as: *le train à destination de...* (while trains coming from a specific place are announced as: *le train en provenance de...*)

2.10   After doing words, do I have *à* or *de* or nothing at all?

'I help grandmother to walk', 'Emma refuses to own up' and 'Jacqueline likes to sing'. In all three of these phrases the English doing words 'help', 'refuses' and 'likes' are accompanied by 'to' alone. However, their counterparts in French: *aider, refuser* and *aimer* are followed by <u>either</u> à, <u>or</u> de <u>or</u> nothing at all? How can we know which word, if any, follows which doing word? Look at the groups of examples below; can you find a general thematic point in common between the sentences in Group a and then contrast it to those in Group b?

GROUP A

Doctor Dubarry helped me to walk after my accident.
Le docteur Dubarry m'a aidé à marcher après mon accident. *(aider à)*

I think that you are going to pass your exams.
Je crois que tu vas réussir à tes examens. *(réussir à)*

Remember, it was me who encouraged you to apply.
Souviens-toi, c'est moi qui t'ai encouragé à poser ta candidature. *(encourager à)*

Watch out! I'm very fond of those old singles!
Fais attention! Je tiens beaucoup à ces vieux 45 tours! *(tenir à)*

The old ladies enjoyed themselves looking at the volleyball players
on the beach.
Les vieilles dames se plaisaient à regarder les joueurs de volley-ball sur la plage. *(se plaire à)*

The old men enjoyed themselves looking at the women who were dancing.
Les vieillards s'amusaient à regarder les femmes qui dansaient. *(s'amuser à)*

I have finally managed to work hard.
Je suis enfin parvenu à travailler dur. *(parvenir à)*

Last night I finally managed to communicate my feelings to him/her.
Hier soir je suis enfin arrivé à lui dire quels étaient mes sentiments. *(arriver à)*

I consent to invite Paul although I am not fond of him. (FORMAL)
Je consens à inviter Paul bien que je ne tienne pas à lui. (FORMAL) *(consentir à)*

There we are Paul, I am inviting you to join us this time.
Voilà Paul, je t'invite à nous rejoindre cette fois. *(inviter à)*

Kamal is going to teach you to ride.
Kamal va t'apprendre à monter à cheval. *(apprendre à)*

In the army I was taught to do very long marches.
Dans l'armée on m'a entraîné à faire de très longues marches. *(entraîner à)*

Isn't this proof enough to convince you?
Cette preuve ne suffit-t-elle pas à vous convaincre? *(suffire à)*

I am going to work at singing that tune well.
Je vais travailler à bien chanter cet air.   *(travailler à)*

Do you persist in believing that piece of news? (FORMAL)
Persistez-vous à croire cette information-là? (FORMAL)   *(persister à)*

Mr. Kalu is always trying to please me. That's very nice of him.
Monsieur Kalu cherche toujours à me plaire. C'est très gentil de sa part.   *(chercher à)*

This company excels in building underground railways.
Cette entreprise excelle à construire des métros.   *(exceller à)*

I expect to see the results of your efforts.
Je m'attends à voir les résultats de tes efforts.   *(s'attendre à)*

At this moment I am preparing to face reality.
En ce moment je me prépare à faire face à la réalité.   *(faire face à)*

The poor little boy was doing his utmost to explain the accident before
the court. (FORMAL)
Le pauvre petit s'évertuait à expliquer l'accident devant la cour. (FORMAL)   *(s'évertuer à)*

Nobody is authorised to smoke in this room. (FORMAL)
Personne n'est autorisé à fumer dans cette salle. (FORMAL)   *(autoriser à)*

This tennis racket belongs to my brother Khaled.
Cette raquette de tennis appartient à mon frère Khaled.   *(appartenir à)*

Yes, ok. Now I am beginning to understand the difficulty of
your position.
Oui d'accord. Maintenant je commence à comprendre la difficulté
de votre situation.   *(commencer à)*

GROUP B

Our department is going to complain about your behaviour in this
matter. (FORMAL)
Notre section va se plaindre de votre comportement dans cette affaire.   *(se plaindre de)*
(FORMAL)

The drunk threatened to hit me on the head.
L'ivrogne a menacé de me frapper sur la tête.   *(menacer de)*

The member of staff at the ticket window flatly refused to give
me information.
L'agent au guichet a carrément refusé de me renseigner.   *(refuser de)*

Yes, that's right; I am accusing you of having stolen my money.
Oui, c'est ça, je vous accuse de m'avoir volé mon argent.   *(accuser de)*

I regret being a witness to the death of your uncle. (FORMAL)
Je regrette d'avoir été le témoin du décès de Monsieur votre oncle. (FORMAL)   *(regretter de)*

Darling, you forgot to flush the loo. (INFORMAL)
Chérie, tu as oublié de tirer la chasse d'eau. (INFORMAL)   *(oublier de)*

The president neglected to inform the government of the measures taken. (FORMAL)
Le président a négligé d'informer le gouvernement des mesures prises. (FORMAL)   *(négliger de)*

Frankly, I am scared of trusting him with my secret.
Franchement, j'ai peur de lui confier mon secret.   *(avoir peur de)*

In the desert the adventurer did without all the usual comforts.
Dans le désert l'explorateur s'est passé de tout le confort habituel.   *(se passer de)*

Do you really suspect her of cheating on her husband for two years?
Tu la soupçonnes vraiment d'avoir trompé son mari pendant deux ans?   *(soupçonner de)*

I blame you for having made an error preparing this order. (FORMAL)
Je vous reproche d'avoir fait une erreur dans la préparation de cette commande. (FORMAL)   *(reprocher de)*

Lilian had to apologise for vomiting in the sink yesterday evening.
Liliane devrait s'excuser d'avoir vomi dans l'évier hier soir.   *(s'excuser de)*

I think that the baby needs to drink now.
Je crois que le bébé a besoin de boire maintenant.   *(avoir besoin de)*

Coming back after the holidays I am afraid of not regaining my natural rhythm.
À mon retour des vacances je crains de ne pas retrouver mon rythme habituel.   *(craindre de)*

Gentlemen, I order you to give up the guilty person to me. (FORMAL)
Messieurs, je vous commande de me livrer le coupable. (FORMAL)   *(commander de)*

Gentlemen, I order you to give up the guilty person to me. (FORMAL)
Messieurs, je vous charge de me livrer le coupable. (FORMAL)   *(charger de)*

Gentlemen, I order you to give up the guilty person to me. (FORMAL)
Messieurs, je vous ordonne de me livrer le coupable. (FORMAL)   *(ordonner de)*

I avoid working too much in the heat.
J'évite de trop travailler par temps chaud.   *(éviter de)*

The children laughed at the bizarre appearance of the clown.
Les enfants ont ri de l'air bizarre du clown.   *(rire de)*

The bouncers prevented us from entering the 'Planet Earth' nightclub last night. (INFORMAL)
Les videurs nous ont empêché d'entrer au Planet Earth hier soir. (INFORMAL)   *(empêcher de)*

The bouncers said that we couldn't go into the 'Planet Earth' nightclub
last night. (INFORMAL)
Les videurs nous ont interdit d'entrer au Planet Earth hier soir. (INFORMAL)   *(interdire de)*

Have you ever pretended to be ill during your career?
As-tu jamais fait semblant d'être malade lorsque tu travaillais?   *(faire semblant de)*

Murielle pretends to sleep when Maurice comes home late stinking
of alcohol.
Murielle feint de dormir quand Maurice rentre tard puant l'alcool   *(feint de)*

Do you doubt the faithfulness of your lover? (FORMAL)
Doutez-vous de la fidélité de votre amant(e)? (FORMAL)   *(douter de)*

Jules, if you drive like that you risk causing an accident.
Jules, si tu conduis comme ça tu risques de causer un accident.   *(risquer de)*

Are you going to stop whining! (INFORMAL)
Vas-tu cesser de pleurnicher! (INFORMAL)   *(cesser de)*

Come on dad, when are you going to get rid of that old hat?
Écoute papa, quand est-ce que tu vas te débarrasser de ce vieux chapeau?   *(se débarrasser de)*

Why does she always want me to be suspicious about Robert's promises?
Pourquoi est-ce qu'elle veut toujours que je me méfie des promesses de Robert?   *(se méfier de)*

Ah you are only seventeen years old. I suspected as much.
Ah, vous n'avez que dix-sept ans? Je m'en doutais.   *(se douter de)*

Well, you are making fun of me there, aren't you? (INFORMAL)
Bon, là vous vous moquez de moi, n'est-ce pas? (INFORMAL)   *(se moquer de)*

I know her, Simone always exploits the kindness of her friends.
Moi je la connais. Simone abuse toujours de la gentillesse des ses amis.   *(abuser de)*

The pirates wanted to seize our boat.
Les pirates voulaient s'emparer de notre navire.   *(s'emparer de)*

It was hilarious. The priest went to the wrong door, twice. (INFORMAL)
C'était trop marrant. Le curé il s'est trompé de porte deux fois. (INFORMAL)   *(se tromper de)*

GROUP C

He's a man who likes telling stories.
C'est un homme qui aime raconter des histoires.   *(aimer)*

Me, go out? I prefer to stay at home and knit. (INFORMAL)
Moi, Sortir? J'aime mieux rester à la maison à tricoter. (INFORMAL)   *(aimer mieux)*

How can you prefer to knit? We're going into town, come with us.
Comment peux-tu préférer tricoter? On sort en ville, viens avec nous.   *(préférer)*

It's obvious this family should complain to the police.
Il est évident, cette famille devrait aller à la police pour déposer plainte.   *(devoir)*

This team dared to break into a bank during the night.
Cette équipe a osé attaquer une banque pendant la nuit.   *(oser)*

'I have always desired to know your opinion on this subject' he declared.
(FORMAL)
'J'ai toujours désiré connaître votre opinion sur ce sujet' déclara-t-il. (FORMAL)   *(désirer)*

This customer wants to be in London before midday, shall we have the
helicopter called out?
Ce client veut être à Londres avant midi, on fait appeler l'hélicoptère?   *(vouloir)*

Jack hopes to be able to win the gold medal at the next Olympic Games.
Jacques espère pouvoir gagner la médaille d'or aux prochains Jeux Olympiques.   *(espérer)*

Come and see me this evening, cutie. (INFORMAL)
Viens me voir ce soir, mignonne. (INFORMAL)   *(venir)*

I am going to do the shopping tomorrow.
Je vais faire les courses demain.   *(aller)*

I beg you sir, let me go. (FORMAL)
Je vous en prie, Monsieur, laissez-moi partir. (FORMAL)   *(laisser)*

What do you count on doing/expect to do during the summer holidays?
Qu'est-ce tu comptes faire pendant les grandes vacances?   *(compter)*

The tightrope walker nearly fell right at the start of his act.
Le funambule a failli tomber juste au début de son numéro.   *(faillir)*

He claims to be a good skier.
Il prétend être un bon skieur.   *(prétendre)*

Can you/do you know how to play the piano?
Savez-vous jouer du piano?   *(savoir)*

That man! he adores being worshipped by the audience.
Celui-là, il adore être adulé par le public.   *(adorer)*

Chloé hates doing the dishes.
Chloë déteste faire la vaisselle.   *(détester)*

He seems not to be intelligent enough to go to the lycée.
Il semble ne pas être assez intelligent pour aller au lycée.   *(sembler)*

Here is one of my basic principles: one has to always tell the truth.
Voilà un de mes principes fondamentaux: il faut toujours dire la vérité.   *(falloir)*

Zoë, listen to me, it's better not to go there.
Zoé, écoute-moi, il vaut mieux ne pas y aller.   *(valoir mieux)*

I don't care; you can do what you want. (INFORMAL)

Cela m'est égal. Tu peux faire ce que tu veux. (INFORMAL)   *(pouvoir)*

Oh no! He has sent Melissa to look for the customers. She will never find them.

Ce n'est pas vrai! Il a envoyé Mélissa chercher les clients. Elle ne les trouvera jamais.   *(envoyer)*

ANSWER

GROUP C

The difference is dictated by how the doing words relate to human feeling. Some of them such as *vouloir*, *sembler* and *savoir* are of course very common, so it is advisable to learn them first in their own right as doing words which are followed by nothing.

GROUPS A AND B

There is a tip to help you to remember whether a doing word takes *à* or *de*; doing words followed by *à* are more <u>positive</u> in feeling; many of them are also concerned with actions in the real world. Contrast this with doing words followed by *de* which are more <u>negative</u> in feeling many of them also refer to people's characters. This distinction between <u>positive</u> and <u>negative</u> feeling is best used as a guideline and not as a hard and fast rule. The table below shows the main exceptions which have been sorted according to theme.

Thematic Table of the Main Exceptions to the 'Feeling' Guideline

à	de
• doing words concerned with wasting time: *tarder à, perdre son temps à, hésiter à*	• Many of the exceptions involve doing words in which the person who does the action is in a disadvantaged or subordinate position compared with other people involved in the sentence. *essayer de* *tenter de* *tâcher de* *offrir de* *remercier de* *accepter de* *promettre de* *se contenter de* *féliciter de* *persuader de*
• doing words concerned with harming: *faire mal à, nuire à*	
• another doing word *renoncer à*	• other doing words *mériter de* *jouir de* *choisir de* *rêver de*

2.11   When do I say *penser* on its own, then *penser à* or *penser de*?

What is the difference in meaning between the groups a, b and c below?

GROUP A

Do you really think that they look so stubborn?
Penses-tu vraiment qu'elles ont l'air si têtues?

I think that I will come tomorrow.
Je pense que je viendrai demain.

GROUP B

While I am absent, think of me.
Pendant mon absence, pense à moi.

I can't remember what I was thinking about this morning.
Je ne peux pas me souvenir de ce à quoi j'ai pensé ce matin.

GROUP C

What did they think about the documentary on Northern Ireland?
Qu'est-ce qu'ils ont pensé du reportage sur l'Irlande du Nord?

So Béatrice, what did he think of your essay?
Alors Béatrice, qu'est-ce qu'il a pensé de ta dissertation?

ANSWER

In the sentences in group a, 'think' is being used in a general sense as 'mental processing', the sense of 'what do you think about something'. Whereas in group b it is a case of 'having someone or something in mind'. In group c, the meaning is more precise and could be translated as 'what is your opinion about that matter' and the matter in question usually has some intellectual content.

2.12 When do I say *manquer* on its own, then *manquer à* or *manquer de*?

Look at the groups of sentences below. Can you work out the different combinations of types of words which accompany *manquer*?

GROUP A

I arrived at quarter past nine so I missed the only train going from Westbridge to the airport.
Je suis arrivé à neuf heures et quart donc j'ai manqué le seul train allant de Westbridge à l'aéroport.

Ah Régis, you made me miss the only session of my favourite group: 'The Tykes.'
Ah Régis tu m'a fait manquer la seule séance de mon groupe préféré: 'The Tykes.'

GROUP B

When I went to university, I missed my boyfriend.
Quand je suis allée à l'université mon petit ami m'a manqué.

But when he went to spend a year abroad he didn't miss his parents.
Mais quand il est allé passer une année à l'étranger ses parents ne lui ont pas manqué.

You know Adrienne, I am going to miss you. That is why I am hesitating to go abroad.
Tu sais Adrienne, tu vas me manquer. C'est pour cette raison que j'hésite à partir à l'étranger.

GROUP C

The problem with my new boss, is that he lacks discretion.
Le problème avec mon nouveau chef, c'est qu'il manque de discrétion.

So many of our fellow citizens lack foodstuffs.
Tant de nos concitoyens manquent de vivres.

ANSWER

When you are taking about missing something like as a train because you arrived too late for it, then use *manquer* just with the thing as in group a. When talking about missing someone in French, you put them first in the sentence because they are so important to you. Used in this way, *manquer* is followed by *à*, so if a certain 'he' or 'she' is missing a person called Luc you say *Luc lui manque* and if 'they' are missing Luke, then you say: *Luke leur manque*. So *manquer à* means 'to be missed by' (it is like a passive, see 10.1). In group c you see that *manquer de* has another meaning: 'to lack.'

2.13   When do I use *décider* on its own, then *se décider à* or *décider de*?

Can you find the difference in the type of meaning below which determines whether the doing word in French is followed by *à* and *de*?

GROUP A
He decided that he would not go to the beach.
Il a décidé qu'il n'irait pas à la plage.

Here are the choices and now decide!
Voilà les choix, et maintenant décide!

GROUP B
Barry decided to turn back and to set off towards the chalet again.
Barry décida de faire demi-tour et de repartir vers le chalet.

Deciding whether to do something always takes me a long time.
Décider de faire quelque chose me prend toujours beaucoup de temps.

GROUP C
The party decided to pursue a policy of co-operation with the EU.
Le parti politique s'est décidé à poursuivre une politique de coopération avec l'Union Européenne.

After thinking about it for a long time Bertha decided to leave her uncle's company.
Après y avoir longtemps réfléchi, Berthe s'est décidée à quitter l'entreprise de son oncle.

ANSWER

In group a, 'decide' is being used in a general sense and can include an element of spontaneity which is not found in the examples in the other group. In the sentences in groups b and c, 'decide' is being used in a strong and clear sense of 'to come to a decision about something after some thought', it's a meaning of 'to make one's mind up' about something. Group c is stronger and clearer than group b.

2.14   When do I use *jouer* on its own, then *jouer* à or *jouer de*?

Take a look at the different ways in which *jouer* is used below, look at all the groups and then see if you can decide on the differences between them.

GROUP A

Our children played together for three hours in the park.
Nos enfants ont joué ensemble pendant trois heures dans le jardin public.

Come on Jack, get up and come and play with me!
Allez Jacques, lève-toi et viens jouer avec moi!

GROUP B

Neither Pierre, Paul, nor Patricia are fit enough to play polo.
Ni Pierre, ni Paul, ni Patricia ne sont pas assez en forme pour jouer au polo.

During the winter they play football in the sports centre.
Pendant l'hiver ils jouent au foot au centre sportif.

GROUP C

We spent the whole evening drinking and playing the guitar.
Nous avons passé toute la soirée à boire et à jouer de la guitare.

Can you/do you know how to play the piano?
Savez-vous jouer du piano?

ANSWER

Group a uses *jouer* in a general way, without specifying which game or sport are being played.

Group b uses *jouer à* and refers to specific sports.

Group c uses *jouer de* and is used only for musical instruments.

2.15   How do I say 'worse': *pire, plus mauvais* or *plus mal*?

Can you distinguish the subtly different ways in which each of the three French words for 'worse' is being used?

GROUP A

It is said that the wound that he received this time is worse than the ones he had before.
On dit que la blessure qu'il a reçue cette fois-ci est pire que les précédentes.

Being disturbed two times for the same thing is worse than having to solve all sorts of different problems.
Être dérangé deux fois pour la même chose est pire que d'avoir à résoudre toutes sortes de problèmes différents.

GROUP B

This soup is worse than the one that we were served yesterday.
Cette soupe est plus mauvaise que celle qu'on nous a servie hier.

In my opinion the last opera by this composer is worse that all his other works.
À mon avis le dernier opéra de ce compositeur est plus mauvais que toutes ses autres œuvres.

GROUP C

Now, alas, after my operation, I sing worse than before.
Maintenant, hélas, après mon opération, je chante plus mal qu'auparavant.

After going through this cloud of toxic smoke my sight is worse than before.
Après avoir traversé ce nuage de fumées toxiques je vois plus mal qu'auparavant.

ANSWER

In group a *pire* refers to something that, from the sense of the phrase, you expect is going to be bad anyway!

The keyword is quality in the sentences in group b, *le plus mauvais* relates to the quality of things which can, and perhaps should, be good. In the group c sentences, *plus mal* describes doing words.

2.16 How do I say 'the worst': *le pire, le plus mauvais* or *le plus mal?*

This section is not difficult if you have looked at the previous one!

GROUP A

Having seen the other students in this year I think that this group is simply the worst.
Par rapport aux autres étudiants de cette année je crois que ce groupe est tout simplement le pire.

The worst thing is that he has never recognised his crimes.
Le pire c'est qu'il n'a jamais reconnu ses crimes.

GROUP B

Daddy, at school today I had to eat the worst lasagne in my life!
Papa, à l'école aujourd'hui, j'ai dû manger les plus mauvaises lasagnes de ma vie!

The main striker of Lens had the worst injury of his career as a first division footballer.
L'attaquant principal de Lens a eu la plus mauvaise blessure de sa carrière de footballeur de première division.

GROUP C

Oh it's funny, that's the worst shaped pumpkin that I have ever seen. (INFORMAL)
Oh c'est marrant, c'est la citrouille la plus mal formée que j'aie jamais vue. (INFORMAL)

In this provincial museum you will find the worst painted pictures that I know.
Dans ce musée de province vous trouverez les tableaux les plus mal peints que je connaisse.

ANSWER

The solution can be summarised as follows: *le pire* refers to something, which is going to be bad anyway. *Le plus mauvais* in group b designates an absence of quality and *le plus mal* (in group c) means 'worse', when referring to doing words.

2.17 How do I say 'would' in French?

How can I say 'would' in French? See if you can distinguish three different types of meaning in the groups of examples below.

GROUP A

During the holidays they would go to a nightclub every Saturday.
Pendant les vacances ils allaient chaque samedi en boîte.

During his youth he would get drunk every weekend.
Quand il était jeune il s'enivrait toutes les fins de semaines.

GROUP B

Would you help me to put away the plates? (INFORMAL)
Tu veux m'aider à ranger les assiettes? (INFORMAL)

Would you like me to be an interpreter for you? (FORMAL)
Voulez-vous que je vous serve d'interprète? (FORMAL)

GROUP C

I would really like to know what the boss said during the meeting.
Je voudrais bien savoir ce que le patron a dit pendant la réunion.

I would like to attend the concert, but unfortunately I have got the flu.
J'aimerais assister au concert mais, malheureusement, je suis grippé.

ANSWER

GROUP A

This group of examples concerns habit in the past. In these types of sentences there will always be an indication that a certain action takes place more than once. Examples of this type are sometimes translated by 'used to' instead of 'would.'

GROUP B

This group of examples always refer to 'you' and are requests phrased as questions. In addition, 'would' is the polite form of another word beginning with 'w': that is 'want'. In this case 'would' simply translates the present tense of the doing word 'to want', *vouloir*. Remember that the order of the doing word and the person is reversed in questions and linked with a dash. So from *vous voulez*, you get *voulez-vous?*

GROUP C

The sentences in this group have two parts arranged either side of a central hinge (*ce que* and *mais*) in this case. One of the parts is dependent, that is to say, conditional on the other.

2.18   How do I say 'number': *nombre, numéro* or *chiffre*?

Look at the groups of sentences below, each presents a different way of saying 'number' in French; can you make out the differences in usage?

GROUP A

A fair number of the students do not attend the lectures.
Un bon nombre d'étudiants manquent aux cours magistraux.

But on Monday morning they arrived in large numbers.
Mais le lundi matin ils sont arrivés en grand nombre.

GROUP B

Do you know what number they live at?
Est-ce que vous savez à quel numéro ils habitent?

I possess all the numbers of this journal.
Je possède tous les numéros de cette revue.

GROUP C

I am lost there with your calculations, you have to show me the precise figures.
Là je suis perdu dans tes calculs, il faut me montrer les chiffres précis.

I cannot read the number that you have written on the envelope.
Je ne peux pas lire le chiffre que tu as écrit sur l'enveloppe.

ANSWER

In group a, *nombre* is the general term and refers to the number of things or people seen as a whole, that is to the quantity. In group b with *numéro* the reference is more precise to the individual numbers as they are distinguished from each other in order, one after another. Group c, with *chiffre* is even more precise and contains references to the appearance of the figure 0 to 9 as they are written down.

3

There are four ways of saying something in French, where there is only one in English

3.1 What are the different words used to say 'time': *une fois, une époque, l'heure* or *le temps*?

In the groups below the sentences show you the four different words for 'time' in French. Can you work out the different segments of meaning which each of the words covers?

GROUP A

Yes, it was that time when we were on holiday in Northern Italy...
Oui, c'était cette fois où on était en vacances dans le Nord de l'Italie...

The same type of crisis has occurred many times in the history of our business. (FORMAL)
Une crise du même genre s'est produite maintes fois dans l'histoire de notre entreprise. (FORMAL)

And then the mathematics teacher said: 'Do I have to repeat it to you for the umpteenth time?'
Et ensuite le professeur de mathématiques a dit: 'est-ce que je dois vous le répéter pour la énième fois?'

GROUP B

Oh yes, at that time this port played an important role in world trade. Now all that is over.
Eh oui, à cette époque-là ce port jouait un rôle important dans le commerce mondial. Maintenant tout cela est terminé.

In the Roman era, there was a series of big roads across Europe.
À l'époque romaine, il y avait un réseau de grandes voies à travers l'Europe.

GROUP C

What time is it?
Quelle heure est-il?

It was dinner time in the castle and so the bell was rung.
C'était l'heure du déjeuner au château et donc on a fait sonner la cloche.

GROUP D

Sorry, I won't go into town with you this evening because I really don't have the time.
Désolé je n'irai pas en ville avec toi ce soir parce que je n'ai vraiment pas le temps.

I know a book where a man asks a woman the following question: 'do you have time this evening?'
Je connais un livre où un homme pose à une femme la question suivante: 'vous avez du temps ce soir?'

ANSWER

In group a, *fois* means a specific occasion which is then often counted with numbers, for example: 'I ran round the hill three times more than you', which translates as: *J'ai fait le tour de la colline trois fois plus que toi* and 'three times two are six' *trois fois deux, six*. In group b, *époque* is a historical period of time which is large-scale. In group c, *l'heure* means 'time of day' with an 'o'clock' or another marker such as dinnertime which divides up the day. Finally, in group d, *le temps* means a period of time which is not defined by numbers; it is the most general and frequent word for 'time'. These are the basic fields of meaning which make the four types clear; you will also find a complementary list in a dictionary.

3.2 When do I use four of the different ways of saying 'to make': *faire, rendre, fabriquer, confectionner*?

In French, there are at least four different words which mean 'to make'. Each of the sentences in the groups below show you how their fields of reference are different from each other.

GROUP A

She made her bed every morning before going to school.
Elle a fait son lit chaque matin avant d'aller à l'école.

Jean, take it easy. Don't make any mistakes please.
Jean, vas-y doucement. Ne fais pas d'erreurs s'il te plaît.

GROUP B

This type of town, always deserted during the winter, tends to make me sad.
Ce genre de ville, toujours déserte pendant l'hiver, a tendance à me rendre triste.

We do not promise anything: to make you happier for example.
Nous ne vous promettons rien: de vous rendre plus heureux par exemple.

GROUP C

Yes it really is true, they make weapons in this large building alone on the hill.
Oui c'est bien vrai, on fabrique des armements dans ce grand bâtiment isolé sur la colline.

In the thirties my family owned a factory where toys were made.
Dans les années trente ma famille a possédé une usine où on fabriquait des jouets.

GROUP D

Mr. Bradley was satisfied to be able to go back to London to have his shirts make by hand.
Mr Bradley était satisfait de pouvoir retourner à Londres pour se faire confectionner ses chemises.

Gentlemen, being a master chocolate maker is more than having the talent for making pralines. (FORMAL)
Messieurs, être maître-chocolatier, c'est plus que de posséder le talent de confectionner des pralines. (FORMAL)

ANSWER

The pattern of the French words for 'make' has similarities with that of the words for 'time'. In group a, *faire* resembles *temps* because it is the most general and the most common word. In group b, *rendre* is used with describing words. You can remember it by the following trigger phrase: *tu me rends si triste* which means 'you make me so sad'. In group c, we have objects which are made in factories, whereas in group d, we have things which are made by hand, by craftsmen and women.

3.3   What are the four ways of writing the French words for 'old' and when do I use them?

There are four ways of writing the French words for 'old'. After studying the groups of examples below, can you work out a pattern which determines the form used? Again you may find it easier to look at groups b, c and d first before considering group a.

GROUP A

The old computer was in the corner of the room.
Le vieil ordinateur se trouvait dans le coin de la pièce.

GROUP B

That is an old wooden bed.
Voilà un vieux lit en bois.

Do you like old cycles?
Aimes-tu collectionner les vieux vélos?

GROUP C

And this is an old table from a French café.
Et ceci c'est une vieille table venant d'un café français.

The old yellowing pages of the family record booklet were on the ground.
Les vieilles pages jaunies du livret de famille se trouvaient par terre.

GROUP D

As there were no more men available the old ladies danced together.
Comme il n'y avait plus de cavaliers de disponibles, les vieilles dames dansaient entre elles.

When I am in Paris, I always look for beautiful old postcards in the secondhand book-sellers.
Quand je suis à Paris je cherche toujours de belles vieilles cartes postales chez les bouquinistes.

ANSWER

There are four options:

The words in group a are used to describe masculine persons/things which start with 'a', 'i', 'e', 'o' or 'u'. These are always the shortest form and always ends in the letter 'l'.

The words in group b are used to describe masculine persons/things which start with letters other than 'a', 'i', 'e', 'o' or 'u' and naming words in the masculine plural.

The words in group c are used to describe feminine persons/things.

The words in group d are used to describe persons/things in the feminine plural.

3.4   How do I say 'all': *tout, toute, toutes,* or *tous*?

Look at the groups of examples below; can you work what determines the form of *tout* that you choose? Perhaps you might look at groups b, c and d before a, which is the most difficult. After each of the sentences in French you will get guidance on how to pronounce the word.

GROUP A
We saw it all since we were very close to the place where the accident happened.
Nous avons tout vu car nous étions très près de l'endroit où l'accident est arrivé. [pronounce as 'TOU']

No point lying to the investigators, they know it all.
Inutile de mentir aux enquêteurs, ils savent tout. [pronounce as 'TOU']

GROUP B
They were on their balcony and they saw the whole scene.
Ils étaient sur leur balcon et ils ont vu toute la scène. [pronounce as 'TUTE']

All the family were there for his marriage.
Pour son mariage, toute la famille était là. [pronounce as 'TUTE']

GROUP C

All cars will be equipped with an airbag in a few years.

Toutes les voitures seront équipées d'un airbag dans quelques années. [pronounce as 'TUTE']

Jean-Paul Sartre? I have read all his plays.

Jean-Paul Sartre? J'ai lu toutes ses pièces de théâtre. [pronounce as 'TUTE']

Last year I went to all the performances of the Comédie-Française.

L'année dernière j'ai assisté à toutes les représentations de la Comédie-Française. [pronounce as 'TUTE']

GROUP D

Not a single one refused the invitation. They all came.

Pas un seul n'a refusé l'invitation. Ils sont tous venus. [pronounce as 'TUS', i.e. with the 's']

You are all responsible.

Vous êtes tous responsables. [pronounce as 'TUS', i.e. with the 's']

We were all on time for the meeting.

Nous étions tous à l'heure au rendez-vous. [pronounce as 'TUS', i.e. with the 's']

He comes here every day.

Il vient ici tous les jours. [pronounce as 'TOU']

I know all Robert's friends.

Je connais tous les amis de Robert. [pronounce as 'TOU']

ANSWER

In group b, c and d you can see that the form of *tout* is simply determined by the naming word to which it refers: add an 'e' for feminine, add 'es' for feminine plural and change it to *tous* for a masculine plural. In group a, *tout* does not refer to something specific; so it works as a general category.

As far as pronunciation is concerned, you only really have a choice with *tous*, the form that accompanies *ils*. In that case pronounce the word as 'TUS', i.e. with an 's', when *tous* is placed **before** a word beginning in 'a', 'e', 'i', 'o', or 'u' describing word (like *responsables* here, or before a part of a doing word (like *venus* here). Or **after** any form and tense of the doing word *être*. Otherwise pronounce it 'TOU', i.e. without an 's', just like you always pronounce *tout*.

3.5 Do I say *de, d', du* or *des* when I mean 'from' when speaking about towns and cities?

When you say 'from' with reference to a town or city you have the choice of three words in French: *de, d', du* or *des*. The first choice (*de*) is by far the most common, but when are the others used? Look through the groups of examples below and try to work out the answer.

GROUP A

Listen John, I have to know when you will be coming back from Lyons.
Écoute Jean, il faut que je sache quand tu vas revenir de Lyon?

Do you hear me, I'm leaving from Garston at three o'clock, whether you like it or not!
Tu m'as bien compris, je pars de Garston à trois heures, que tu le veuilles ou non!

GROUP B

Once the festival was finished, they returned from Avignon immediately.
Le festival terminé, ils sont tout de suite rentrés d'Avignon.

During the Second World War many soldiers did not return from Germany.
Pendant la Deuxième Guerre mondiale de nombreux soldats ne sont pas revenus d'Allemagne.

GROUP C

I could immediately see that he was an enemy paratrooper. He was coming from Le Havre and asked me for directions to Le Havre.
J'ai tout de suite vu qu'il s'agissait d'un parachutiste ennemi. Il venait du Havre et m'a demandé la direction du Havre.

The troops left Cairo at exactly two o'clock in the morning.
Les troupes sont parties du Caire à deux heures pile du matin.

GROUP D

In 2000 a stage of the Tour de France left des Andelys towards Rouen.
En 2000 une étape du Tour de France une étape est partie des Andelys en direction de Rouen.

He only got back from les Arcs (a famous skiing centre in the Savoie *département*) at six o'clock in the morning.
Il n'est rentré des Arcs qu'à six heures du matin.

ANSWER

You will probably use *de* in the majority of cases, as in group a; but watch out for the names of towns and cities which start with 'a', 'e', 'i', 'o', or 'u'. These shorten *de* to *d'*, as in group b, and then there are the cases of towns with *Le* and *Les* in their names. These follow the usual pattern and combine with *de* with *le* and *les* to make *du* and *des*.

3.6   Do I say *à, au, aux* or *dans* when I mean 'in' when speaking about towns and cities?

When you say 'in' with reference to a town or city you have the choice of three words in French: *à, au, aux* or *dans*. The first choice (*à*) is by far the most common, but when are the others used? Look through the groups of examples below and try to work out the answer.

GROUP A

David, when were you in Paris?
David, quand est-ce que tu as été à Paris?

I was born in Minithorpe, a small village near Leeds.
Je suis né à Minithorpe, un petit village près de Leeds.

I think that you are mistaken. Ali has never been in La Rochelle.
Il me semble que vous faites erreur. Ali n'est jamais allé à La Rochelle.

GROUP B

The Churchill family spent three days in Cairo in 1922.
La famille Churchill a passé trois jours au Caire en 1922 (mil neuf cent vingt-deux).

All of our company's factories are situated in Le Havre.
Les usines de notre entreprise se trouvent toutes au Havre.

GROUP C

Yes, they have also got a branch in Les Arcs.
Oui, ils ont également une succursale aux Arcs.

GROUP D

On Friday evenings, traffic is always very heavy in the city of Boston.
Le vendredi soir, la circulation est toujours très dense dans Boston.

Traffic is always very heavy in Paris, that is inside the ring road.
La circulation est toujours très dense dans Paris, c'est-à-dire à l'intérieur du boulevard périphérique.

ANSWER

As you can see, *à* is used in the vast majority of cases. *Au* and *aux* refer to those names of cities and towns which start with *le* and *les*. The sentences in group d use *dans* has a sense of 'within the city limits'.

It is also possible to use *sur* with towns and cities, but this has the special meaning of 'in the region' or of a town or city.

Then the boss hurriedly announced: 'we need more staff in the Rennes region.'
Alors le patron s'est exprimé précipitamment: nous avons besoin de plus de personnel sur Rennes.

Abdel was a young high school teacher. At first he had been allocated a post in the South of France, but he feared being allocated a post in the Paris region.
Abdel était jeune professeur de lycée. Il avait été nommé au début dans le Midi. Il craignait d'être nommé sur Paris.

3.7   *Il s'est lavé*, the base form of *se laver* in the 'have' tense (the perfect), frequently changes, adding 'e', 's' or 'es', but when?

Understanding why the base form changes is quite easy, but it is more difficult to remember to make the change.

GROUP A

He washed in the bathtub.
Il s'est lavé dans la baignoire.

As usual Max got up before his school friends.
Comme d'habitude, Max s'est levé avant ses camarades.

GROUP B

Karine washed herself the next day because she was too tired in the evening.
Karine s'est lavée le lendemain matin car elle était trop fatiguée le soir.

Ingrid realised that she was wrong.
Ingrid s'est rendue compte qu'elle avait tort.

GROUP C

Jim, Karine and the others washed in the river because there was no water in the village.
Jim, Karine et les autres se sont lavés dans la rivière puisque il n'y avait pas d'eau dans le village.

The other children got by without my help.
Les autres enfants se sont débrouillés sans mon aide.

GROUP D

Jocelyne and Karine washed in the waterfall.
Jocelyne et Karine se sont lavées sous la chute d'eau.

Your girlfriends continuously made fun of me.
Tes copines se sont sans cesse moquées de moi.

ANSWER

Every time you see *s'est*, check for feminine. If you see a *se sont*, you can be sure that the base form is going to change depending on whether you have a group of women (when you add 'es') on the one hand, or a group of men or a mixed group on the other (when you add 's').

The same pattern as above applies to the 'had' tense (the pluperfect): *il s'était lavé*, and with the 'would have' tense (the conditional perfect): *il se serait lavé*.

3.8   How do I say 'some': *de la, du, de l'* or *des*?

Look at the sentences in the groups below; you will probably be able to work out when to use the four different forms of *de* quite quickly.

GROUP A

Would you like some fresh cream with your strawberries? (FORMAL)
Voudriez-vous de la crème fraîche avec vos fraises? (FORMAL)

Hey, Jean-Paul look, there is snow on the summits.
Tiens, Jean-Paul, regarde, il y a de la neige sur les sommets.

GROUP B

Yes there is wood behind the house.
Oui il y a du bois derrière la maison.

I am going to buy some bread and wine for this evening, ok?
Je vais acheter du pain et du vin pour ce soir, d'accord?

GROUP C

I beg your pardon Madam? You put schnapps into your coffee at breakfast!
Comment Madame? Vous mettez de l'eau-de-vie dans votre café au petit déjeuner!

What? You are drinking alcohol at breakfast.
Quoi? Tu bois de l'alcool au petit déjeuner.

GROUP D

Mr Stein: What would you like Madam?
Mrs. Egger: I will have some roses please.
M. Stein: Madame, vous désirez?
Mme Egger: Je vais prendre des roses, s'il vous plaît.

ANSWER

Whether you use *de la*, *du*, *des* or *de l'* depends on whether the naming word to which it refers takes *la*, *le*, *les* or starts with 'a', 'e', 'i', 'o', or 'u' (for *de l'*). All that is not really very difficult, but the main thing to remember is that sometimes in English you don't have any word for 'some', you just have the naming word (there is one of these examples in each group). This means you have to check that the meaning is 'some', before you know whether you have to use: *de la*, *du*, *des* or *de l'*.

In negative sentences 'some' changes to 'any'. For example: 'I will have some roses' is translated as *je vais prendre des roses*, but 'I will not have any roses' is translated as *je ne vais pas prendre de roses*. 'Any' in negative sentences is always translated by *de*, it does not matter if the naming word takes *le*, *la* or *les*.

3.9 Usually words like *joué*, *fini* and *rendu* (and other simple past participles) don't change, but sometimes they take 'e' 's' or 'es'? When?

Look at the sentences in group a, they represent the usual state of affairs, then there are three additional positions. All the deviations from the usual state of affairs happen for the same reason and that reason is reflected in the form of the sentences in groups b, c and d. Then the differences between the groups b, c and d are a result of the words involved. Can you work it out?

GROUP A

He played in the village football team.
Il a joué dans l'équipe de football du village.

Clarissa has finally finished her maths homework.
Clarisse a enfin fini son devoir de maths.

I did give you the change, didn't I?
Je t'ai bien rendu la monnaie, n'est-ce pas?

I saw the sun rise this morning.
J'ai vu le soleil se lever ce matin.

GROUP B

What story would you have told?
Quelle histoire aurais-tu racontée?

How did you spot me? She said smiling.
Comment m'as-tu aperçue? dit-elle en souriant.

GROUP C

How many games had you played?
Combien de parties avais-tu jouées?

Here are the letters you wrote.
Voilà les lettres que vous avez écrites.

GROUP D

I looked at the ducks, which stayed near the pond.
J'ai regardé les canards restés près du bord de l'étang.

How many rabbits did you see?
Combien de lapins avez-vous vus?

ANSWER

The state of affairs where words like *joué*, *fini* and *rendu* are written without 'e', 's' or 'es' is the base position of group a. The deviation from this form happens when there is a reversal in word order and that happens when the person or thing who does the action (the subject) is put in second position. This causes the words to change and is a process which is similar to the passive; see 10.1. The way that the words change is determined by the naming word or person to which the doing word refers. If the naming word is feminine singular (*la*/*une*) then you add an 'e', as in group b. You can avoid the most common mistake made by English-speakers by remembering that these agreements are frequently accompanied by inversion with a hyphen (-). If the naming word is feminine plural, then you find 'es' added to the base form as in group c. If the naming word is a masculine or mixed plural then 's' is added as in group d.

There is no agreement with *en*:

Have you seen any French films? Yes, I've seen some.
As-tu vu des films français? Oui, j'en ai vu un certain nombre.

There is also no agreement when *me*, *te*, *se*, *nous*, *vous*, mean 'for the benefit of' or when there is a reference to an exchange between two people:

She bought a gold bracelet for herself.
Elle s'est acheté un bracelet en or.

They waved at each other.
Elles se sont fait un signe de la main.

4

There are five ways of saying something in French, where there is only one in English

4.1 What are the five ways of writing the French words for 'soft', 'new', 'mad', 'beautiful' and when do I use them?

There are five ways of writing the French words for 'soft', 'new', 'mad' and 'beautiful'. After studying the groups of examples below, can you work out a pattern which determines the form used.

GROUP A

You have a very beautiful cat, Madam Gobain.
Vous avez un très beau chat, Madame Gobain.

Denise, have you seen the new book that has just been bought by the library?
Denise, as-tu vu le nouveau livre que la bibliothèque vient d'acheter?

It's like being the victim of a crazed killer.
C'est comme le fait d'être victime d'un tueur fou.

This stormy weather makes me listless.
Ce temps orageux me rend mou.

GROUP B

Maurice thinks he is a beautiful man.
Maurice se croît bel homme.

Anne has bought a new bird of paradise.
Anne s'est acheté un nouvel oiseau de paradis.

Have you seen the film *Dr Strangelove* by Stanley Kubrick?
Vous avez vu le film Dr Folamour de Stanley Kubrick?

In my opinion, counselling is a false paradise which does not change fundamental problems.
À mon avis, l'aide psychosociale est un mol oreiller, qui ne change pas les problèmes fondamentaux.

GROUP C

The town of Chartres has a beautiful cathedral.
La ville de Chartres possède une belle cathédrale.

Alice also bought a new car.
Alice s'est également acheté une nouvelle voiture.

Gaby shouted at her sister: 'You're crazy!'
Gaby cria à sa sœur: 'Tu es folle!'

How can one describe Goutrin? Above all, it is a soft cheese.
Comment décrire le Goutrin? Avant tout, c'est un fromage à pâte molle.

GROUP D

The melons are too ripe, touch them, look at how soft they are.
Les melons sont trop mûrs, touche-les, regarde comme ils sont mous.

These antiques are now being sold for crazy prices.
Ces antiquités se vendent maintenant à des prix fous.

In Versailles there are very beautiful gardens.
À Versailles il y a de très beaux jardins.

GROUP E

As there were no more gentlemen available the beautiful ladies danced together.
Comme il n'y avait plus de cavaliers de disponibles, les belles dames dansaient entre elles.

When I am in Paris, I always look for new postcards in the secondhand booksellers.
Quand je suis à Paris je cherche toujours de nouvelles cartes postales chez les bouquinistes.

ANSWER

There are four options:

The words in group a are used to describe masculine persons/things which start with letters other than 'a', 'e', 'i', 'o', or 'u'.

The words in group b are used to describe masculine persons/things which start with 'a', 'e', 'i', 'o', or 'u' and some words starting with 'h', see 8.4. These are always the shortest form and always end in the letter 'l'.

The words in group c are used to describe feminine persons/things.

The words in group d are used to describe persons/things in the masculine plural.

The words in group e are used to describe persons/things in the feminine plural.

5

There are seven ways of saying something in French, where there is only one in English

5.1 What are the seven words meaning 'what' in French?

You will probably be familiar with many of them, but look through the groups of sentences below and see if you can understand the different ways in which the words for 'what' are functioning.

GROUP A

What's important, therefore, is to start as soon as possible.
Ce qui est important, c'est donc de commencer aussi vite que possible.

What happened is not yet clear.
Ce qui est arrivé n'est pas encore clair.

What (on earth) is moving down there?
Qu'est-ce qui bouge là-bas?

GROUP B

What you are saying to me is very strange.
Ce que tu me dis est très bizarre.

What I see is that we are going to encounter big problems.
Ce que je vois, c'est que nous allons rencontrer de gros problèmes.

I know what you are going to say, but please let me explain...
Je sais ce que vous allez dire, mais permettez moi de m'expliquer...

What on earth can they be doing upstairs?
Qu'est-ce qu'ils peuvent bien faire en haut?

GROUP C

What are they doing upstairs? (FORMAL)
Que font-ils en haut?(FORMAL)

What can you say, faced with such behaviour?
Que dire devant un tel comportement?

What do you mean by that remark?
Que voulez-vous dire par cette remarque?

GROUP D

He knows exactly what you need.
Il sait exactement ce dont tu as besoin.

That's not what we need.
Ce n'est pas ce dont nous avons besoin.

He doesn't tell us what he remembers any more.
Il ne nous dit plus ce dont il se souvient.

GROUP E

What a life!
Quelle vie!

They are made for each other! What a beautiful couple they would make!
Ils sont faits l'un pour l'autre! Quel beau couple ils feraient!

What are the difficulties of this choice?
Quelles sont les difficultés de ce choix?

GROUP F

'What?' (VERY INFORMAL)
Quoi? (VERY INFORMAL)

FREDDIE: Jack has been in prison since yesterday.
SAMMIE: You're joking, what did he do? (VERY INFORMAL)
FREDDIE: Jacques est en prison depuis hier.
SAMMIE: Sans blague, il a fait quoi?(VERY INFORMAL)

I know what I am talking about; he doesn't!
Je sais de quoi je parle; lui, non!

What are you referring to?
À quoi faites-vous allusion?

What did they dance around?
Elles ont dansé autour de quoi?

The gangsters smashed up the bar, after which they left in a hurry.
Les gangsters ont saccagé le bar, après quoi ils sont partis à toute vitesse.

What did you put the sculpture on?
Tu as posé la sculpture sur quoi?

GROUP G
The female telephone operator: Mr. Ng is the head of after-sales service.
The Customer: What (excuse me?)?
La standardiste: Le chef du service après-vente est Monsieur Ng.
Le client: Comment?

ANSWER

You can use *ce qui* or *ce que*. If the person or thing is doing the action (the subject) then use *ce qui* as in group a.

If it receives the action then use *ce que* as in group b. Use these when 'what' stands for something which is not named. The last example in both groups a and b have an additional *qu'est-* this makes the sentence stronger; one of the ways of translating this is to say 'what **on earth**.' If you want to be even more indignant and ask WHAT!?, then you can make *qu'est-ce que* even stronger and say: *Qu'est-ce que c'est que ça?* What on earth is that? This refers to something specific of which you violently disapprove.

When the word 'what' comes at the start of a phrase and you are describing a doing word such as *faire*, then, as in group c, you can use *que*.

In group d *dont* is used just like *ce que*, but when the doing word is followed by *de*. For example *se souvenir de, avoir besoin de*.

The sentences in group e use *quel* and its relations (*quelle*, *quels* and *quelles*) when 'what' refers to something which is named.

Group f. If you use *quoi* to indicate extreme surprise it can be considered impolite. *Quoi* can also refer to a thing not named and accompanies words like *à*, *de*, *autour de*, *sur*. *Après quoi* concerns one event which follows another.

In group g you will find *comment*, the polite way of letting a person know that you haven't heard or understood what they have said.

6

There are eight ways of saying something in French, where there is only one in English

6.1   What are the eight different ways to say 'half' in French?

The sentences in the groups below will tell you how.

GROUP A

When we got back the dog had already eaten half of the roast.
Quand on est revenu le chien avait déjà mangé la moitié du rôti.

Mum told me that I could take half the dessert!
Maman m'a dit que je pourrais prendre la moitié du dessert!

It seems to me that the builders have only done half the job.
Il me semble que les maçons n'ont fait que la moitié du travail.

GROUP B

Do you know that Dorothy is half-Austrian and half-French?
Sais-tu que Dorothée est mi-autrichienne mi-française?

The well is found halfway between our house and the neighbour's barn.
Le puits se trouve à mi-chemin entre notre maison et la grange du voisin.

GROUP C

Do you have any half priced seats?
Est-ce que vous avez des places à demi-tarif?

During his sabbatical he will only have half his salary.
Pendant son année sabbatique il n'aura qu'un demi-salaire.

I need half a glass of wine to prepare this dish.
Il me faut un demi-verre de vin pour préparer ce plat.

GROUP D

Fifty years ago, we were only paid twelve rupees per half-day.
Il y a cinquante ans, on ne nous payait que douze roupies la demi-journée.

The police entered the apartment and there was still half a cup of warm coffee on the table.
La police est entrée dans l'appartement et il y a avait encore une demi-tasse de café tiède sur la table.

Are you fine with a half bottle of Clos-Trigonelles?
Tu es d'accord pour une demi-bouteille de Clos-Trigonelles?

GROUP E

This summer our cousin Farid will be ten and a half years old.
Cet été notre cousin Farid aura dix ans et demi.

Dad definitely wants us to be back before half past midnight.
Papa veut absolument que nous soyons rentrés avant minuit et demi.

GROUP F

I want to set off before half past six.
Je veux me mettre en route avant six heures et demie.

GROUP G

(to a waiter in a restaurant or bar) Half a Pelforth (beer) please.
Un demi Pelforth s'il vous plaît.

GROUP H

A half-bottle of red wine please (in a restaurant or bar).
Une demie de vin rouge s'il vous plaît.

ANSWER

Group a. When you mean 'the half' in the sense that there is some understanding of the whole object, idea or group **from which the half was taken** or **to which the half belongs,** then use *la moitié*. In everyday conversation it is sometimes said that you can tell whether someone is a pessimist or an optimist by the way that he or she might describe a glass with liquid as either half-empty (the pessimist) or half-full (the optimist). You can also think of the use of *la moitié* in the same way because it looks at the fraction in terms of the whole (the optimist) or in terms of nothing (the pessimist). If you look at the examples which refer to the builders in group a, you can see, in your mind's eye, the whole of the job of which the builders have only done half. So *à moitié* is used where you have doing words. According to the most strict rules of grammar it is also possible to say *à demi* in these cases; however, this book prefers *à moitié* for the simple reason that it is always right to say *à moitié*, but only sometimes correct to say *à demi* and what is the point of having to needlessly learn exceptions? Group b *mi...mi* is normally found together (except in set phrases such as *mi-chemin*). This way of saying half stresses the harmoniousness of the combination of the two halves, rather than the individuality of each fifty percent. If one does indeed want to stress the dual nature of the thing and its two halves the *moitié*, being a longer word will point it up.

In the rest of this unit different forms of the word *demi* will be used. Here what is meant is 'a half' in the sense that you are focusing on a half as a **quantity in itself** then use *demi*, which is never used on its own. In groups c and d there is *demi* with a dash (*demi-*) is joined to the front of all words to which it refers. It takes *un* or *une* depending on the gender of the word to which it is stuck: *un demi-* in group c and *une demi-* in group d. In groups e and f we have *demi* preceded by *et*. In these two groups, in contrast to c and d, *et demie* is written with an 'e' when the naming words to which it refers takes *la* or *une*, as in the case of *heure*. Groups g and h are specialist vocabulary which relate to drinking! *Un demi* is a half a glass because the French say *le verre* and *une demie* is a half of *la bouteille* of wine.

7

French is the exact opposite
of English

7.1 Do I use a capital letter when writing the names of months in French?

In the film he was born on the fourth of July.
Dans le film il est né le quatre juillet.

My birthday is on the seventeenth of August.
Mon anniversaire est le dix-sept août.

ANSWER

Where you write a capital letter in English, they write a simple letter in French.

7.2 Do I use a capital letter when writing the names of days of the week in French?

Just another manic Monday.
Encore un lundi de fous.

Do you want to go out with me on Saturday?
Est-ce tu veux sortir avec moi samedi?

ANSWER

Where you write a capital letter in English, they write a simple letter in French. The word 'on' in the term 'on Saturday' is not translated into French; you just say the day.

7.3   Do I use a capital letter when writing the names of languages in French?

Do you speak Czech?
Parlez-vous tchèque?

Yes, I speak fluent French.
Oui, je parle le français couramment.

ANSWER

Where you write a capital letter in English, they write a simple letter in French. In the second sentence *le* is used; this is optional. When referring to the inhabitants of a country both languages use capitals (as in English):

Are you English? (addressing a woman)
Êtes-vous Anglaise, Madame?

Are they Japanese?
Est-ce qu'ils sont Japonais?

7.4   Do I use a capital letter for describing words which refer to a particular town or city?

This is a very interesting Parisian restaurant.
C'est un restaurant parisien très intéressant.

This facade is typical for a London building
Cette façade est typique pour un bâtiment londonien.

ANSWER

Describing words which refer to a particular town or city in French have a simple letter, this is the opposite from the capital letter which is written in English. When referring to a person, French uses a capital in the same way as English.

The people of Toulouse must not miss this chance.
Il ne faut pas que les Toulousains manquent cette occasion.

7.5   When some words are singular in French, how are they written in English?

My former Director of Studies in Cambridge taught physics and spoke French fluently.
Le directeur d'études que j'avais à Cambridge enseignait la physique et parlait couramment le français.

Laëtitia did not realise that she had to study statistics in her geography lessons.
Laëtitia n'était pas au courant qu'elle devait étudier la statistique dans ses cours de géographie.

The image of the Indian woman is at the crossroads of European colonisation.
L'image de la femme indienne est au carrefour des colonisations européennes.

The thermometer shows that it is zero degrees Celsius in the garden this morning.
Le thermomètre indique zéro degré dans le jardin ce matin.

ANSWER

Here you can see that the English looks like a plural where the French looks like a singular. The word 'physics' is not a real plural in English because we say: 'physics is a fascinating subject' and the same applies to all fields of study, which end in *-ique* in French such as *la linguistique*. However, the important thing is to remember to use a *la* in front of the French words in the examples above. In the last example with 'degrees', only one and zero take the singular in French, all other numbers would be accompanied by *degrés*.

7.6   When some words are plural in French, how are they written in English?

This book is going to increase and enrich your knowledge of French.
Ce livre va augmenter et enrichir vos connaissances en français.

He bought all of his furniture at auction.
Il a acheté tous ses meubles dans les ventes aux enchères.

I am so tired that I will be happy to go on holiday next week.
Je suis si fatigué que je serai contente de partir en vacances la semaine prochaine.

ANSWER

In the cases above you have a word which is singular in English and plural in French.

7.7   How do I write family names in the plural in French?

Were you aware of this difference between English and French usage?

I saw the Smiths in town this afternoon.
J'ai vu les Smith en ville cet après-midi.

The countess invited the Pierrons.
La comtesse invita les Pierron au bal.

ANSWER

Unlike English, French does not add an 's'. The plural is indicated with *les* and therefore family names do not need to be altered.

7.8   Do I use *le, la* and *l'*, when writing job titles?

Captain Montsouris is now forty.
Le capitaine Montsouris a maintenant quarante ans.

Senior member of the Council of State, Madame Poutre stated that she was satisfied on seeing the new embassy.
La conseillère d'État, Madame Poutre, a exprimé sa satisfaction en voyant la nouvelle ambassade.

ANSWER

In French the titles of jobs take *le, la* or *l'*; to English-speaking people it makes the French job holder sound very grand!

7.9   Do I use *le, la* and *l'*, when writing the names of countries in French?

England was the greatest colonial power in the nineteenth century.
L'Angleterre était la plus grande puissance coloniale au dix-neuvième siècle.

Canada is partly a francophone country.
Le Canada est un pays qui est en partie francophone.

'Lagania encourages respect for human rights' the president stated.
'La Laganie encourage le respect des droits de l'homme' a déclaré le président.

Scotland is the land, which makes the best whiskies.
L'Ecosse, c'est le pays qui fabrique les meilleurs whiskies.

ANSWER

When writing the names of countries in French, you need to put in a *le, la* or *l'*.

7.10   Must I repeat *à, de* and *en* in lists?

Look at the lists in French below and their English translations. What is the obvious difference between them?

GROUP A

You can now benefit from this service in many European countries, in France, Germany, Spain and Portugal.
Vous pouvez maintenant bénéficier de ce service dans plusieurs pays européens, en France, en Allemagne, en Espagne et au Portugal.

Coaches full of demonstrators came from Marseilles, Lyons, Avignon and Toulouse.
Des cars pleins de manifestants sont venus de Marseille, de Lyon, d'Avignon et de Toulouse.

While we cross the desert we will have to give up: fine food, television, a daily shower and conversations with our friends.
Pendant notre traversée du désert nous devrons renoncer à la bonne cuisine, à la télévision, à une douche quotidienne et aux conversations avec nos amis.

GROUP B

I don't like Jeannette much and yet I get on very well with her brother, her friend and even her dog! (INFORMAL)

Je n'aime pas trop Jeanette et pourtant je m'entends très bien avec son frère, avec son ami Maurice et même avec son chien! (INFORMAL)

I hate Jean and yet I get on very well with Henri, Louise, Pierre and Magali; that is to say all his friends.

Je déteste Jean et pourtant je m'entends très bien avec Henri, Louise, Pierre et Magali; c'est-à-dire avec tous ses amis.

ANSWER

GROUP A

French tends to repeat *à*, *de* and *en* before each item in the list.

GROUP B

Position words (other than *à*, *de* or *en*) are repeated if the writer wants to stress the individuality of all the items in the list, and not repeated if the item, are being considered as a group.

7.11 Do I use *le*, *la* and *l'*, when writing general, non-specific statements?

'Money is not everything' said the tramp.
'L'argent n'est pas tout dans la vie' a dit le clochard.

Basically, surrealism allows dreams and the irrational to enter the arts and literature. (FORMAL)
Au fond, le surréalisme laisse entrer les rêves et l'irrationnel dans les arts et les lettres. (FORMAL)

ANSWER

Be on the look out for general statements which are intended to have value outside the specific story that is being told in the paragraph where they appear. If they are generally relevant, for example such sentences are often found in conclusions, then the main naming word in the sentence takes nothing in English, but has *le*, *la*, or *l'* in front of it in French.

7.12 With the names of jobs and professions in French, should I translate the English 'a' or 'the'?

She is an accountant.
Elle est agent-comptable.

Mr. Gironde was the mayor of Bordeaux during the Second World War.
Monsieur Gironde a été maire de Bordeaux pendant la Seconde Guerre mondiale.

ANSWER

When referring specifically to the jobs that a person does in French, you just write the name of the job without 'a' or 'the' as above. However, when you add a word describing how the person did the job, then you need to add the word for 'the': *le, la,* or *l'*. For example:

Jack G. is the best trainer in this region.
Jacques G. est le meilleur entraîneur dans cette région.

Estelle is a talented bass guitarist.
Estelle est une bassiste de talent.

7.13 With persons belonging to religions in French, should I translate the English 'a'?

'Is he a Protestant?', wondered Jack.
'Est-il protestant?', se demanda Jacques.

Tina Turner has been a Buddhist for about twenty years.
Tina Turner est bouddhiste depuis une vingtaine d'années.

'I am a Moslem', Omar told us with pride.
'Je suis musulman', nous dit Omar avec fierté.

ANSWER

When describing a person belonging to a specific religion, you use a capital letter and the word 'a' in English; in French, only the describing word is used, without 'a' or a capital letter.

7.14   With the names of monarchs and popes with a number in French, should I say 'the' as in English?

One day, Louis the Fourteenth, the Sun King, exclaimed 'I am the state'.
Un jour, Louis XIV (Louis quatorze), le Roi Soleil, s'est exclamé: 'L'Etat, c'est moi'.

John-Paul the Second is the first Slav pope.
Jean-Paul II ("deux") est le premier pape slave.

ANSWER

In French, you just say the number without using 'the'. When writing use the Roman numbers. The one exception to this is the first king, queen or pope: *Charles Ier*, which is pronounced *'Charles premier'*.

7.15   How do I translate the words for decades such as: 'the fifties', 'the nineties', 'the sixties' into French?

Look at the sentences below; you will see that the contrast between the French and the English is small but significant.

Europe underwent drastic change in the forties.
L'Europe a subi un bouleversement considérable dans les années quarante.

Greenpeace continued to highlight ecological problems in the nineties.
Greenpeace a continué d'attirer l'attention sur les problèmes écologiques dans les années quatre-vingt-dix.

Come on old man, stop talking about your nostalgia for the sixties!
Allez mon vieux, ne parle plus de ta nostalgie des années soixante!

ANSWER

Here the number stays 'pure' and doesn't change to follow the plural *années*. On the other hand, in English, the plural is clear. Note that the word 'in' with individual years, written as numbers, is always translated as *en* in French. For example:

The Second World War broke out in 1939.
La Seconde Guerre mondiale a éclaté en 1939.

8

French has unique forms which are not found in English

8.1 How do I say 'on Mondays' and 'on Tuesdays'?

Since I began working full-time, I am always tired on Mondays.
Depuis que j'ai commencé à travailler à plein-temps je suis toujours fatigué le lundi.

We never go to the gym on Sundays.
Nous n'allons jamais à la salle des sports le dimanche.

ANSWER

When English refers to a habit which takes place on, or which refers to, several days of the week, it logically puts the day in the plural; whereas French uses the singular with the word *le*.

8.2 How is it possible to say whether some words take *la* or *le*?

Look at the highlighted ending of the keyword in each sentence below.

GROUP A
I saw a slug in your salad!
*J'ai vu une lim**ace** dans ta salade!*

I would like to walk by the river.
*J'aimerais faire une promen**ade** le long de la rivière.*

A hedge marked the limit of his garden.
*Une **haie** indiquait la limite de son jardin.*

Oh what a villain!
*Ah, quelle **canaille**!*

The queen is on holiday this week.
*La **reine** est en vacances cette se**maine**.*

The rainy season takes place twice a year in Sri Lanka.
*La **saison** des pluies a lieu deux fois par an au Sri Lanka.*

At that point Christ was in an olive grove.
*Le Christ se trouvait alors dans une olive**raie**.*

The Cathedral, is a novel by J.-K. Huysmans.
*La Cathéd**rale** est un roman de J.-K. Huysmans.*

We celebrated the birth of our son.
*On a fêté la nais**sance** de notre fils.*

Do you like dance?
*Aimez-vous la **danse**?*

The queen's cousin was killed by an arrow.
*Le cousin de la **reine** fut tué par une flè**che**.*

Have you done the dictation with the other students?
*Est-ce que vous avez fait la dic**tée** avec les autres étudiants?*

Do you see the difference between both paintings?
*Voyez-vous la diffé**rence** entre les deux peintures?*

We commit ourselves to the defence of this country.
*Nous nous engageons pour la dé**fense** de ce pays.*

I cannot study in the university library.
*Je ne peux pas étudier dans la bibliothè**que** de la fac.*

I do not like cooked meat and sausages.
*Je n'aime pas la charcu**terie**.*

How can one be a university teacher without having done a thesis?
*Comment peut-on être professeur de fac sans avoir fait une **thèse**?*

She is a goddess!
*C'est une dé**esse**!*

Does Michi's flat only have a kitchenette?
*L'appartement de Michi n'a qu'une kitche**nette**?*

Deslauriers, this uniform jacket is in a lamentable state.
*Deslauriers, cette var**euse** est dans un état lamentable.*

The baddie in the film said: I ate his liver with a broad bean.
Le méchant dans le film a dit: j'ai mangé son foie avec une fève.

Oh, me, I love good grub. (INFORMAL)
Oh, moi, j'adore la bonne bouffe. (INFORMAL)

You should only take the soft part of the bread.
Il ne faut prendre que la mie du pain.

Where is the teapot?
Où est la théière?

Marcel ate a madeleine cake.
Marcel a mangé une madeleine.

What a surprise to see this medieval church in a district like this.
Quelle surprise de voir cette église médiévale dans un quartier pareil.

Be careful of the spelling of the French word 'comparaison'.
Faites attention à l'orthographe française du mot 'comparaison'.

To get off a car ferry you have to use a gangway.
Pour descendre d'un car ferry il vous faut utiliser une passerelle.

You have to say 'une personne' in French even if you are speaking about a man.
Il faut dire une personne en français, même s'il s'agit d'un homme.

Wild oats no longer grow in the fields near our house.
La folle avoine ne pousse plus dans les champs près de chez nous.

Madame Bovary got into a cart.
Madame Bovary est montée dans une carriole.

Beware of the trapdoor!
Attention à la trappe!

I regret the tension which still exists between us.
Je regrette la tension qui subsiste entre nous.

Do you have to say 'Votre Altesse' when you are speaking to the Pope?
Est-ce qu'il faut dire 'Votre Altesse' quand vous vous adressez au Pape?

I freely admit it; it's beauty that directs my life.
Je l'admets volontiers, c'est la beauté qui dirige ma vie.

I hope that our friendship will last all our lives.
J'espère que notre amitié durera toute notre vie.

The game is over and what emotion on the field of the Stade de France!
Ça y est, le match est terminé et quelle émotion sur le terrain du Stade de France!

Here we often see a seagull on our roof.
Ici nous voyons souvent une mouette sur notre toit.

What a negative attitude!
Quelle attitude négative!

It has been years since there has been an interlude between programmes.
Ça fait des années qu'il n'y a plus d'interlude entre les émissions.

In the times when people used to heat with coal there used to be soot in the houses.
À l'époque où l'on chauffait au charbon il y avait de la suie dans les maisons.

This coat is unfortunately not lined.
Ce manteau n'a malheureusement pas de doublure.

GROUP B

What a miracle!
Quel miracle!

His courage is magnificent.
Son courage est magnifique.

The broom was behind the door.
Le balai se trouvait derrière la porte.

Gardenal, that is a medicine, which can be dangerous when taken in large doses.
Le gardénal, ça c'est un médicament qui lorsqu'il est pris à haute dose peut être dangereux.

His sarcasm troubles me a great deal.
Ses sarcasmes me gênent beaucoup.

My daughter only eats chocolate.
Ma fille ne mange que du chocolat.

The duke went through into the dining room.
Le duc passa dans la salle à manger.

He walked on my foot.
Il m'a marché sur le pied.

My uncle owns a castle.
Mon oncle possède un château.

I fear that there is no remedy for this illness.
Je crains qu'il n y ait pas de remède contre cette maladie.

I was a part-time assistant in a collège in France.
J'ai été assistant à temps partiel dans un collège en France.

What is the problem in the system that you explained to us?
Quel est le problème dans le système que vous nous avez exposé?

They are going to pay for our lunch and dinner.
Ils vont nous payer le déjeuner et le dîner.

The trial finished in a verdict of 'case dismissed'.
Le procès s'est terminé par un non-lieu.

The lawyer used to have lunch in his chambers.
L'avocat déjeunait dans son cabinet.

My uncle was hiding in a shelter.
Mon oncle se cachait dans un abri.

John Burrough is a novelist who also writes short stories.
John Burrough est un romancier qui écrit également des nouvelles.

My car is in the car park behind the supermarket.
Ma voiture se trouve sur le parking derrière le supermarché.

This patient had one iris which was larger than the other.
Ce patient avait un iris qui était plus grand que l'autre.

Communism guides the future of two or three states in the world.
Le communisme guide l'avenir de deux ou trois États dans le monde.

The government has failed in its attempts to improve the situation.
Le gouvernement a échoué dans sa tentative d'améliorer la situation.

Whatever happens, Great Britain will see at least one more king.
Quoi qu'il advienne, la Grande-Bretagne verra au moins encore un roi.

They should install a urinal near this club.
Ils devraient installer un urinoir près de cette boîte.

Do you watch the telethon each year?
Est-ce qu tu regardes le téléthon chaque année?

Cabbage is my favourite vegetable.
Le chou est mon légume préféré.

ANSWER[1]

There is no straight answer because there are exceptions (for instance *musée* and *lycée* take *le*), but the endings in the two groups above give an indication of which words take *le* and which take *la*. The main thing is to understand an ending as more than a single letter (except in the case of c and d) and consider them as an ending sound. The endings have been arranged in alphabetical order here. It is particular difficult to spot gender in words which begin with a, e, i, o, or u such as *espoir*, which is an 'oir' ending and takes *le*.

---

1. This list builds on the one found in Glanville Price's complete revised version of *L. S. R. Byrne and E.L. Churchill's*, *A Comprehensive French Grammar*, Oxford, Blackwells, 1993, pp. 42-60.

8.3   Which naming words take *-aux* in the plural?

Below you can see words which are normal in the singular, but which all take *-aux* in the plural.

There were many animals which were hiding in the undergrowth.
Il y a avait beaucoup d'animaux qui se cachaient dans la broussaille.

I have been told that there are roadworks on the A1 motorway.
On m'a dit qu'il y a des travaux sur l'autoroute A1.

I was able to see magnificent paintings in the museums of this town.
J'ai pu voir des tableaux magnifiques dans les musées de cette ville.

Excuse me? You bought me two cakes on my birthday.
Comment? Tu m'as acheté deux gâteaux pour mon anniversaire.

ANSWER
- -

Above you will find some of the naming words which take *-aux* in the plural. There are other naming words which are always written with *-aux*.

The interest rates of this bank are very disappointing.
Les taux d'intérêt de cette banque sont très décevants.

Finally we have been able to reorganise our premises to improve the service for our customers.
Enfin on a pu réaménager nos locaux pour améliorer le service pour nos clients.

- -

8.4   What are the two ways to say and write words beginning with a letter 'h' in French?

Look at the two groups of sentences below and also say them out loud as well. What is the difference?

GROUP A
The axe was under the table.
La hache se trouvait sous la table.

Chance dictated that there were no owls in the hamlet this year.
Le hasard a fait qu'il n'y avait pas de hiboux dans le hameau cette année.

When I am in Le Havre, I have the boldness to breathe in the see breeze.
Quand je suis au Havre j'ai la hardiesse de humer la brise marine.

Of course French beans cannot be grown on the high ground around the town.
Bien sûr que l'on ne peut pas cultiver des haricots sur les hauteurs autour de la ville.

I hate this type of film: *La Haine* is an example.
Je hais ce genre de film: La Haine en est un exemple.

GROUP B

Honour, humility and honesty: those are the qualities of our organisation.
L'honneur, l'humilité et l'honnêteté: voilà les qualités de notre organisme.

The homosexual and the heterosexual are still not equal in our society.
L'homosexuel et l'hétérosexuel ne sont pas encore égaux dans notre société.

I used to live on the third floor with my Aunt Julie.
J'habitais au troisième avec ma tante Julie.

This habitat is unfortunately becoming extinct.
Cet habitat est malheureusement en voie de disparition.

ANSWER

In French 'h' words fall into two categories. When they say the words in group a, the French make a very short pause between the *le* or the *la* and the word. Although they do not say the 'h' sound as you would in English. So the nonsense phrase *des haricots sur les hauteurs* is pronounced as five separate words, not as three, which would be the case if they were run into each other. This hardness, independence and separation is confirmed in the way that the 'h' words in group a are written. They stay separate in writing from the *le* and the *la* which come before them.

In group b, 'h' words behave as you would expect them to do in French. That is to say they behave like a, e, i, o and u, so the French use *cet* to mean 'this' when referring to them. They are also pronounced differently from the words in group b because the *le* or the *la* or the *je* are shortened and run into the 'h' word. Overall, there are fewer group a words than group b ones. This is one of those cases where you have to learn the words that belong to each category. Thankfully, far fewer words begin with 'h' in French than in English.

8.5   When is there an *é* at the start of a word and when not?

Can you see the pattern which distinguishes the use of accents at the beginning of
the highlighted words below?

GROUP A

Yes, I recognise that they have made a great effort.
Oui, je reconnais qu'ils ont fait un gros effort.

My father has kept his hope for the future.
Mon père a gardé son espoir pour l'avenir.

At the moment I cannot see any example to give to you.
Pour l'instant je ne vois pas d'exemple à vous donner.

People generally have a lot of confidence in the euro.
On a généralement beaucoup de confiance dans l'euro.

He did not want to employ foreigners.
Il ne voulait pas embaucher des étrangers.

GROUP B

Of course this painter's sketches must evolve to become complete works.
Les ébauches de ce peintre doivent bien sûr évoluer pour devenir des œuvres achevées.

I write two thousand word per day.
J'écris deux mille mots par jour.

I think it is very important to be well brought up.
Je crois que c'est très important d'avoir de l'éducation.

John and Jim never change.
John et Jim sont égaux à eux-mêmes.

We got thrown out of the restaurant. What a scandal!
On s'est fait éjecter du restaurant. Si ce n'est pas scandaleux!

How to work out such a plan?
Comment élaborer un tel plan?

They are experiencing some difficulties in the realisation of this project.
Ils éprouvent des difficultés dans la réalisation de ce projet.

I have been studying French for five years.
J'étudie le français depuis cinq ans.

There will be classical music and possibly jazz.
Il y aura de la musique classique et éventuellement du jazz.

Women's emancipation is one of the principal gains of the twentieth century.
L'émancipation de la femme est un des principaux acquis du vingtième siècle.

Pancakes with maple syrup are a treat.
Des crêpes au sirop d'érable c'est un régal.

ANSWER

The two groups here summarise the use of accents with words beginning with the letter 'e'. Certain sequences of letters, those in group b, are always accompanied by an 'é', those in group a take 'e'. The few exceptions concern foreign words such as: *edam*.

8.6 What is the unique pattern of describing words with *gens*?

GROUP A
Look at those nasty people. What a sad way to behave.
Regardez ces méchantes gens. Quel triste façon de se comporter.

It's often old people who have the experience that has to be used to solve such a problem.
C'est souvent les vieilles gens qui ont l'expérience à laquelle il faut avoir recours pour régler un problème semblable.

GROUP B
All the less well-off people in this part of town live in either ground-floor living quarters or in single attic rooms.
Tous les gens peu fortunés du quartier habitent soit dans des logements situés au rez-de-chaussée soit dans des chambres de bonne.

You are wrong, there are happy people all over the world.
Vous avez tort, il y a des gens heureux dans le monde entier.

ANSWER

The pattern of describing words with *gens* is highly unusual. When using, *vilain, bon, petit, vieux, méchant* and *mauvais*, you put them before *gens* and the word is temporarily transformed into a feminine. However, with all other describing words, it is considered as masculine.

8.7 On occasions the *vous* and *tu* form are mixed, in a form which is neutral.

Go for it little brother. (INFORMAL)
Allez mon petit frère.(INFORMAL)

ANSWER

Normally the *tu* and the *vous* forms cannot be interchanged. However, there is one set expression, which has established itself and which uses the *vous* form of *aller* in informal contexts, where one would not usually expect to see it. To recap the difference between *tu* and *vous*, see 1.35.

8.8 Which French doing words have 'ç', an extra 'e', an 'è', a double letter, or a change from 'y' to 'i' and when?

GROUP A

The parents of the young girl were beginning to worry, when they saw that their daughter hadn't returned.
Les parents de la jeune fille commençaient à s'inquiéter quand ils ont vu que leur fille n'était pas rentrée.

We started asking ourselves questions when our son left home to live with his friends.
Nous commencions à nous poser des questions quand notre fils a quitté la maison pour aller vivre avec ses amis.

The killer dismembered the body of his victim.
Le tueur a dépecé le corps de sa victime (both male and female victims in French are *la victime*).

M. Dort has the pleasure of announcing the engagement of his daughter Fatima.
M. Dort a le plaisir d'annoncer les fiançailles de sa fille Fatima.

GROUP B

He ate everything.
Il mangea tout.

He ate some chocolate covered fried grasshoppers.
Il a mangé des sauterelles frites et nappées de chocolat.

He picked the blackberries and ate them without taking a single one home.
Il a cueilli des mûres et les a mangées sans en amener une seule à la maison.

It is true that we eat a lot of fried food.
Il est vrai que nous mangeons beaucoup de fritures.

GROUP C

Do you think that you will be able to get up at six o'clock every day?
Crois-tu pouvoir te lever tous les jours à six heures?

At the week-end I get up at eleven.
Le week-end, je me lève à onze heures.
Le week-end, tu te lèves à onze heures.
Le week-end, il se lève à onze heures.
Le week-end, elle se lève à onze heures.
Le week-end, nous nous levons à onze heures.
Le week-end, vous vous levez à onze heures.
Le week-end, ils se lèvent à onze heures.
Le week-end, elles se lèvent à onze heures.

GROUP D

Do you think that you can call him back immediately?
Crois-tu pouvoir le rappeler tout de suite?

I call him back.
Je le rappelle.
Tu le rappelles.
Elle le rappelle.
Nous le rappelons.
Vous le rappelez.
Ils le rappellent.

These machines always reject 100 euro notes.
Ces machines rejettent toujours les billets de cent euros.

GROUP E

Every year I send him a card at Christmas.
Tous les ans je lui envoie une carte pour le Noël.

Claude cleans the inside of his car on Sunday afternoons.
Claude nettoie l'intérieur de sa voiture le dimanche après-midi.

They use drills to do the work.
Elles emploient des perceuses pour faire le travail.

This time it's me who is paying for the drinks.
Cette fois c'est moi qui paye/paie les boissons.

Are you bored?
Tu t'ennuies?

ANSWERS

Group a. In doing words which end with '-cer', c changes to 'ç' when followed by 'a' or 'o'. For example: *agacer, lancer, avancer* and *menacer*.

Group b. In doing words which end in '-ger', the 'g' is followed by an 'e' to soften its sound before 'a' and 'o'.

Group c. In doing words with two 'e's the first one changes to 'è' except with *nous* and *vous*.

Group d. With doing words like *appeler*, the first and second consonants are doubled with *je, tu, il, elle, ils* and *elles*; but not with *nous* and *vous*.

Group e. In doing words which end with '-uyer' and '-oyer', 'y' changes to 'i' when the ending is silent (*je, tu, il, ils* and *elles*). With doing words ending in '-ayer' you do not have to change from 'y' to 'i'.

8.9   Am I sure about the tenses which follow *venir de*?

Look at the sentences below to remind yourself about the pattern of tenses following *venir de* in French and how they are translated into English.

That's really strange, I have just met Louise in town, when she should be in the office.
Voilà quelque chose de vraiment étrange, je viens de rencontrer Louise en ville, alors qu'elle devrait être au bureau.

Newcastle United had just won the championship when I came back from my walk in the park.
L'équipe de Newcastle United venait de remporter le championnat quand je suis rentrée de ma promenade au jardin public.

ANSWER

French has a present tense where English uses 'has/have just' and French uses 'was' where English writes 'had just.' *Venir de* with a place just means 'to come from.' For example: *si j'avais mon sifflet, cela indiquerait que je viendrais d'un match de football.*

8.10   Am I sure about the tenses which follow *depuis*?

See if you can isolate the differences between the tenses which follow *depuis* and *depuis que* in French and English.

The team had been playing for about twenty minutes when it began to hail.
L'équipe jouait depuis une vingtaine de minutes quand la grêle a commencé à tomber.

This company hasn't changed since 1990.
Cette entreprise n'a pas changé depuis mil neuf cents quatre-vingt-dix.

ANSWER

French has a present tense where English has 'has been' or French uses 'was' where English writes 'had been'. When *depuis* refers **broadly** to a time 'since when' it is translated as 'since', but when it refers more **narrowly** to the point in time when an imaginary stopwatch started ticking, then it is translated as 'for.'

There is another way of saying 'since' in spoken French if you have a quantity of time that is countable (such as a 'half an hour'); use *ça fait* then the amount of time, then *que* followed by the same tense pattern as with *depuis*.

There you are late again, we have been in this restaurant for half an hour.
Te voilà en retard encore une fois, ça fait une demi-heure que nous sommes dans ce restaurant.

What about sentences which imply a negative?

It will soon be ten years since I have seen him.
Ça fait bientôt dix ans que je ne l'ai pas vu.

Depuis must come before an expression of duration, it never follows it and that is why the *ça fait...que* construction is the only option in the last sentence.

8.11 Which tenses accompany both parts of sentences with *si* meaning 'if'?

French has a strict sequence of tenses, whereas English is more relaxed. Moreover, the short forms in English ('I'd've' etc.) can conceal the tenses.

1.

If I do not clean my flat, I'll get criticized by my neighbours.
Si je ne nettoie pas mon appartement, je me ferai critiquer par mes voisins.

If you see him you will understand me.
Si tu le vois, tu me comprendras.

2.

If I was/were in your position, I'd complain directly to the managing director (MD) chief executive offices (CEO).
Si je me trouvais dans ta situation, je me plaindrais directement au président-directeur général (P.-D.G.).

3.

If I'd known, I'd have warned him.
Si je l'avais su, je l'aurais prévenu.

If Farid and his father had come, we would have been happy.
Si Farid et son père étaient venus, nous aurions été contents.

ANSWER

Here is the sequence of tenses:

the content of the part of the sentence with *si*	the content of the part of the sentence without *si*, complementing it
present tense	future tense
'was' tense in English (imperfect)	'would' tense in English (conditional)
'had' tense in English (pluperfect)	'would have' tense in English (conditional perfect)

This rhyming phrase may help you to remember.
"with *si* future and conditional never, only when the meaning's 'whether'".

In French schools they used to say: *les scies n'aiment pas les raies*, literally translated, this means 'saws don't like scratches', but the way it sounds may remind you **not** to put *si* and '...*rais*' the 'would' tense ending together.

8.12   When is *aurait dit* not translated by 'would have said'?

We usually translate *aurait dit* and forms related to it by 'would have'; but the sentences below have a different meaning, what is it?

He seems to have taught them how to build explosive devices.
Il semble qu'il leur aurait appris comment fabriquer des engins explosifs.

The prime minister is said to be outraged by Mr Smith's words.
On dit que le premier ministre serait outré par les propos de M. Smith.

The president's spokeswoman appears to have gone too far with her declarations on the role of the secret service.
Il semble que la porte-parole du président serait allée trop loin avec ses déclarations sur le rôle des services secrets.

There may well be old mine shafts under the village.
Il y aurait peut-être des anciennes galeries de mine sous le village.

ANSWER

Aurait and forms related to it are being used here to report something, about which the speaker is slightly in doubt. It is being used to report a hypothesis.

9

French uses this form frequently, where English hardly uses it at all

9.1   What is the subjunctive in French and how do I use it?

The subjunctive is a little like a parallel universe. Most doing words also have separate subjunctive forms! Fortunately, though, you will have to know only the present tense (in the *je*, *tu*, *il*, *nous*, *vous* and *ils* forms) and the *il/elle* form of the 'was' tense (the imperfect)! The subjunctive is used much more frequently in French than in English (the words 'might' and 'may' are the only traces of the subjunctive which remain in English).

In these examples you **have to** use the subjunctive in three cases:

- after expressions of feeling and emotion with *que*. See 9.1.1.

- after expressions concerned with argumentation with *que*. See 9.1.2.

- after a group of expressions of emotion and argumentation with *que*. See 9.13.

This means that you will be looking out for certain types of meaning. The aim of this point is to make you aware of these types of meaning **and** to give you a way of remembering trigger words which prompt you to use the subjunctive.

Perhaps you will also notice that there are two different people (or groups) of people involved in each of the sentences below; one before the subjunctive and a different one after the subjunctive. When you have a sentence with the same person in both parts, you do **not** use the subjunctive, but the 'to' form of the doing word, the form that is listed first in dictionary entries. Examples of this are found after 'BUT' at the end of each group of sentences.

9.1.1   After which type of expressions of feeling and emotion do I **have to** use the subjunctive?

Try and think of a heading which is appropriate for each of the ten categories of sentences below.

I.

I am happy that you have come so soon.
Je suis content que tu sois venu si tôt.

I am glad/happy that you have finally got your driving licence.
Je suis heureuse que tu aies enfin ton permis de conduire.

He is delighted that she has decided to go on holiday with him.
Il est ravi qu'elle ait accepté de partir en vacances avec lui.

It would be good if you paid before the end of the month.
Il serait bon que vous payiez avant la fin du mois.

It is a good thing that he left.
C'est une bonne chose qu'il soit parti.

I would not be unhappy that she knows what we think about her. (FORMAL)
Je ne serais pas mécontente qu'elle sache ce que nous pensons d'elle. (FORMAL)

BUT

I am happy to be here (i.e. 'I am happy that I am here').
Je suis content d'être ici.

Fortunately, they warned us that the flight was cancelled.
Heureusement qu'ils nous ont prévenu que le vol était annulé.

II.

I permit you to read my diary.
Je permets que vous lisiez mon journal intime.

They agree to our making music on the terrace. (FORMAL)
Ils veulent bien que nous fassions de la musique sur la terrasse. (FORMAL)

I see no reason why they should not come this Sunday.
Je ne vois pas d'inconvénient à ce qu'ils viennent dimanche prochain.

How are you going to prevent her from coming this time?
Comment allez-vous empêcher qu'elle ne vienne cette fois?

BUT

What is going to stop me from telling the others what I think of them?
Qu'est-ce qui m'empêcherait de dire aux autres ce que je pense d'eux?

III.

He is sad that his team lost four nil.
Il est triste que son équipe ait été battue quatre à zéro.

I am sorry that your mother died far from home. (FORMAL)
Je regrette que Madame votre mère soit morte loin de chez elle. (FORMAL)

She is not happy that her friends went out without her.
Elle n'est pas contente/heureuse que ses copines soient sorties sans elle.

I am sorry that my son cannot baby-sit for you tonight.
Je suis désolé que mon fils ne puisse pas garder vos enfants ce soir.

We are sorry that our employees treated you in this way.
Nous sommes navrés que nos employés vous aient traité ainsi.

It is a pity that my family was unable to attend the ceremony at the church.
C'est dommage que ma famille n'ait pas pu assister à la cérémonie à l'église.

It is shameful that he abandoned his family in this way.
Il est honteux qu'il ait abandonné sa famille de cette manière.

BUT

I deeply regret having treated him like that.
Je regrette profondément de l'avoir traité ainsi.

IV.

Her husband was angry that the milkman behaved in this way.
Son mari était fâché que le laitier se soit comporté ainsi.

Giles is furious that she exposed herself to such danger.
Gilles est furieux qu'elle se soit exposée à un pareil danger.

BUT

We are annoyed at missing the appointment with the car mechanic.
Nous sommes fâchés d'avoir manqué le rendez-vous avec le garagiste.

V.

He fears that we are not going to be on time. (FORMAL)
Il craint que nous ne soyons pas à l'heure. (FORMAL)

I am afraid that she's got lost in the forest.
J'ai peur qu'elle ne se soit égarée dans la forêt (ne required if it's positive*).*

Take an umbrella for fear that it might rain. (FORMAL)
Prends un parapluie de peur qu'il ne pleuve (ne required*). (FORMAL)*

You have to find another club, unless the owner wants to accept you.
Vous devez trouver un autre club, à moins que le propriétaire ne veuille vous accepter (ne required*).*

BUT

Madam, I fear that I am disturbing you, but do you know where the exit is? (FORMAL)
Madame, je crains de vous déranger mais savez-vous où se trouve la sortie? (FORMAL)

VI. (THE LARGEST SECTION IN THIS GRAMMAR POINT)

I doubt that his brother has visited Japan.
Je doute que son frère ait visité le Japon.

It is not certain that there will be sun tomorrow.
Il n'est pas certain que nous ayons du soleil demain.

I don't think that there is a misunderstanding.
Je ne pense pas qu'il y ait un malentendu.

Mum doesn't think that he said that. (INFORMAL)
Maman ne croit pas qu'il ait dit cela. (INFORMAL)

I cannot believe that this gang was able to escape.
Je n'arrive pas à croire que ce gang ait pu s'évader.

BUT

By themselves, words meaning 'to think' *penser* and *croire* do **not** express doubt in French, therefore they are **not** followed by the subjunctive. The French are positive when they think something and then express it, not surprising in the light of the famous words of the French philosopher Descartes: *Je pense, donc je suis*, 'I think, therefore I am.' However, doubt and the subjunctive do come in when this certainty of thought and statement is turned negative, with *ne...pas* for example. This means that the French for 'I don't think that...' is followed by the subjunctive.

NO DOUBT

I think we're going to see them tonight.
Je pense que nous allons les voir ce soir.

He thinks that he knows that their house is wonderful.
Il croit savoir que leur maison est superbe.

DOUBT

I do not think we're going to see them tonight.
Je ne pense pas que nous les voyions ce soir.

Our parents do not think that these were his last words.
Nos parents ne croient pas que celles-ci aient été ses dernières paroles.

NO DOUBT

I think that his grandfather is more than seventy years old.
Il me semble que son grand-père a plus de soixante-dix ans.

DOUBT

It seems that his grandfather is/might be more than seventy years old.
Il semble que son grand-père ait plus de soixante-dix ans.

NO DOUBT

It seems to us that she often betrays her friends' secrets.
Il nous semble qu'elle trahit souvent les secrets de ses amies.

DOUBT

Il seems that she (may) often betray(s) her friends' secrets.
Il semble qu'elle trahisse souvent les secrets de ses amies.

NO DOUBT

It seems to me that she is providing information to an official of a foreign embassy.
(FORMAL)
Il me semble qu'elle fournit des renseignements à un fonctionnaire d'une ambassade étrangère.
(FORMAL)

DOUBT

It would seem that she is providing information to an official of a foreign embassy.
Il semblerait qu'elle fournisse des renseignements à un fonctionnaire d'une ambassade étrangère.

AN EXCEPTION

It seems that he is the richest man in the village.
Il paraît qu'il est l'homme le plus riche du village.

In the following examples we move into a domain where it is possible either to use or not to use the subjunctive, depending on what the speaker wanted to say. So, if you want to indicate that something is virtual, that is, **if you want to raise a doubt concerning the real existence of something in a particular time and place, you use the subjunctive** in your sentence. As with the examples above, if there is no doubt, then there is no subjunctive.

NO DOUBT

Our boss is looking for a technician who can do this repair (The speaker is sure there is a technician who can do the repair).
Notre patron cherche un technicien qui peut faire cette réparation.

DOUBT

Our boss looking for a technician who can do this repair
Notre patron cherche un technicien qui puisse faire cette réparation.

(In this case the speaker doubts whether there really is a technician out there who can do that repair. Perhaps it's a really difficult one. Or, perhaps, there is not a technician available at that particular moment in time).

At first sight, the following examples seem to be full of certainty and therefore we might suspect that they do not take the subjunctive. However, in these cases, the speaker is opening what he or she is saying to **doubt** from the listener. The 'you may doubt me' element of in these sentences takes away their absolute certainty and allows the subjunctive in.

Julie is the most intelligent woman I know.
Julie est la femme la plus intelligente que je connaisse.

Michel is the only one to trust her.
Michel est le seul qui lui fasse confiance.

This unique experience was appreciated in the world of work.
Cette expérience unique fût appréciée dans le monde du travail.

VII.

This civil servant has denied that his boss signed the authorisation.
Ce fonctionnaire a nié que son chef ait signé l'autorisation.(we don't know if the boss signed it or not)

Robert denies that his wife saw them arrive.
Robert nie que sa femme les ait vus arriver. (we don't know if they arrived or not)

VIII.

The young supporters wanted the match to be postponed until the following day.
Les jeunes supporters ont désiré que le match soit reporté au lendemain.

This evening I prefer you to go out with your girlfriends. (INFORMAL)
Ce soir j'aime mieux que tu sortes avec tes copines. (INFORMAL)

I would like him to pay more attention to his work.
J'aimerais qu'il fasse plus attention à son travail.

I would want/wish him to come with me.
Je souhaiterais qu'il vienne avec moi.

I would like him to do all the homework that he is given.
J'aimerais bien qu'il fasse tous les devoirs qu'on lui donne.

It would be preferable if this change came about as soon as possible. (FORMAL)
Il serait souhaitable que ce changement advînt aussitôt que possible. (FORMAL)

I would prefer her not to drink so much at the weekend.
Je préférerais qu'elle ne boive pas autant le week-end.

I insist that you do it yourself. It will take you ten minutes.
Je tiens à ce que vous le fassiez vous-même. Ça va vous demander dix minutes.

I do not want André to be punished.
Je ne veux pas qu'André soit puni.

BUT

'I want to do what I want all the time' he affirmed. (INFORMAL)
'Je veux faire ce que je veux tout le temps' a-t-il affirmé. (INFORMAL)

IX.

The marshal ordered his soldiers to attack the fort. (FORMAL)
Le maréchal ordonna que ses soldats prennent d'assaut le fort. (FORMAL)

We demand that he recognises his mistakes.
On exige qu'il reconnaisse ses fautes.

Why does he speak about things of which he is ignorant? He should keep his peace. (FORMAL)
Pourquoi parle-t-il de choses qu'il ne connaît pas? Qu'il se taise. (FORMAL)

She should tell me what she wants.
Qu'elle me dise ce qu'elle veut.

Let him go to Hell! (INFORMAL)
Qu'il aille au Diable! (INFORMAL)

Yes, I agree, it is time he tells me the truth.
Oui, je suis d'accord, il est temps qu'il me dise la vérité.

BUT

The general ordered the soldier to go and fetch his horse.
Le général ordonna au soldat d'aller lui chercher son cheval.

X.

It is necessary that you warn him beforehand.
Il est nécessaire que tu le mettes en garde auparavant.

I have to tell you something important.
Il faut que je vous dise quelque chose d'important.

It is indispensable that an interpreter accompanies the minister at all times.
Il est indispensable qu'un interprète accompagne le ministre en permanence.

It was essential that he finished the task before the other group.
Il était essentiel qu'il terminât le travail avant l'autre groupe.

BUT

Come on Annick, on Sunday you absolutely have to visit Aunt Gladys.
Écoute Annick, dimanche il faut absolument aller voir tante Gladyse.

XI.

It is possible that he may go to New York next week.
Il se peut qu'il aille à New York la semaine prochaine.

It is possible that the aircraft passengers are already dead.
Il est possible que les passagers de l'avion soient déjà morts.

BUT

Today, it is possible to go around the world in less than thirty hours.
Aujourd'hui, il est possible de faire le tour du monde en moins de trente heures.

ANSWER

The phrase made up of the trigger words will help you to remember when to use the subjunctive. French uses it frequently, English hardly at all. Here are the trigger words:

i.   happy
ii.   permission
iii.   sad
iv.   angry
v.   fear
vi.   doubt
vii.   denial
viii.   want
ix.   command
x.   possibly…
xi   necessary

Here is the phrase: 'she was **happy** with his **permission**,
        but **sad** and **angry** about his **fear**, **doubt** and **denial**,
        she still **wanted** to **command** the things that
        would be **possibly** be **necessary**.'

9.1.2   After which type of expressions of argumentation do I **have to** use the subjunctive?

If we want to convince others with argument, we need to position ideas and expressions in relation to each other and also in relation to the real world. The following phrases which all do that, end in *que* and are followed by the subjunctive. They frequently refer to actions in the real world. Most speakers of French consider that using the subjunctive in your speech and writing is a badge of sophistication, a sign that you can move ideas around in the complex ways. See if you can work out possible names for each of the categories by finding a common element across the meaning of the sentences. Answers are given below.

i. (SEE ALSO **1.4**)

We acted in this way so that the owner takes us seriously.
Nous avons agi ainsi pour que le propriétaire nous prenne au sérieux.

The staff on the boat will act in such a way that your needs will be catered for.
Le personnel du navire fera en sorte que vos besoins soient satisfaits.

Professor Simon speaks more loudly so that the students at the back of the hall can hear him. (INFORMAL)
Le professeur Simon parle plus fort afin que les étudiants au fond de l'amphi puissent l'entendre.(INFORMAL)

Your office should prepare this report in a such a way that it can be read by non-specialists.
Votre service devrait préparer ce rapport de telle sorte qu'il puisse être lu par des non-spécialistes.

II.

The match starts at three, unless the referee is late.
Le match commence à trois heures, à moins que l'arbitre ne soit en retard.

We will get there before the other group, provided that we leave early.
Nous y arriverons avant l'autre groupe, à condition que nous partions de bonne heure.

Suppose that it rains this afternoon, our guests are not going to be able to go for a walk in the park.
À supposer qu'il pleuve cet après-midi, nos invités ne vont pas pouvoir se promener dans le parc.

Supposing that it rains this afternoon, our guests are not going to be able to go for a walk in the park.
En supposant qu'il pleuve cet après-midi, nos invités ne vont pas pouvoir se promener dans le parc.

Suppose that it rains this afternoon, our guests are not going to be able to go for a walk in the park.
Supposez qu'il pleuve cet après-midi, nos invités ne vont pas pouvoir se promener dans le parc.

The fact that he believes himself to be better than others does not stop me from being his friend.
Le fait qu'il se croie supérieur aux autres ne m'empêche pas d'être son ami.

III.

Although he works forty hours a week, he is never tired.
Bien qu'il travaille quarante heures par semaine, il n'est jamais fatigué.

Although everybody is there, the boss has still not arrived.
Quoique tout le monde soit là, le patron n'est toujours pas arrivé.

IV. (SEE ALSO 2.1 AND 2.2)

Watch out sir, hold your child before he falls!
Attention monsieur, tenez votre enfant avant qu'il ne tombe!

Your brother is going to remain here until you have finished your homework.
Ton frère va rester ici jusqu'à ce que tu aies terminé ton devoir.

It is time that he admits his role in this matter.
Il est temps qu'il admette sa participation dans cette affaire.

It is urgent that you are there before your team arrives.
Il est urgent que vous soyez là avant l'arrivée de votre équipe.

Francine started to cry after the sentence was passed.

EITHER

Francine s'est mise à pleurer après que la peine ait été prononcée.

OR

Francine s'est mise à pleurer après que la peine a été prononcée.

(You have a choice whether or not to use the subjunctive here because usage is changing, *après que* is becoming like *avant que* which is already followed by the subjunctive).

V.

It is of no consequence that he is very old, this man must be judged.
Peu importe qu'il soit très âgé, cet homme doit passer en jugement.

It is not that he is unpleasant all the time, but he is moody all the same.
Ce n'est pas qu'il soit désagréable tout le temps, mais il est quand même lunatique.

We can find nothing which proves that this suspect knows the victim.
Nous ne trouvons rien qui nous prouve que ce suspect connaisse la victime.

There is no one who is capable of running the hundred metres in less than eight seconds.
Il n'y a personne au monde qui soit capable de courir un cent mètres en moins de huit secondes.

That's it, there's nothing that we can do for him.
C'est fini, il n'y a rien que nous puissions faire pour lui.

It is impossible that there is a cuboid planet.
Il est impossible qu'il y ait une planète cubique.

The thief was able to get into the house without us realising anything.
Le voleur a pu s'introduire chez nous sans que nous nous soyons aperçus de quelque chose.

It is false that she is sixteen.
Il est faux qu'elle ait seize ans.

It is rare that one sees this bird around here.
Il est rare qu'on voie cet oiseau par ici.

As far as I know one has to be a member to enter this club. (FORMAL)
Autant que je sache il faut être membre pour entrer dans ce club. (FORMAL)

ANSWER

Here are the names of the individual categories. How close were your guesses? You could now go back and fill the names in and to look through the examples again.

i.   goals and results
ii.   just imagine…
iii.   contrasts with although
iv.   time and time distinctions
v.   imagining a negative or a near negative

9.1.3   Which other expressions of emotion and argument also take the subjunctive?

ANSWER

It is important that you know what you have to do.
Il est important que tu saches ce que tu dois faire.

It is surprising that he went to Paris so soon.
Il est surprenant qu'il soit allé à Paris si tôt.

As for me, it is enough that he says he loves her.
Quant à moi, il suffit qu'il dise qu'il l'aime.

Is it fair that you are always first?
Est-ce qu'il est juste que vous soyez toujours le premier?

Is it normal that he can't stop swearing?
Est-il normal qu'il ne puisse pas s'arrêter de jurer?

It is better that he knows nothing about what we did yesterday.
Il vaut mieux qu'il ne sache rien de ce que nous avons fait hier soir.

9.2 What is the 'historic present' and when do I use it?

Look through the three paragraphs below, paying particular attention to the use of tense. What effect is the author trying to achieve?

Il s'appelle le Chevalier de Maine et il veut séduire la favorite du Prince de Lorné. D'abord il lui fait parvenir des billets doux par l'intermédiaire de son laquais Fronton. Mais le Chevalier se trouve renvoyé par la dame sans autre forme de procès. Et bientôt il renonce à son projet. (FORMAL)

1859. Les habitants de l'île de Bolon sont inquiets. Nuit et jour le volcan gronde, ils savent très bien qu'il sont en danger. Très vite ils se rassemblent devant la case du chef. Le grand Mutou sort et se tient devant ses tribus. Il lit l'inquiétude sur leurs visages et il en est bouleversé. Il leur dit d'une voix affaiblie qu'il ne reste plus qu'à quitter leur île bien-aimée.

Vous voulez une information technique sur les ordinateurs Megaoctet dans les années soixante-dix ? Alors vous rendez-vous compte qu'une pareille demande est difficile à satisfaire ? Le lendemain vous vous adressez à la direction, qui vous informe par courrier que la société est en voie de restructuration et qu'il est absolument impossible de vous renseigner.

ANSWER

Therefore this tense is called the historic present; here the present tense describes events which took place in the past. The author's aim in each case is to make a story about the past come alive. The important thing to note is that the French doing words should be translated into the past in English. Whenever you see a present tense in a story in French with clear indications that it took place in the past (such as dates), check whether the author is using the present tense for effect. The historic present is very different from the past historic (*il alla*), which refers to actions in the past which have no effect on the present (see 1.18).

9.3   What are the frequent differences in word order between French and English?

Appreciated by specialists for its excellent bouquet, this wine has broken all records for price. (FORMAL)

Apprécié par les spécialistes pour son excellent bouquet, ce vin a battu tous les records de prix. (FORMAL)

Although she has many family responsibilities, Mrs. Béranger continues to attend classes at the conservatory.

Bien qu'ayant beaucoup d'obligations familiales, Mme Béranger continue à suivre les cours du conservatoire.

We went home full of joy.

Tout joyeux, nous sommes rentrés chez nous.

Simple and fun, this children's game comes from the USA.

Simple et amusant, ce jeu pour enfants vient des Etats-Unis.

ANSWER

Standard word order in French and English consists of a person who does an action (the subject), the doing word which describes the action and then the thing which receives the action which is done (the object), then there are optional words which may describe how the action was done (the complement). However, French departs from this word order much more frequently than English. Indeed, it is possible to make your writing sound French by interspersing your sentences with examples where the word order varies, for instance by beginning the sentence with the complement. Watch out, though, because the overuse of this technique is considered pretentious.

9.4 How can simple naming words in French be used to translate rarer English doing words?

Look at how the way the French phrase is built up, they mean the same thing as their English translations, but what is the difference in the number of words used in each case?

GROUP A
Slowly and with much scraping, the audience rose to its feet.
Lentement, et accompagnée par plusieurs bruits de chaise, l'assistance s'est levée.

The queen reviewed the regiments who had assembled in front of her palace.
La reine a passé en revue les régiments qui s'étaient assemblés devant son palais.

From afar, I saw a person waving at me. (FORMAL)
De loin, j'ai vu une personne qui me faisait signe de la main. (FORMAL)

The children shook their heads.
Les enfants ont fait non de la tête.

ANSWER

French frequently has simple naming words translating the richness of English expressions with doing words. Therefore, when translating from English to French, think first of a simple combination of words to translate single doing words in English.

10

English uses this form frequently, where French uses it hardly at all

10.1 What are the ways of avoiding the frequently-occurring English passives? and what is their effect on tense in French?

What is the passive? Look at this table that shows what changes in the passive.

Normal order		Passive order	
first position	section position	first position	second position
The dog bit	him	he was bitten by	the dog

ANSWER

It is a reversal, where the person or thing which receives the action is put in first position. In normal order in English we would expect the person or thing which does the action to come first and the person or thing which receives the action to come second.

Take a look at the sentences below; they are examples of how the passive is avoided in French.

GROUP A

What was said in the meeting?
Qu'est-ce qu'on a dit à la réunion?

It seems that you have not been informed.
J'ai l'impression qu'on ne vous a pas informé.

GROUP B

My argument is based on the statistics on a report from 1999.
Je me suis basé sur les statistiques d'un rapport de 1999.

This record is so successful that thousands of copies of it will be sold.
Ce disque a un tel succès qu'il va se vendre à des milliers d'exemplaires.

ANSWER

— —

The sentences in group a avoid the passive by using *on*. Those in group b, avoid the passive by using doing words with *se* (reflexives). It is usually best to avoid the passive in French, unless it seems that the reversal of normal order is at the heart of the meaning of the sentence.

What is the different effect on tense when a passive in French is an action or a state? Look at the sentences below and you should be able to allocate the tenses to action and to state quite easily.

— —

GROUP A

He was bitten by a Pitbull Terrier.
Il a été mordu par un pitbull.

OR *Il fut mordu par un pitbull.* (see also 1.18 when to use past historic)

In this sentence you can also use *se faire* and the 'to' form of the doing word 'to bite'. In any case, the pattern of tenses stays the same:

Il s'est fait mordre par un pitbull.

OR *Il se fit mordre par un pitbull.*

Samuel was run over by a car.
Samuel a été renversé par une voiture.

OR *Samuel fut renversé par une voiture.*

GROUP B

The butter was kept in the fridge.
Le beurre était rangé dans le frigo.

Jack was very hurt by Mary's comments.
Jacques était très blessé par les remarques de Marie.

ANSWER

If the passive describes an action, then use the 'have' tense if the context is informal, and the past historic when it is formal. If the passive conveys a state, then only use the 'was' tense. The ways that actions and states relate to tense here is identical to the tense differences in section 1.18.

10.2   How to I translate English doing words ending in '-ing'?

Have a look at the sentences in groups a, b and c below; what is the type of word which recurs in English and what are the different ways in which is it translated into French?

GROUP A

Karen is getting craftier as the years go by.
Karen devient plus rusée au fil des années.

I am feeling better now.
Je me sens mieux maintenant.

Commercial translating is not easy.
La traduction commerciale n'est pas facile.

I'll be seeing you again soon, don't worry.
Je te reverrai bientôt, ne t'inquiètes pas.

No smoking.
Défense de fumer.

No Parking.
Défense de stationner.

After finishing his speech, he left.
Son discours terminé, il partit.

Do you like swimming?
EITHER Est-ce que vous aimez nager?
OR Est-ce que vous aimez la natation?
OR Aimez-vous la natation? (FORMAL)
OR Aimez-vous nager? (FORMAL)
(*natation* has a sense of swimming as a sport).

GROUP B

'Flying saucers have landed behind the library' exclaimed Willy before he fell over.
'Des soucoupes volantes se sont posées derrière la bibliothèque' s'est exclamé Willy avant de tomber sur le dos.

He told a touching story.
Il a raconté une histoire touchante.

She made several moving testimonies to the court.
Elle a fait plusieurs témoignages émouvants à la cour.

GROUP C

Isabelle always dances listening to the radio.
Isabelle danse toujours en écoutant la radio.

I have a friend who broke four ribs playing rugby.
J'ai un copain qui s'est cassé quatre côtes en jouant au rugby.

The little boy says he hurt himself falling from the top of the stairs.
Le petit dit qu'il s'est fait mal en tombant du haut de l'escalier.

Drinking makes people talkative!
C'est en buvant qu'on devient bavard!

Practising one's sport every day makes success possible.
C'est en s'entraînant tous les jours qu'on rend la réussite possible.

Although I respect your opinion, I realise that you are often wrong.
Tout en respectant ton opinion, je me rends compte que tu as souvent tort.

Although I am a Christian, I recognise the value of other religions.
Tout en étant chrétien, je reconnais la valeur des autres religions.

ANSWER

In these sentences we are dealing with words which almost all end with '-ing' in English. In most of the sentences in group a, the 'ing' is not translated into French. You can see that this group is large and has a variety of different types of language, ranging from everyday sentences, such as 'I am feeling better', to signs such as: 'No Parking'. This is an indication of how often '-ing' words occur in English where they cannot be translated directly into French. Group b is a smaller group; it uses the word ending in '-ing' as a describing word! In these cases it is always translated by a word ending in *-ant* in French. And describing a person or thing, it changes according to whether the person or thing is feminine, masculine plural or feminine plural, thus adding *e, s* or *es*. Group c is different again. Here the '-ing' word is translated because it conveys the idea of one thing happening at the same time as another in English. Here is another translation tip related to group c: when you have to translate sentence like: 'he ran down the street' and even more complicated ones such as 'he slammed the door behind him', you can use the *-ant* form and *en* in French because these two actions of 'running' and the direction 'down' happen at the same time. Or they are almost simultaneous in the case of 'slammed' and 'behind'.

He ran down the street.
Il descendit la rue en courant.

OR il a descendu la rue en courant.

He slammed the door behind him.
Il est sorti en claquant la porte.

--- --- --- --- --- --- --- --- --- --- --- --- --- --- --- --- --- ---

10.3 Do the colours in French change to follow *le, la* and *les*, when I add *clair* and *sombre*, the words for 'light' and 'dark'?

'He's called Mario and he's got brown eyes', said Elisabeth.
*'Il s'appelle Mario et il a les yeux **bruns**' a dit Elisabeth.*

CHANGES TO...

'He's called Mario and he's got dark brown eyes' says Elisabeth.
*'Il s'appelle Mario et il a les yeux **brun** foncé' a dit Elisabeth.*

There was a blue carpet in the room.
*Il y avait une moquette **bleue** dans la pièce*

CHANGES TO...

There was a light blue carpet in the room.
*Il y avait une moquette **bleu** clair dans la pièce.*

ANSWER

When they are written with 'light' and 'dark', both *clair* and *foncé* and the colours themselves do not change.

11

There are two words, or ways of saying something in English, where there is only one in French

11.1 How do I translate 'it' and 'them' with doing words with *à*?

Look at the sentences below; 'it' and 'them' in English are only translated into French in one way. Can you detect the trigger in the doing words which sets this off?

Tomorrow is Henri's party. You are invited to it, are you?
Demain c'est la fête d'Henri. Vous y êtes invitée, n'est-ce pas?

Do you remember Antoine and Antoinette's parties last year; but no, you were not invited to them, were you?
Vous vous rappelez les fêtes d'Antoine et d'Antoinette l'année dernière; mais non, vous n'y étiez pas invitée, n'est-ce pas?

ANSWER

If you have already mentioned a thing or things once in the sentence and then use a doing word which takes *à* (see 2.10), then both 'it' and 'them' are translated by *y*.

11.2   How do I translate 'it' and 'them' with doing words with *de*?

Look at the sentences below; 'it' and 'them' in English are only translated into French in one way. Can you detect the trigger in the doing words which sets this off?

Your behaviour in class is awful and I am going to complain about it to the headmistress. (FORMAL)
Votre tenue en classe est déplorable et je vais m'en plaindre à la directrice.(FORMAL)

The drinks were past their 'sell by' date and I am going to complain about them.
Les boissons étaient périmées et je vais m'en plaindre.

Our team has been beaten and we are completely infuriated about it.
Notre équipe a été battue et nous en sommes complètement indignés.

What a long series of defeats! We are sick of them. (INFORMAL)
Quelle longue série de défaites! Nous en avons marre. (INFORMAL)

ANSWER

If you have already mentioned a thing or things once and then use a doing word which takes *de* (see 2.10.), then both 'it' and 'them' are translated by *en*.

11.3   When does *même* mean 'same' and when does it mean 'even'?

In the two groups of sentences below there is a basic difference in the way that *même* is being used, can you see it?

GROUP A

We want the same thing; we have the same dream.
Nous voulons la même chose; nous rêvons à la même chose.

He doesn't know that twins have the same birthday!
Il ne sait pas que des jumeaux ont le même anniversaire!

GROUP B

You don't even love your dog.
Tu n'aimes même pas ton chien.

Even I could do a painting like that!
Même moi, je pourrais faire une peinture comme ça!

ANSWER

Use this test: if *même* is used with naming words, then it is translated as 'same'; otherwise it is translated by 'even'.

11.4   When does *son* mean 'his' and when 'her'?

Look at the sentences below, *son* is a basic word, but can you work out what determines its usage?

Simon is Jeanne's brother, therefore Simon is her brother.
Simon est le frère de Jeanne, donc Simon est son frère.

Simon is Paul's brother, therefore Simon is his brother.
Simon est le frère de Paul, donc Simon est son frère.

There's Ginette, her cousin plays football for France.
Voilà Ginette, son cousin joue dans l'équipe nationale de France de football.

ANSWER

Son is used before a masculine word; it can mean both 'his' and 'her.' It is determined by the thing or person possessed and not by the possessor as in English.

11.5　When does *sa* mean 'his' and when 'her'?

Sa, too is a basic word, but what determines when it is used?

And the farmer's sister, what's she called?
Well, his sister is called Gertrude. (INFORMAL)
Et la sœur du fermier, comment s'appelle-t-elle?
Eh bien, sa sœur s'appelle Gertrude. (INFORMAL)

Amir told us that his cousin does a lot of sport.
Amir nous a dit que sa cousine fait beaucoup de sport.

The official: So, Madam, whose aunt are you?
Aunt Angélique: Sir I am his aunt (she says pointing at her nephew).
The nephew: Yes sir, you are looking at my Aunt Angélique.
Le fonctionnaire: Alors, Madame vous êtes la tante de qui?
Tante Angélique: Monsieur, je suis sa tante (dit-elle en montrant son neveu).
Le neveu: Oui monsieur, c'est ma tante Angélique que vous avez devant vous.

ANSWER

Sa is used before a feminine word; it can mean both 'his' and 'her.' It too is determined by the thing or person possessed and not by the possessor as in English.

11.6　When does *aussi* mean 'also' and when does it mean 'therefore'?

When you look at the sentences in the two groups below, what is it about *aussi* which makes it change meaning?

GROUP A

'I too have work to do', he answered.
'Moi aussi, j'ai du travail à faire', lui a-t-il répondu.

But is it true that Jean came as well? How happy I am!
Mais est-ce que c'est vrai que Jean est venu aussi? Comme je suis contente!

But you too found it difficult to translate this letter.
Mais vous aussi, vous avez eu du mal à traduire cette lettre.

GROUP B

He had health problems, therefore he wouldn't do sport at school.
Il avait des problèmes de santé, aussi ne faisait-il pas de sport à l'école.

Her father sees how she got lost in the park. Therefore he says that she is too young to go out without him.
Son père voit comme elle se perd dans le parc. Aussi dit-il qu'elle est trop jeune pour sortir sans lui.

ANSWER

The form and meaning of the sentences in group a will already be familiar to you. So what is the difference between groups a and b? You can see that in group b *aussi* comes at the start of the phrase (after a comma) or sentence, that it means 'therefore' and that after it the normal order of the person followed by the doing word are reversed.

11.7   How does a change in position affect the words *ancien, anciens, ancienne* and *anciennes*?

How does the position of *ancien* (and *anciens, ancienne* and *anciennes*) affect how it is translated into English?

GROUP A

I have been told that they are ancient buildings.
On m'a dit que ce sont des bâtiments anciens.

An ancient temple dominates the town of Tourel.
Un temple ancien domine la ville de Tourel.

In the corner of the room you will see an ancient tapestry.
Au coin de la pièce vous verrez une tapisserie ancienne.

Look at the ancient ruins of the temple of Maba, they date from 1348.
Regardez les ruines anciennes du temple de Maba, elles datent de 1348.

GROUP B

Seeheim's new arts centre was built in the town's former abattoirs.
On a construit le nouveau centre culturel de Seeheim dans les anciens abattoirs de la ville.

On Saturday I met my former French teacher at the municipal theatre.
Samedi j'ai rencontré mon ancien professeur de français au théâtre municipal.

The former headmistress of our school now works in the Ministry of Education.
L'ancienne directrice de notre école travaille maintenant au Ministère de l'Education Nationale.

After leaving the firm I hardly see my former women colleagues.
Depuis mon départ de l'entreprise je ne vois guère mes anciennes collègues de travail.

ANSWER

In each group you can see how the meaning of *ancien* and its relations changes according to whether it precedes or follows the naming word. This phrase may help you to remember the difference: if it's 'old' it drags along behind the naming word (otherwise it means 'former').

11.8   When does *faire* mean to 'make', to 'do' and when does it mean to 'have something done'?

What is the difference between the use of *faire* between groups a, b and c?

GROUP A
You did it very well, congratulations!
Tu l'as fait très bien, félicitations!

GROUP B
Sir I am sorry to say that you have made a mistake. (FORMAL)
Monsieur je regrette de vous dire que vous avez fait une erreur. (FORMAL)

GROUP C
I had a new garage built.
J'ai fait construire un nouveau garage.

After hearing a strange noise, I had my car checked.
Après avoir entendu un bruit anormal, j'ai fait contrôler ma voiture.

My wife went to town to have a new ball gown made for herself.
Ma femme est allée en ville pour se faire confectionner une nouvelle robe de bal.

ANSWER

You will be familiar with the forms in groups a and b; however, in group c there is a shift in meaning, the action is no longer performed by the person speaking, but by another, usually a tradesperson with specialist skills. In English, this corresponds to the phrase: 'to have something made or done.'

11.9   When is there one form of the present tense in French and two forms in English?

What is the difference in the time frame of the actions described in groups a and b below?

GROUP A

I see what you mean.
Je vois ce que vous voulez dire.

I do what I want to here, ok?
Je fais ce que je veux ici, d'accord?

GROUP B

We are still seeing pictures of animal carcasses on television.
On voit encore des images de carcasses d'animaux à la télévision.

Look, I am doing exactly what you said.
Regardez, je fais exactement ce que vous m'avez dit de faire.

ANSWER

Group a contains sentences with a straightforward present tense in English and French. In group b, the form of the word is no different in French. However, English has another type of present tense that uses the parts of 'to be' and the '-ing' from the doing word in question. This form of the present conveys the idea of an action that has been going on for some time. So, when translating from French to English, be aware that you can use the forms in group b if they fit into the context of the sentence. There is always the possibility of two forms of the present tense in English.

11.10 What is the one word in French which means both 'thank you' and 'no thank you'?

Have a look at these exchanges between two people in groups a and b below and see if you can understand the difference between the situations in which the offer takes place.

GROUP A

Mrs Dufour: Here is your new bank card, sir.
Mr Jeanneret: Thank you madam.
Mme Dufour: Voici votre nouvelle carte bancaire, monsieur.
M. Jeanneret: Merci madame.

GROUP B

Mr. Black: More spinach?
Jacqueline: No thanks.
M. Noir: Tu reprends des épinards?
Jacqueline: Merci.

ANSWER

In group b, there is a clear choice, the person offering does not know whether the other person is going to accept or refuse the offer, so the choice is open and genuine. The word *merci*, thanks the person for the offer and refuses it, in fewer words than the English 'no thank you'. It is frequently accompanied by a gesture to underline that it is a refusal, either a shake of the head or a 'stop' gesture (palm outwards and vertical).

11.11 What is the one word in French which means both 'expensive' and 'dear' to a person?

What is the decisive difference in the use of *cher* and its relations in the groups below?

GROUP A

In this boutique they only sell very expensive products.
Dans cette boutique on ne vend que des produits très chers.

It is said that England is an expensive country.
On dit que l'Angleterre est un pays où la vie est chère.

GROUP B

My dearest niece.
Ma très chère nièce.

Dear Jean, I am going to miss you!
Cher Jean, que tu vas me manquer!

ANSWER

The difference is one of word order: *cher* meaning 'expensive' follows the naming word and *cher* meaning 'dear to someone' precedes it. You can remember it in this way, many things in life are expensive and therefore, just like most describing words, *cher* with this meaning follows the naming word. Being 'dear to a person' is much rarer and therefore it comes before the naming word, just like a few special describing words (such as *bon* and *vieux*).

11.12 What is the one word in French, which means both 'poor, pitiable' and 'poor, with no money'?

In the sentences in groups a and b below, you will see a familiar pattern of difference in meaning developing.

GROUP A

Oh my poor friend, we are in a fine mess now.
Oh mon pauvre ami, nous voilà maintenant dans de beaux draps.

He has been terrible to his wife, he is really a sad bloke. (VERY INFORMAL)
Il a été odieux envers sa femme, c'est vraiment un pauvre type. (VERY INFORMAL)

GROUP B

They are poor countries and very few people live there
Ce sont des pays pauvres et très peu de gens y vivent.

Most of the poor countries are found south of the equator.
La plupart des pays pauvres se trouvent au sud de l'équateur.

ANSWER

───

Pauvre changes meaning according to word order; when it comes before the naming word it means 'pitiable' and when it comes after it means 'poor' in the sense of lacking in money and material things.

───

11.13 What is the one word in French which means both 'clean' and 'own'?

What determines the meaning of *propre*?

GROUP A

Yes of course they have their own apartment.
Oui bien sûr qu'ils ont leur propre appartement.

I am sure that Fiona has her own mobile. (INFORMAL)
Je suis sûr que Fiona a son propre portable.(INFORMAL)

GROUP B

Henry lives in a clean apartment in the centre of Perpignan.
Henri habite un appartement propre au centre de Perpignan.

Here you are, a clean glass.
Tiens, voici un verre propre.

ANSWER

───

Propre follows the same pattern. When it comes before the naming word it means 'own' and when it comes after it means 'clean'.

───

11.14 What is the one word in French, which means 'look at' in English?

How are the two elements of the English doing word to 'look at' translated into French?

Look at me attentively, I am going to surprise you.
Regardez moi très attentivement, je vais vous surprendre.

Jeanne sat down in a café and looked at the people going past in the street for two hours.
Jeanne s'est installée dans un café et a regardé les passants dans la rue pendant deux heures.

There, look at that bird of prey on the post.
Tenez, regardez cet oiseau de proie sur le poteau.

ANSWER

French uses the doing word *regarder* alone, where English needs an 'at', when there is a specific object or individual to be observed. This includes the 'people going past in the street for two hours' because this is considered to be a specific episode.

11.15 What is the one word in French, which means 'pay for' in English?

In the sentences below the 'for' in the English 'to pay for' is not translated.

Who's going to pay for the drinks this time? (INFORMAL)
C'est qui qui va payer les boissons cette fois-ci?(INFORMAL)

My parents cannot afford to pay for foreign holidays for their children every year.
Mes parents n'ont pas les moyens de payer des vacances à l'étranger à leurs enfants tous les ans.

Oh no, I've left my wallet at home, who can pay my bill for me?
Oh zut, j'ai oublié mon porte-monnaie à la maison, qui pourrait régler l'addition à ma place?

ANSWER

This is an extremely common mistake and it is important to recognise that you only need *payer* in French, this always applies because there is always a specific object to pay for in French and in English.

11.16 What is the one word in French, which means to 'wait for' in English?

In the sentences below the 'for' in the English 'to wait for' is not translated.

'Wait for me under the oak tree behind the barn' Marie whispered to me.
'Attends-moi sous le chêne derrière la grange' me chuchota Marie.

You always have to wait for the traffic light to change before putting your foot down. (INFORMAL)

Il faut toujours attendre que le feu passe au vert avant d'appuyer sur le champignon. (INFORMAL)

One of the most famous plays of the twentieth century is *Waiting for Godot*.

Une des pièces les plus célèbres du vingtième siècle, c'est En Attendant Godot.

ANSWER

This is another case of recognising that you only need one word – *attendre* in French when you want to express waiting for a specific person. However, when a phrase accompanies 'wait' then use *que* plus the subjunctive (see subjunctive 9.1.2, iv and 'until' at 2.2), as in the following example:

We are waiting for him to leave the theatre / until he leaves the theatre.

Nous attendons qu'il quitte le théâtre.

11.17 What is the one word in French, which means 'listen to'?

In the sentences below the 'to' in 'listen to' is not translated.

Please Janine, listen to what I am going to tell you.

Janine s'il te plaît, écoute bien ce que je vais te dire.

We were in the process of listening to the news on the radio when Siobhan came in.

On était en en train d'écouter les informations à la radio quand Siobhan est entrée.

We went out onto the balcony to listen to the waves crashing on the beach.

Nous sommes sortis sur le balcon pour écouter les vagues déferler sur la plage.

Listen, you have to understand that I have had enough of it now.

Écoute, il faut que tu comprennes que j'en ai assez maintenant.

ANSWER

Once again, it is a case of remembering that English has two words, where French has one. This applies in the vast majority of cases, only appeals for attention (such as in the final example) and direct appeals to hearing as a sense have both one word in English and in French. For example: 'Chut, écoute!' which is translated as 'Shh, listen!'

11.18 What is the one word in French, which means 'ask for'?

Take a look at the sentences below, the 'for' in 'to ask for' in English is not translated into French.

Believe me, in that hotel, you shouldn't ask for room 101.
Crois-moi, dans cet hôtel-là, il ne faudrait pas demander la chambre 101.

Are you sure that you are going to ask for a reduction?
Es-tu sûr que tu vas demander un rabais?

ANSWER

You only need *demander* in French in those cases (the vast majority) where a person is asking for something specific which is mentioned in the sentence. The pattern is different in both French and English if the thing being asked for is a phrase with a doing word as in the following sentences:

When you arrive at his office ask to see me.
Quand tu arrives à son bureau demande à me voir.

In the first example above 'ask' is followed by 'to' in English and *à* in French. In the example below 'ask' is not followed by anything in French or in English.

If you need anything do not hesitate to ask me for it.
Si vous avez besoin de quelque chose n'hésitez pas à me le demander.

12

There are three ways of saying something in English, where there is only one in French

12.1 How do I translate *il y a*?

How are the words *il y a* working in different ways below?

GROUP A
A hundred years ago, the study of foreign languages was reserved for a minority of pupils.
Il y a cent ans, l'étude des langues étrangères était réservée à une minorité d'élèves.

GROUP B
There is some cake in the kitchen, if you want some, just help yourself.
Il y a du gâteau dans la cuisine, si tu en veux, n'hésite pas à te servir.

GROUP C
There are a hundred years in a century.
Il y a cent ans dans un siècle.

ANSWER
─ ─
In the first example *il y a* means 'ago'. In the examples in group b, *il y a* means 'there is' and in group c it means 'there are'.
─ ─

12.2   How do I translate *lui*?

Looking at the sentences in the groups below, can you deduce when you have the choice whether to translate *lui* with either 'him' or 'her' or 'it' and when there is only one correct translation? A subsidiary question is: what is the difference between groups b and c?

GROUP A

Eve gave the apple to him/to her.
Ève lui donna la pomme.

Do you think that she will write to him/her?
Pensez-vous qu'elle lui écrira?

The monster went away when Dennis gave it a kick.
Le monstre partit quand Denis lui donna un coup de pied.

I advised him/her to go to the prefecture straightaway and show his /her documents.
Je lui ai conseillé d'aller tout de suite présenter ses papiers à la préfecture.
(conseiller à quelqu'un de faire quelque chose)

Sir, I cannot allow him/her to speak in that way.
Monsieur, je ne peux pas lui permettre de s'exprimer ainsi.
(permettre à quelqu'un de faire quelque chose)

His teachers forbid him/her from running beside the swimming pool.
Ses professeurs lui défendent de courir sur le bord de la piscine.
(défendre à quelqu'un de faire quelque chose)

The general ordered him/her to contact the reinforcements in the southern sector.
Le général lui a donné l'ordre de contacter les renforts dans le secteur sud.
(commander à quelqu'un de faire quelque chose)

GROUP B

Are you going to go out with him?
Est-ce que tu vas sortir avec lui?

The children gathered around him.
Les enfants se sont rassemblés autour de lui.

Yes, my confidence in him does not stop growing.
Oui, ma confiance en lui ne cesse d'augmenter.

GROUP C

Yes, he's the robber, no doubt about it. (INFORMAL)
Oui, c'est lui le voleur, aucun doute. (INFORMAL)

Well really! she is stronger than him.
Décidément elle est plus forte que lui

No, I am not like him at all.
Non, je ne suis pas du tout comme lui.

ANSWER

In group a, *lui* means 'him', 'her' or 'it' with doing words which take *à* (see 2.10). It is handy to remember that these doing words generally **regulate human behaviour** and have a set pattern with *me*, *te*, *lui*, *se*, *nous*, *vous* and *leur* (when the person is not mentioned, otherwise *à* is used with the person's name). Groups b and c share the fact that *lui* is translated by 'him' alone. In group b, *lui* is used when 'him' follows a position words such as 'around', *autour de*, 'on', *sur*, 'above' *au-dessus de*, and 'below' *au-dessous de*. In group c, *lui* means 'him' when the word 'him' is emphasised; for example when it follows *c'est* or when it is used in comparisons.

12.3   When do I use *leur* (and *leurs*)?

Look at the sentences in the three groups below; can you piece together the ways in which *leur* is being used in group a and how and why *leur* and *leurs* is used in group b?

GROUP A

I am telling them the truth.
Je leur dis la vérité.

He seems to have taught them how to make explosive devices.
Il leur aurait appris comment fabriquer des engins explosifs.

GROUP B

The president gave his opinion to them.
Le président de la République leur a donné son avis.

What did you say to them?
Qu'est-ce que vous leur avez dit?

GROUP C

The two young pupils threw their briefcases on the ground.
Les deux jeunes élèves ont jeté leur cartable par terre.

The baseball players put on their caps.
Les joueurs de base-ball ont mis leur casquette.

I saw their socks next to their shoes on the river bank.
J'ai vu leurs chaussettes à côté de leurs chaussures sur la rive.

Coming back from holiday, they found their house completely wrecked.
En rentrant de vacances, ils ont trouvé leur maison entièrement saccagée.

ANSWER

In group a *leur* means 'them' and appears with the doing words which take *à*. 'In these cases *leur* comes immediately before the main doing word in French; whereas in English 'them' immediately follows the doing word. The examples in group b appear with doing words which take *à*, just as in group a, but they are translated by 'to them' in English. The main thing to be aware about is that both 'them' and 'to them' can be translated into French by *leur*. In group c *leur* refers to singular naming words and also to things, which people either only have one of (for example, 'head'), or only possess one of at any one particular time; for example, 'hat'. You will also find *leurs* used in the plural when referring to things of which people have more than one. So in French we identify the plural in the normal way here by the addition of an 's'.

13

There are five ways of saying something in English, where there is only one in French

13.1   How do I translate *on*?

English speakers of French often underuse *on* and do not realise its versatility; some of the sentences below may contain uses which are new to you.

GROUP A
You can affirm that the English are patriotic.
On peut affirmer que les Anglais sont patriotes.

In the evening you can always go to the local pub.
Le soir, on peut toujours aller au pub du coin.

GROUP B
One does what one says.
On fait ce qu'on dit.

In this situation one feels powerless.
Dans cette situation on se sent impuissant.

GROUP C
Soon we are going to get near the town.
Bientôt on va s'approcher de la ville.

Come on, we're going to have a great time. (VERY INFORMAL)
Allez viens, on va s'éclater.(VERY INFORMAL)

GROUP D

So lads, are you all settled in well ?
Alors les gars, on est bien installé ?

GROUP E

They seldom eat horsemeat in France.
On mange très rarement du cheval en France.

They are talking of putting up taxes in Great Britain.
On parle d'augmenter les impôts en Grande-Bretagne.

They tell me that you do not like it here.
On me dit qui vous ne vous plaisez pas chez nous.

ANSWER

On is used very frequently in French and is versatile. Its meanings of 'you' and 'one' are interchangeable, but 'one' is more formal than 'you' of course. On meaning 'we' and 'you' in the plural are similar and are used in spoken French. The final meaning 'they' is the rarest, but also the one that is most frequently overlooked.

13.2 There is one word in French which means 'nil', 'o', 'zero', 'love' and 'nought'?

Look at the richness of the English language in expressing 'nothing'!

GROUP A

Lens beat Paris-Saint-Germain four nil.
Lens s'est imposé quatre à zéro face au Paris-Saint-Germain.

GROUP B

In the fourth game of the second set, Yvette Rocher is leading Lyndsey Dodds by thirty to love.
Dans le quatrième jeu du deuxième set, Yvette Rocher mène trente-zéro contre Lyndsey Dodds.

GROUP C

The thermometer shows that it is zero degrees Celsius in the garden this morning.
Le thermomètre indique zéro degré dans le jardin ce matin.

GROUP D
Yes the last two figures in my telephone number are 'o' and six.
Oui les deux derniers chiffres de mon numéro de téléphone sont zéro et six.

GROUP E
Don't forget that the code ends in a nought.
N'oubliez pas que le code se termine par un zéro.

ANSWER

Group a; this is a way of saying *zéro* which belongs to the specialist vocabulary of football.

Group b: this is a way of translating *zéro* which belongs to the specialist vocabulary of tennis (combine *quinze-*, *trente-* and *quarante-* with *zéro*, to form 'fifteen-love', 'thirty-love' and 'forty love'.

Group c: this is a fixed expression which translates *zéro* in the domain of temperature.

Group d: here *zéro* comes in a series of numbers (three or more). You could say 'zero' in English too of course, but there is another more frequent way of translating it.

Group e: this is an older, rarer way of saying *zéro* in English.

PART TWO

THE GRAMMAR WORKBOOK

1

There are two ways of saying something in French, where there is only one in English

1.1 When do I say *si* and when *oui*, meaning 'yes'?

Fill the blank spaces below with either *si* or *oui*.

Questions 1.1	Explanations 1.1	Answers 1.1
1. Max: Non, Sam ne l'aurait pas pris. Nathalie: Mais ___!	1. The first sentence is in the negative. There is disagreement.	1. Max: Non, Sam ne l'aurait pas pris. Nathalie: Mais si!
2. James: Ce prof arrive toujours en retard. Sunil: ___, nous nous y sommes habitués.	2. The first sentence is positive. There is no disagreement.	2. James: Ce prof arrive toujours en retard. Sunil: oui, nous nous y sommes habitués.
3. Andrée: Je ne crois pas qu'on se revoie avant Noël. Steven: ___, à la fête de Joaquin.	3. The first sentence is in the negative. There is disagreement.	3. Andrée: Je ne crois pas qu'on se revoie avant Noël. Steven: Si, à la fête de Joaquin.
4. Manou: Je vois que tu ne te sens pas bien... Rachid: Mais ___! Je vais bien.	4. The first sentence is in the negative. There is disagreement.	4. Manou: Je vois que tu ne te sens pas bien... Rachid: Mais si! Je vais bien.
5. Samuel: Tu penses que papa sera d'accord là-dessus? Jennifer: ___ je crois.	5. The first sentence is not a negative sentence and there is no disagreement.	5. Samuel: Tu penses que papa sera d'accord là-dessus? Jennifer: oui je crois.

1.2 How do I say 'to know': *savoir* or *connaître*?

Using the present tense, put the correct doing word in the blank.

Questions 1.2	Explanations 1.2	Answers 1.2
1. Je ___ où il a caché son argent. 2. ___-vous qu'il a été très malade? 3. Je ___ bien Monsieur Proust. 4. Il ___ très bien l'Arabie Saoudite. 5. Ce gars-là, il ne ___ pas sa force. 6. Je ___ à quelle heure le train doit arriver. 7. Ma mère ___ quel jour et quel mois il est né. 8. ___-vous qu'il est interdit de se baigner ici? 9. Écouter de la musique sublime pendant des heures, c'est une habitude que je ___ bien! 10. Je ___ les vins d'Alsace parce j'en bois toutes les semaines.	1. Hard fact. 2. Also a fact. 3. Knowing a person. 4. Experience based knowledge. 5. Experienced based knowledge, or rather a lack of it. 6. A fact. 7. Two facts. 8. A fact, hard knowledge. 9. Experience-based knowledge. 10. Knowledge amassed through experience.	1. Je sais où il a caché son argent. 2. Savez-vous qu'il a été très malade? 3. Je connais bien Monsieur Proust. 4. Il connaît très bien l'Arabie Saoudite. 5. Ce gars-là, il ne connaît pas sa force. 6. Je sais à quelle heure le train doit arriver. 7. Ma mère sait quel jour et quel mois il est né. 8. Savez-vous qu'il est interdit de se baigner ici? 9. Écouter de la musique sublime pendant des heures, c'est une habitude que je connais bien! 10. Je connais les vins d'Alsace parce que j'en bois toutes les semaines.

1.3 Do I say *sans* or *sans que*?

Put either *sans* or *sans que* into the blanks below.

Questions 1.3	Explanations 1.3	Answers 1.3
1. Le catastrophe de Marsala a eu lieu ___ personne n'ait pu l'enregistrer. 2. Il faut que j'aille la voir ___ lui. 3. Le cambrioleur a pu fausser compagnie aux gendarmes (give them the slip) ___ ceux-ci s'en aperçoivent toute de suite. 4. Comment a-t-il bien pu lire la lettre ___ ouvrir l'enveloppe? 5. ___ vous, nous aurions renoncé à notre projet.	1. A phrase after the blank with a subjunctive. 2. Only one word after the blank. 3. A phrase after the blank with a subjunctive. 4. No complete phrase after the blank. 5. The comma marks the end of the phrase; therefore there is only one word after the blank.	1. Le catastrophe de Marsala a eu lieu sans que personne n'ait pu l'enregistrer. 2. Il faut que j'aille la voir sans lui. 3. Le cambrioleur a pu fausser compagnie aux gendarmes sans que ceux-ci s'en aperçoivent toute de suite. 4. Comment a-t-il bien pu lire la lettre sans ouvrir l'enveloppe? 5. Sans vous, nous aurions renoncé à notre projet.

1.4   Do I say *pour* or *pour que*?

Put either *pour* or *pour que* into the blanks below.

Questions 1.4	Explanations 1.4	Answers 1.4
1. Ce manuel de grammaire est trop simple ___ moi. 2. ___ comprendre ce qu'il dit, il faut l'écouter attentivement. 3. ___ ne pas t'abîmer la santé, il faut que tu arrêtes de boire. 4. Nous avons tout fait ___ il mène à bien ses études. 5. On a utilisé des graphiques ___ ils comprennent la situation de l'entreprise.	1. Only one word after the blank. 2. Several words after the blank, but not a complete sentences with a person doing the action. 3. Only two words after the blank before the comma. 4. Full sentence after the blank. 5. Full sentence after the blank.	1. Ce manuel de grammaire est trop simple pour moi. 2. Pour comprendre ce qu'il dit, il faut l'écouter attentivement. 3. Pour ne pas t'abîmer la santé, il faut que tu arrêtes de boire. 4. Nous avons tout fait pour qu'il mène à bien ses études. 5. On a utilisé des graphiques pour qu'ils comprennent la situation de l'entreprise.

1.5   Do I say *plus de* or *plus que*?

Choose either *plus de* or *plus que* for the blank spaces below.

Questions 1.5	Explanations 1.5	Answers 1.5
1. D'habitude, il a plus ___ six voitures chez lui. 2. Je vois là plus ___ une simple erreur. 3. Plus ___ la taille, c'est la couleur de la robe qui me gêne. 4. Sa façon d'agir est plus ___ choquante. 5. Il y a plus ___ vingt personnes ici.	1. Cars are countable. 2. Non-countable, a naming word accompanied by a describing word. 3. *La taille* is being used in a non-countable way. 4. Non-countable. 5. Countable.	1. D'habitude il a plus de six voitures chez lui. 2. Je vois là plus qu'une simple erreur. 3. Plus que la taille, c'est la couleur de la robe qui me gêne. 4. Sa façon d'agir est plus que choquante. 5. Il y a plus de vingt personnes ici.

1.6 Normally doing words use *avoir*, but how can I remember which words use *être*?

Using the 'have' tense, put the either *avoir* or *être* into the blank.

Questions 1.6	Explanations 1.6	Answers 1.6
1. Est-ce que Marie ___ déjà descendue?	1. 'D' is the first letter of 'draper's van'	1. Est-ce que Marie est déjà descendue?
2. Oui, nous ____ arrivés à l'heure.	2. 'A' is also in the 'van' and it is a doing word which describes movement.	2. Oui, nous sommes arrivés à l'heure.
3. En voyant l'autre homme, il ___ pensé à mon père.	3. A doing word with 'p', but one which does not denote movement.	3. En voyant l'autre l'homme, il a pensé à mon père.
4. Simon ___ entré dans la préfecture.	4. Movement is present in this doing word.	4. Simon est entré dans la préfecture.
5. Je ___ rentrée en bus.	5. This doing word includes movement and is related to the previous one.	5. Je suis rentrée en bus.
6. Mon oncle ___ devenu comptable.	6. This doing word is related to *venir*, which clearly has movement.	6. Mon oncle est devenu comptable.
7. Peter ___ tombé par terre.	7. This is a doing word which refers to ↓ (down).	7. Peter est tombé par terre.
8. Mon père ___ descendu les poubelles.	8. This is a 'van' word, but is being used to carry out an action on an object.	8. Mon père a descendu les poubelles.
9. Il ___ remonté le clignotant sur ta bicyclette.	9. This is a 'van' word, but is being used to carry out an action on an object.	9. Il a remonté le clignotant sur ta bicyclette.
10. Jean ___ monté pour voir s'il était là.	10. This is a doing word which refers to ↑ (up).	10. Jean est monté pour voir s'il était là.

1.7   What is the right word order if I start a phrase with *peut-être*?

Translate the following English sentences into French using both ways that you have learnt.

Questions 1.7	Explanations 1.7	Answers 1.7
1. Perhaps they have already left for (*partir en*) town. 2. Perhaps we will have good weather (*du beau temps*) tomorrow. 3. Perhaps they are going to come to our party (*notre fête*).	For each question. The first way includes *que* with normal word order. The second type includes a reversal of word order between the person and the doing word.	1. Peut-être qu'ils sont déjà partis en ville. Peut-être sont-ils déjà partis en ville. 2. Peut-être que nous aurons du beau temps demain. Peut-être aurons-nous du beau temps demain. 3. Peut-être qu'ils vont venir à notre fête. Peut-être vont-ils venir à notre fête.

1.8   How do I say 'good': *bon* or *bien*?

You have to insert either *bon* or *bien* into the gaps below.

Questions 1.8	Explanations 1.8	Answers 1.8
1. Ah Janine, ce parfum sent très ___! 2. L'Autriche possède un ___ réseau de transports en commun. 3. Ce serait ___ si on pouvait aller le voir. 4. Est-ce que tu trouves que cet hamburger est ___? 5. Oui nous pensons qu'il est ___ comme professeur.	1. This is a good smell. 2. This is a judgement presented as a fact. 3. This is a judgement. 4. Here 'good' refers to food. 5. This is a judgement.	1. Ah Janine, ce parfum sent très bon! 2. L'Autriche possède un bon réseau de transports en commun. 3. Ce serait bien si on pouvait aller le voir. 4. Est-ce que tu trouves que cet hamburger est bon? 5. Oui nous pensons qu'il est bien comme professeur.

1.9   How do I say 'better': *mieux* or *meilleur*?

Choose between *mieux* or *meilleur* for the gaps below.

Questions 1.9	Explanations 1.9	Answers 1.9
1. Personne ne chante ___ que Georges. 2. Ma statue est ___ que la tienne. 3. Ce violon est ___ que celui-là. 4. Je joue ___ que vous au badminton. 5. Cette peinture est la ___ de ce musée.	1. 'Better' refers to a doing word here. 2. 'Better' refers to a naming word here. 3. 'Better' refers to a naming word here. 4. 'Better' refers to a doing word here. 5. 'Better' refers to a naming word here.	1. Personne ne chante mieux que Georges. 2. Ma statue est meilleure que la tienne. 3. Ce violon est meilleur que celui-là. 4. Je joue mieux que vous au badminton. 5. Cette peinture est la meilleure de ce musée.

1.10   How do I say 'best': *le mieux* or *le meilleur*?

Select *le mieux* or *le meilleur* to fill the gaps below.

Questions 1.10	Explanations 1.10	Answers 1.10
1. Voilà le choriste qui chante ___. 2. Je vous prie d'agréer, Madame, l'expression de mes ___ sentiments. 3. Nous avons fait de notre ___. 4. Mon oncle m'a dit que les Bochiman sont les ___ coureurs du monde. 5. C'est là qu'on trouve les ___ vins de la région. 6. Quel est le ___ tableau de Picasso à votre avis?	1. 'Best' refers to a doing word here. 2. 'Best' refers to a naming word here. 3. 'Best' refers to a doing word here. 4. 'Best' refers to a naming word here. 5. 'Best' refers to a naming word here. 6. 'Best' refers to a naming word here.	1. Voilà le choriste qui chante le mieux. 2. Je vous prie d'agréer, Madame, l'expression de mes meilleurs sentiments. 3. Nous avons fait de notre mieux. 4. Mon oncle m'a dit que les Bochiman sont les meilleurs coureurs du monde. 5. C'est là qu'on trouve les meilleurs vins de la région. 6. Quel est le meilleur tableau de Picasso à votre avis?

1.11   How do I say 'whatever': *quel... que* or *quoi...que*?

Choose between *quel... {que}* or *quoi... {que}* to fill the gaps below.

Questions 1.11	Explanations 1.11	Answers 1.11
1. ___ que soient tes soucis, tes amis te soutiendront.	1. 'Whatever' refers to a naming word.	1. Quels que soient tes soucis, tes amis te soutiendront.
2. ___ qu'elle fasse, elle ne réussit que rarement.	2. 'Whatever' refers to a doing word.	2. Quoi qu'elle fasse, elle ne réussit que rarement.
3. ___ que soit la chose qu'on lui donne, il n'est jamais satisfait.	3. 'Whatever' refers to a naming word.	3. Quelle que soit la chose qu'on lui donne, il n'est jamais satisfait.
4. ___ que vous fassiez, vous n'arriverez jamais à le convaincre.	4. 'Whatever' refers to a doing word.	4. Quoi que vous fassiez, vous n'arriverez jamais à le convaincre.
5. ___ que soit le résultat, nous savons, de toute façon, que tu as fait de ton mieux.	5. 'Whatever' refers to a naming word.	5. Quel que soit le résultat, nous savons, de toute façon, que tu as fait de ton mieux.

1.12   How do I say 'each': *chaque* or *chacun(e)*?

Which is correct for the blank spaces below, *chaque* or *chacun(e)*?

Questions 1. 12	Explanations 1.12	Answers 1.12
1. ___ devrait connaître ses limites.	1. 'Each' is being used with a doing word here.	1. Chaque personne devrait connaître ses limites.
2. ___ fois que je sors de la baignoire je glisse sur le carrelage.	2. 'Each' is describing a naming word here and does not change.	2. Chaque fois que je sors de la baignoire je glisse sur le carrelage.
3. ___ d'entre nous a droit à un emploi.	3. 'Each' is being used with a doing word here.	3. Chacun(e) d'entre nous a droit à un emploi.
4. A ___ son goût.	4. 'Each' here is being used with a set phrase.	4. A chacun son goût.
5. Un jour viendra où ___ devra prendre soin de ses parents.	5. 'Each' is being used with a doing word here.	5. Un jour viendra où chacun devra prendre soin de ses parents

1.13   How do I use negatives in French?

Translate the following sentences into French.

Questions 1.13	Explanations 1.13	Answers 1.13
1. Karima hasn't read this book.	1. A two-part negative.	1. Karima n'a pas lu ce livre.
2. I am only nineteen years old.	2. A virtual two-part negative.	2. Je n'ai que dix-neuf ans.
3. It is hardly possible to see the mountains.	3. A two-part negative.	3. Il n'est guère possible de voir les montagnes.
4. I find that a bit surprising: you didn't want to buy anything in that town.	4. Not....anything in English is translated by 'nothing', a standard two-part negative.	4. Je trouve ça un peu surprenant; tu n'as rien voulu acheter dans cette ville.
5. Andrew hasn't said anything all evening (*toute la soirée*).	5. Not....anything in English is translated by 'nothing', a standard two-part negative.	5. Andrew n'a rien dit de toute la soirée.
6. Not one of the team members (*joueurs de l'équipe*) came (*est venu*) to the training session (*à la séance d'entraînement*).	6. A negative which relates to the absence of people.	6. Aucun des joueurs de l'équipe n'est venu à la séance d'entraî-nement.
	7. A negative which relates to the absence of people.	7. Je n'avais entendu personne.
7. I had heard nobody.	8. Although this relates to the absence of people, normal word order applies here.	8. Jacques a crié son nom. Personne n'a répondu.
8. Jack shouted his name. No one answered.		
9. That is a glass and not a vase.	9. Negation of a naming word alone.	9. Cela est un verre et non pas un vase.
10. I think (*pour moi*) this sculpture is beautiful and not ugly.	10. Negation of a describing word alone.	10. Pour moi cette sculpture est belle et non laide.
11. We cannot find the proof (*la preuve*) here.	11. One of the doing words (*savoir, pouvoir, oser* and *cesser de*) which negate differently in formal contexts.	11. Nous ne pouvons trouver la preuve ici.
12. We do not know how to make wines of such quality (*des vins d'une telle qualité*).	12. One of the doing words (*savoir, pouvoir, oser* and *cesser de*) which negate differently in formal contexts.	12. Nous ne savons comment fabriquer des vins d'une telle qualité.
13. I am not going to repeat it to you.	13. Informal negation.	13. Je ne vais pas vous le répéter deux fois.
14. Neither Pierre, nor Paul want to go out (*sortir*).	14. The translation of the negative 'neither...nor' has one more part in French than in English.	14. Ni Pierre, ni Paul ne veulent sortir.
15. He doesn't say anything to anybody.	15. A combination of two negatives: 'nothing' and 'nobody.'	15. Il ne dit rien à personne.

1.14 How do I translate and use *quelque chose*, meaning 'something'?

Translate the following sentences into French.

Questions 1.14	Explanations 1.14	Answers 1.14
1. There is something behind the door. 2. There is something unpleasant in the drawer (*le tiroir*). 3. Was there (*Y avait-t-il*) something interesting on telly (*à la télé*) yesterday evening? 4. If you (*vous*) hear something suspicious, warn me immediately. 5. I have something to tell you.	1. *Quelque chose* written in two words. 2. *Quelque chose* written in two words and followed by a masculine describing word. 3. *Quelque chose* written in two words and followed by a masculine describing word. 4. *Quelque chose* written in two words and followed by a masculine describing word. 5. *Quelque chose* written in two words.	1. Il y a quelque chose derrière la porte. 2. Il y quelque chose de désagréable dans le tiroir. 3. Y avait-t-il quelque chose d'intéressant à la télé hier soir? 4. Si vous entendez quelque chose de suspect, prévenez-moi immédiatement. 5. J'ai quelque chose à vous dire.

1.15 How do I translate 'who...to', 'who...about', 'who...around' and 'who...with'?

In the questions you have an English sentence and the first possible translation. In each case, the answer is the second way of expressing the sentence in English.

Questions 1.15	Explanations 1.15	Answers 1.15
1. The woman who he was speaking with is my aunt. *La femme avec laquelle il parlait est ma tante.* 2. The footballer who the youths gathered around, fainted. *Le footballeur autour de qui tout le monde s'est pressé, s'est évanoui.* 3. You're the man who I want to live with. *Tu es l'homme avec qui je veux vivre.*	1. Translate 'who'. 2. Translate 'which'. 3. Translate 'which'.	1. La femme avec qui il parlait est ma tante. 2. Le footballeur autour duquel tout le monde s'est pressé, s'est évanoui. 3. Tu es l'homme avec lequel je veux vivre.

1.16 Do I use *en* or *dans* to mean 'in' when taking about a duration of time?

Fill the gaps below with either *en* or *dans*.

Questions 1.16	Explanations 1.16	Answers 1.16
1. ___ deux mois son état s'est aggravé. 2. Je vous donnerai les copies ___ dix jours. 3. Mardi ___ huit nous serons de retour à Paris. 4. J'aurai l'argent ___ deux jours, je te le jures. 5. ___ huit jours il a pu apprendre le cha-cha-cha.	1. Here 'in' refers to duration, to the whole span of the time. 2. Here 'in' points to the end of the period of time and the future tense is used. 3. Here 'in' points to the end of the period of time and the future tense is used. 4. Here 'in' points to the end of the period of time and the future tense is used. 5. Here 'in' refers to duration, to the whole span of the time.	1. En deux mois son état s'est aggravé. 2. Je vous donnerai les copies dans dix jours. 3. Mardi en huit nous serons de retour à Paris. 4. J'aurai l'argent dans deux jours, je te le jures. 5. En huit jours il a pu apprendre le cha-cha-cha.

1.17 When do I say *jour* and when is it right to say *journée* and *soir/soirée*, *an/année* and *matin/matinée*?

Fill the blanks in each sentence with one of the two options in brackets at the end.

Questions 1.17	Explanations 1.17	Answers 1.17
1. Ils ont passé toute ___ ___ à danser. (le soir/ la soirée) 2. ___ ___ nous descendrons en ville pour voir les monuments illuminés. (Un soir/ Une soirée) 3. ___ ___ avec trois enfants, ça fatigue, vous savez. (Un jour/ Une journée) 4. Cornelius se lève à midi tous ___ ___. (les jours/ les journées) 5. Je vous ai déjà souhaité ___ ___ ___, il me semble? (le bon an/ la bonne année)	1. *Toute* indicates that the whole of the evening is meant here. It is also in the feminine! 2. This is a general reference to 'one' evening. 3. The sentence implies that the whole of the day was spent with the children. 4. A general reference. No duration here. 5. This is a fixed expression, which although it is general, uses the longer form.	1. Ils ont passé toute la soirée à danser. 2. Un soir nous descendrons en ville pour voir les monuments illuminés. 3. Une journée avec trois enfants, ça fatigue, vous savez. 4. Cornelius se lève à midi tous les jours. 5. Je vous ai déjà souhaité une bonne année, il me semble?

1.18   Which past tense should I use in French, and when?

Analyse the type of event and reference in the past, so that you can then say whether it is either the 'have' tense/ the past historic OR the 'was' tense.

Questions 1.18	Explanations 1.18	Answers 1.18
1. England didn't win the football World Cup in 1998. 2. At this time my uncle's business was not going very well. 3. They looked at each other, they began to smile and they fell in love. 4. Before we got married you never gave me flowers. 5. He thought that he knew everything about cars. 6. You used to say all the time that my father knew everything about gardening. 7. I felt that he was useless. 8. I got up, got dressed and then went out to have breakfast in a café. 9. My grandfather died at the age of thirty nine. 10. While the adults talked, she played chess with her sister.	1. This a historically complete action, does it have an effect on the present? 2. Is the beginning and the end of this state of affairs clear? 3. How do the events in this sequence follow each other? 4. Do we have a fixed point in time here, a beginning or an end? 5. What sort of representation of time occurs here; is this a state? 6. This is a repeated action. 7. What sort of representation of time occurs here; is this a state? 8. How do the events in this sequence follow each other? 9. What is the pattern of this doing word in time? Is it a point or a duration? 10. Do we have a fixed point in time here, a beginning or an end? Or is this a continuum?	1. The 'have' tense or the past historic is used: L'Angleterre n'a pas gagné la Coupe du Monde en 1998. 2. The 'was' tense is used: A cette époque l'entreprise de mon oncle ne marchait pas très bien. 3. The past historic or the 'have' tense is used: Ils se regardèrent, se sourirent, et ils tombèrent amoureux l'un de l'autre. 4. The past historic or the 'have' tense is used: Avant notre mariage tu ne m'a jamais offert de fleurs. 5. The 'was' tense is used: Il croyait tout connaître sur les voitures. 6. The 'was' tense is used: Vous disiez tout le temps que mon père connaissait tout sur le jardinage. 7. The 'was' tense is used: Je sentais qu'il ne valait pas grand chose. 8. The 'have' tense is used: Je me suis levé, je me suis habillé et ensuite je suis sorti pour prendre un petit déjeuner dans un café. 9. The 'have' tense is used: Mon grand-père est mort à l'âge de trente-neuf ans. 10. The 'was' tense is used: Pendant que les adultes discutaient, elle jouait aux échecs avec sa sœur.

1.19 When do I say *voici* and when *voilà,* meaning 'here'?

Insert *voici* or *voilà* into the blanks below.

Questions 1.19	Explanations 1.19	Answers 1.19
1. Regardez, ___ le laitier qui ouvre la porte du jardin. 2. ___ la bouteille de vin que tu as entamée. 3. Fais attention, ___ le contrôleur qui arrive de l'autre wagon. 4. La ___! 5. Bon, j'en ai assez, je te le donne, ___.	1. The milkman is probably close to the speaker. 2. The speaker seems to be pointing at the bottle, which is close by. 3. The speaker is pointing at something which is further away 'over there' i.e. *là-bas.* 4. Here the speaker could be both referring to something close by or further away. 5. The speaker seems very close to the object and the addressee.	1. Regardez, voici le laitier qui ouvre la porte du jardin. 2. Voici la bouteille de vin que tu as entamée. 3. Fais attention, voilà le contrôleur qui arrive de l'autre wagon. 4. La voilà!/la voici! 5. Bon, j'en ai assez, je te le donne, voici.

1.20 When do I say *celui-ci* and when *celui-là?*
1.21 When do I say *celle-ci* and when *celle-là?*

Put the either *celui-ci, celui-là, celle-ci* or *celle-là* into the gaps below.

Questions 1.20 and 1.21	Explanations 1.20 and 1.21	Answers 1.20 and 1.21
1. Lequel des pains veux-tu? Je pense que je vais prendre ___; Ce pain complet. 2. Quelle est la meilleure raquette dans ce magasin? Je vous recommande ___ sans la moindre hésitation. 3. Lequel des poissons vous plaît le plus? J'aime ___, tout au fond (right at the back) de l'étalage. 4. Choisissez une boisson différente, puisque ___ a un taux d'alcool très élevé.	1. It is *le pain* and the bread seems near the speaker. 2. You say *la raquette* and it seems further away from the speaker. 3. It is *le poisson* and the fish is further away from the speaker. 4. You say *la boisson* and the drink is very close to the speaker.	1. Lequel des pains veux-tu? Je pense que je vais prendre celui-ci; Ce pain complet. 2. Quelle est la meilleure raquette dans ce magasin? Je vous recommande celle-là sans la moindre hésitation. 3. Lequel des poissons vous plaît le plus? J'aime celui-là, tout au fond de l'étalage. 4. Choisissez une boisson différente, puisque celle-là a un taux d'alcool très élevé.

1.22 How do I say 'it' in phrases like 'it is difficult to…', with *il* or *ce*?

Insert *il est* or *c'est* into the gaps below.

Questions 1.22	Explanations 1.22	Answers 1.22
1. Un bon esprit de groupe, ___ une de ces choses qui me fait vraiment plaisir. 2. ___ facile de proposer de telles conclusions. 3. ___ impossible d'évaluer le chiffre d'affaires de cette entreprise en ce moment. 4. Comme je vous l'ai déjà expliqué, il faut éviter de traverser cette région, ___trop dangereux. 5. Voici Malik, ___un bon gardien de but.	1. The blank concerns a reference back to *un esprit de groupe*. 2. This is a reference forward. 3. This is also a reference forward. 4. The meaning of the sentence indicates that this is a reference back. 5. This is an example of a reference back to a person which follows the same pattern as the sentences above.	1. Un bon esprit de groupe, c'est une de ces choses qui me fait vraiment plaisir. 2. Il est facile de proposer de telles conclusions. 3. Il est impossible d'évaluer le chiffre d'affaires de cette entreprise en ce moment. 4. Comme je vous l'ai déjà expliqué, il faut éviter de traverser cette région, c'est trop dangereux. 5. Voici Malik, c'est un bon gardien de but.

1.23 Do I say *dans le* or *en* when I mean 'in' with *départements* and counties?

Use either *dans le* or *en* to fill the blanks below.

Questions 1.23	Explanations 1.23	Answers 1.23
1. Chartres se trouve ___ Eure-et-Loir. 2. Moi, je ne suis pas né ___ Yorkshire! 3. Est-ce que Torquay se trouve dans le Devon? 4. Nous vivions alors ___ Var. 5. De nos jours, le nombre de voitures ___ Corrèze va en augmentant.	1. This French *département* has two words. 2. This is an English county. There is only one possibility here. 3. This is an English county. There is only one possibility here. 4. This is an English county. There is only one possibility here. 5. This is a French *département* with only one word.	1. Chartres se trouve en Eure-et-Loir. 2. Moi, je ne suis pas né dans le Yorkshire! 3. Est-ce que Torquay se trouve dans le Devon? 4. Nous vivions alors dans le Var. 5. De nos jours, le nombre de voitures en Corrèze va en augmentant.

1.24   Do I say *dans le* or *en*, when I mean 'to' with, *départements* and counties?

Use either *dans le* or *en* to fill the blanks below.

Questions 1.24	Explanations 1.24	Answers 1.24
1. Ce chauffeur veut toujours aller ___ Jura. 2. On va __ Maine-et-Loire ce soir. 3. Je vais également ___ Tarn-et-Garonne. Veux-tu venir ___ Staffordshire avec nous? 4. Marie ne voulait pas aller ___ Kent. 5. Au bout de trois ans cette famille en avait assez de vivre ___ Yorkshire.	1. This French *département* has one word. 2. This French *département* has two words 3. This French *département* has two words 4. This is an English county. There is only one possibility here. 5. This is an English county. There is only one possibility here.	1. Ce chauffeur veut toujours aller dans le Jura. 2. On va en Maine-et-Loire ce soir. 3. Je vais également en Tarn-et-Garonne. Veux-tu venir dans le Staffordshire avec nous? 4. Marie ne voulait pas aller dans le Kent. 5. Au bout de trois ans cette famille en avait assez de vivre dans le Yorkshire.

1.25   Do I say *dans le* or *en*, when I mean 'in' with US states, Canadian provinces and geographical regions?

Use either *dans le* or *en* to fill the blanks below.

Questions 1.25	Explanations 1.25	Answers 1.25
1. Il est domicilié ___ Louisiane 2. ___ Saskatchewan on cultive beaucoup de blé. 3. A présent, nous estimons qu'il se trouve ___Colombie-britannique. 4. En hiver ___Arizona il fait assez froid. 5. Quelque part ___ Floride. Je ne sais pas où.	1. *Louisiane* modifies the English name, is feminine and ends in 'e'. 2. *Saskatchewan* is not a modification of the English name and is masculine. 3. *Colombie-britannique* modifies the English name, is feminine and ends in 'e'. 4. *Arizona* is not a modification of the English name and is masculine. 5. *Floride* modifies the English name, is feminine and ends in 'e'.	1. Il est domicilié en Louisiane 2. Dans le Saskatchewan on cultive beaucoup de blé. 3. A présent, nous estimons qu'il se trouve en Colombie-britannique. 4. En hiver dans l'Arizona il fait assez froid. 5. Quelque part en Floride. Je ne sais pas où.

1.26   Do I say *dans le* or *en*, when I mean 'to' with US states, Canadian provinces and geographical regions?

Use either *dans le* or *en* to fill the blanks below.

Questions 1.26	Explanations 1.26	Answers 1.26
1. Je ne veux pas partir ___ Vermont. 2. Ils voulaient aller ___ Alberta. 3. En 1848 les premiers colons américains étaient déjà partis ___ Californie. 4. Est-ce que nous allons ___ Nevada cet hiver? 5. Si vous voulez voir Disneyland il ne faut pas aller ___ Floride.	1. *Vermont* is not a modification of the English name and is masculine. 2. *Alberta* is not a modification of the English name and is masculine. 3. *Californie* is a modification of the English name, ends in an 'e' and is feminine. 4. *Nevada* is not a modification of the English name and is masculine. 5. *Floride* is a modification of the English name, ends in an 'e' and is feminine.	1. Je ne veux pas partir dans le Vermont. 2. Ils voulaient aller dans l'Alberta. 3. En 1848 les premiers colons américains étaient déjà partis en Californie. 4. Est-ce que nous allons dans le Nevada cet hiver? 5. Si vous voulez voir Disneyland il ne faut pas aller en Floride.

1.27   Do I say *aux* or *dans les*, when I mean 'in' with countries and regions which have plural names like the 'The Netherlands'?

Use either *dans les* or *aux* to fill the blanks below.

Questions 1.27	Explanations 1.27	Answers 1.27
1. Je n'ai pas de maison de vacances ___ Maldives. 2. Il existe encore des problèmes politiques ___ Balkans. 3. Ce whisky est fabriqué ___ Hébrides, en Écosse. 4. J'habite ___ Pays-Bas depuis dix ans. 5. On dit qu'il y a du pétrole ___ Malouines.	1. The Maldives is a group of islands. The same form applies to independent countries. 2. The Balkans is a geographical region which is not an independent country. 3. The Hebrides is a group of islands. The same form applies to independent countries. 4. The Netherlands are an independent country; the same form applies to groups of islands. 5. *Les Malouines* (The Falklands) are a group of islands; the same form applies to an independent country.	1. Je n'ai pas de maison de vacances aux Maldives. 2. Il existe encore des problèmes politiques dans les Balkans. 3. Ce whisky est fabriqué aux Hébrides, en Écosse. 4. J'habite aux Pays-Bas depuis dix ans. 5. On dit qu'il y a du pétrole aux Malouines.

1.28   Do I say *aux* or *dans les*, when I mean 'to' with countries and regions which have plural names like the 'The Netherlands'?

Use either *dans les* or *aux* to fill the blanks below.

Questions 1.28	Explanations 1.28	Answers 1.28
1. Je vais ___ Açores pour passer les vacances. 2. Je quitte Bordeaux pour retourner ___ Landes. 3. Avant 1500 les navigateurs n'allaient pas jusqu'___ Philippines. 4. Les Français vont souvent ___ Comores. 5. Demain, nous allons nous rendre ___ Pyrénées.	1. *Les Açores* is a group of islands. The same form applies to independent countries. 2. *Les Landes* is a geographical region which is not a independent country. 3. *Les Philippines* is the name of an independent country and the same form applies to groups of islands. 4. *Les Comores* is a group of islands. The same form applies to independent countries. 5. *Les Pyrénées* is a geographical region which is not a independent country.	1. Je vais aux Açores pour passer les vacances. 2. Je quitte Bordeaux pour retourner dans les Landes. 3. Avant 1500 les navigateurs n'allaient pas jusqu'aux Philippines. 4. Les Français vont souvent aux Comores. 5. Demain, nous allons nous rendre dans les Pyrénées.

1.29   What is difference between *en plus* and *de plus*?

The blanks below have to be filled with either *en plus* or *de plus*.

Questions 1.29	Explanations 1.29	Answers 1.29
1. J'ai dix ans __ plus que mon frère. 2. On nous a demandé deux euros __ plus pour un envoi recommandé. 3. __ plus de sa carrière de pilote elle a élevé trois enfants. 4. __ plus je trouve que vous exagérez. 5. Celui-ci mesure deux mètres __ plus que celui-là.	1. In this sentence there is an element of comparison with a number or a quantity. 2. Here the sense of en plus is, 'in excess of', 'on top of' or 'a step too far'. 3. Here the sense of en plus is, 'in excess of', 'on top of' or 'a step too far'. 4. This is a fixed expression meaning 'furthermore.' 5. In this sentence there is an element of comparison with a number or a quantity.	1. J'ai dix ans de plus que mon frère. 2. On nous a demandé deux euros en plus pour *un envoi* recommandé. 3. En plus de sa carrière de pilote elle a élevé trois enf*ants*. 4. De plus je trouve que vous exagérez. 5. Celui-ci mesure deux mètres de plus que celui-là.

1.30   How do I say 'to remember': *se rappeler or se souvenir de*?

Formulate a translation for the part of these sentences with the doing words 'remember' and 'remind'.

Questions 1.30	Explanations 1.30	Answers 1.30
1. What? You don't remember me? 2. Remind me of the name of the first person on the list please. 3. Do you remember the first time you drove a car? 4. I only vaguely remember her. 5. Now I remem*ber that he* did *talk about an* old lady that he knew.	1. Here a person is remembered. 2. Here someone wants to be reminded, not of a person, but a name on a list. 3. Here, an event is being remembered. 4. This time it is a person who is being remembered. 5. Here, the speaker is recalling how someone talked about another person.	1. Quoi? Vous ne vous souvenez pas de moi? 2. Rappelle-moi le nom de la première personne sur la liste, s'il te plaît. 3. Rappelez-vous la première fois que vous avez conduit une voiture? 4. Je ne me souviens que vaguement d'elle. 5. Maintenant je me rappelle qu'il a parlé d'une vieille dame qu'il connaissait.

1.31   What is the difference between *rendre visite à* and *visiter*?

Translate the sentences below into French, paying special attention to the doing word 'visit'.

Questions 1.31	Explanations 1.31	Answers 1.31
1. Please visit me when I am in London. 2. When I am (use the future in French) in London I will visit the main museums (*musées principaux*). 3. (Something said as Jack says goodbye to his friend John) 'I'll visit, ok?' 4. The Queen's Gallery? I visited that yesterday. 5. Bognor. If you are (use *allez*) on the coast, you really (*absolument*) have to (use *il faut*) visit it (use *la ville*).	1. A person is being visited here. 2. A place is being referred to here. 3. 'Visit' refers to a person. 4. Here 'visit' refers to a place. 5. 'Visit' refers to a place here.	1. Rends-moi visite quand je serai à Londres, s'il te plaît. 2. Quand je serai à Londres je visiterai les musées principaux. 3. Je te rendrai visite, d'ac? (INFORMAL) 4. La Galerie de Peinture Royale? Je l'ai visitée hier. 5. Bognor: Si vous allez sur la côte il faut absolument visiter la ville.

1.32　When to I use *offrir* and when *donner*, meaning to 'give'?

Translate these sentences into French, paying particular attention to the doing word 'give'.

Questions 1.32	Explanations 1.32	Answers 1.32
1. Give me the telephone directory (*l'annuaire*), please (said to a friend).	1. This is a general use of give.	1. Donne-moi l'annuaire s'il te plaît.
2. I managed to give him the project details.	2. This is also a general use of give.	2. Je suis parvenu à lui donner les détails du projet.
3. I was given (use *on*) five presents on my birthday (*le jour de mon anniversaire*).	3. The person was given gifts.	3. On m'a offert cinq cadeaux le jour de mon anniversaire.
4. What are you going to give them for Christmas?	4. This example also refers to giving gifts.	4. Qu'est-ce que vous allez leur offrir pour Noël?
5. Please give me what I want (said to a friend)!	5. In this example it is not possible to say whether a gift is involved. Therefore use the general French word for 'to give'.	5. S'il te plaît, donne-moi ce que je veux.

1.33　When do I use *dépenser* and when *passer*, meaning 'to spend'?

Choose between the correct form of either *dépenser* or *passer* to fill in the blanks below.

Questions 1.33	Explanations 1.33	Answers 1.33
1. J'ai ___ une demi-heure assise devant le musée.	1. This sentence refers to spending time.	1. J'ai passé une demi-heure assise devant le musée.
2. Où est-ce que tu vas ___ les grandes vacances cette année?	2. This sentence refers to spending time.	2. Où est-ce que tu vas passer les grandes vacances cette année?
3. On a ___ trop d'argent en Suisse cet hiver.	3. This sentence refers to spending money.	3. On a dépensé trop d'argent en Suisse cet hiver.
4. J'ai ___ plus de cent euros dans ce magasin.	4. This sentence refers to spending money.	4. J'ai dépensé plus de cent euros dans ce magasin.
5. Combien avez-vous ___ cette fois-ci?	5. This sentence also refers to spending money.	5. Combien avez-vous dépensé cette fois-ci?

1.34 What is the difference between *la langue* and *le langage*?

Choose the correct word for language and, if necessary, the correct form of the describing word.

Questions 1.34	Explanations 1.34	Answers 1.34
1. Le langage familier/La langue familière ne me pose aucun problème. 2. Ma mère croit parler deux langues/deux langages couramment. 3. On croit que le russe est un langage/ une langue qui est difficile à apprendre. 4. Si on est fonctionnaire on doit pouvoir maîtriser le langage administratif/ la langue administrative. 5. J'ai toujours aimé étudier les langues vivantes/ les langages vivants.	1. This is a specific subdivision of language. 2. Here the reference is to two whole languages. 3. The reference here is to a whole language. 4. This is a specific subdivision of 'language'. 5. This is an exception which is a set phrase.	1. Le langage familier ne me pose aucun problème. 2. Ma mère croit parler deux langues couramment. 3. On croit que le russe est une langue qui est difficile à apprendre. 4. Si on est fonctionnaire on doit pouvoir maîtriser le langage administratif. 5. J'ai toujours aimé étudier les langues vivantes.

1.35 What is the difference between *tu* and *vous*, meaning 'you'?

Translate the sentences below into French, the phrases in brackets will help you; the main thing is to choose the correct option between *tu* and *vous*.

Questions 1.35	Explanations 1.35	Answers 1.35
1. 'If you would kindly listen to me now (use *vouloir bien m'écouter*)' – that is what you say when you want to speak to (*vous adresser à*) a group. 2. You are my friend. 3. Oh Fido, you are a clever dog! 4. Come on, Mum, you never let me go out after nine! 5. Sir, I fear that you are wrong (use *faire erreur*).	1. 'You' here refers to more than one person. 2. The speaker is necessarily close to the other speaker here. 3. Here the speaker is addressing an animal. 4. Here the speaker is talking to a member of his or her family. 5. The is a highly formal sentence where the speaker is being polite.	1. 'Si vous voulez bien m'écouter maintenant' est ce que vous dites quand vous voulez vous adresser à un groupe. 2. Tu es mon ami 3. Ah Fido, comme tu es un chien intelligent. 4. Allez, maman, tu ne me laisses jamais sortir après neuf heures du soir. 5. Monsieur je crains que vous ne fassiez erreur.

2

There are three ways of saying something in French, where there is only one in English

2.1 How do I say 'before' *avant, avant que* or *avant de*?

Insert either *avant* or *avant que* in the single blank provided below.

Questions 2.1	Explanations 2.1	Answers 2.1
1. ___ te rencontrer je ne savais pas ce que c'était que l'amour. 2. 'Rentre ___ minuit' cria papa, mais Julie était déjà partie. 3. Il faut agir ___ il ne soit trop tard. 4. Je me maquille toujours ___ sortir en boîte (INFORMAL). 5. S'il te plaît, préviens-nous, ___ tu ne le lui dises.	1. *Rencontrer* is the first form of the doing word you find in the dictionary. 2. The gap is followed by only one word to make a sense unit. 3. *Soit* is a subjunctive and there is a *ne*. 4. *Sortir* is the first form of the doing word you find in the dictionary. 5. *Dises* is a subjunctive and there is a *ne*.	1. Avant de te rencontrer je ne savais pas ce que c'était que l'amour. 2. 'Rentre avant minuit' cria papa, mais Julie était déjà partie. 3. Il faut agir avant qu'il ne soit trop tard. 4. Je me maquille toujours avant de sortir en boîte (INFORMAL). 5. S'il te plaît, préviens-nous, avant que tu ne le lui dises.

2.2   Do I use *que, jusque* or *jusqu'à ce que*, meaning 'until'?

Use either *que*, *jusque* or *jusqu'à ce que* to fill the blanks below.

Questions 2.2	Explanations 2.2	Answers 2.2
1. Bon, nous devons attendre ___ elle soit revenue de l'étranger (INFORMAL). 2. Combien de coureurs vont passer, ___ on le voie? 3. Pendant l'été ils jouent au foot ___ à neuf heures du soir. 4. La police attend ___ le suspect se présente. 5. Oui, tu as été méchant ___ il quitte ta fête, à laquelle tu l'avais invité.	1. To wait until. 2. *Voie* is a subjunctive, in a whole phrase, there is no waiting. 3. *À neuf heures du soir* is not a whole phrase. 4. To wait until. 5. *Soit* is a subjunctive, in a whole phrase, there is no waiting.	1. Bon, nous devons attendre qu'elle soit revenue de l'étranger (INFORMAL). 2. Combien de coureurs vont passer, jusqu'à ce qu'on le voie? 3. Pendant l'été ils jouent au foot jusqu'à neuf heures du soir. 4. La police attend que le suspect se présente. 5. Oui, tu as été méchant jusqu'à ce qu'il quitte ta fête, à laquelle tu l'avais invité.

2.3   How do I say 'ago': *il y a, voilà* or *voici*?

Translate the following sentences into French using the form of 'ago' and the other hints in brackets to help you.

Questions 2.3	Explanations 2.3	Answers 2.3
1. I broke my leg (*me suis cassé la jambe*) two years ago (*il y a*). 2. They saw each other (*se sont vus*) ten years ago (*il y a*). 3. I went sledging (*faire de la luge*) for the first time two years ago (*voilà*). 4. We were married (*on s'est marié*) seven years ago (*voilà*). 5. The Bondis invaded (*ont envahi*) this country two centuries ago (*voici*).	1. Common form. 2. Common form. 3. Rarer form. Use it to enrich your French. 4. Rarer form. Use it to enrich your French. 5. Rarer form. Use it to enrich your French.	1. Je me suis cassé la jambe il y a deux ans. 2. Il se sont vus il y a deux ans. 3. J'ai fait de la luge pour la première fois voilà deux ans. 4. On s'est marié voilà sept ans. 5. Les Bondi ont envahi ce pays voici deux siècles.

2.4   How do I express measurements in French?

Insert the right doing word into the spaces provided in the sentences below. Note that in some cases there is more than one correct choice.

Questions 2.4	Explanations 2.4	Answers 2.4
1. La traîne de sa robe ___ longue de dix mètres. 2. Cette planche à voile est énorme! Elle ___ presque trois mètres de haut! 3. La table dans mon appartement ___ un épaisseur de trente centimètres. 4. Ces falaises ___ une hauteur de plus de trois cent mètres. 5. La piscine ___ cinq mètres de large.	1. There is only one correct answer here. The describing word agrees, so it is the form which most closely resembles English usage. 2. *Profond* and *épais* are not being used here and so there are two valid choices. 3. Here there is only one choice as a naming word has been used to express a measurement. 4. Here there is only one choice as a naming word has been used to express a measurement. 5. *Profond* and *épais* are not being used here and so there are two valid choices.	1. La traîne de sa robe est longue de dix mètres. 2. Cette planche à voile est énorme! Elle fait presque trois mètres de haut! OR Elle a presque trois mètres de haut. 3. La table dans mon appartement a un épaisseur de trente centimètres. 4. Ces falaises ont une hauteur de plus de trois cent mètres. 5. La piscine a cinq mètres de large. OR La piscine fait cinq mètres de large.

2.5   With a doing word do I say *tout, toute,* or *toutes*?

Insert *tout, toute,* or *toutes* to fill the blank spaces in the sentences below.

Questions 2.5	Explanations 2.5	Answers 2.5
1. Nos filles sont toujours ___ émues la veille de Noël. 2. Elle avait l'air ___ drôle quand elle faisait des grimaces. 3. Claire peut préparer ce plat ___ seule. 4. Tu aurais dû voir Maurice, il était ___ seul sur la piste. 5. Cette édition est ___ neuve.	1. *Emues* begins with a vowel and not a consonant. 2. *Drôle* begins with a consonant **and** is feminine singular. 3. *Seule* begins with a consonant **and** is clearly a feminine singular. 4. Here we are concerned with a man. 5. The feminine singular *neuve* begins with a consonant.	1. Nos filles sont toujours tout émues la veille de Noël. 2. Elle avait l'air toute drôle quand elle faisait des grimaces. 3. Claire peut préparer ce plat toute seule. 4. Tu aurais dû voir Maurice, il était tout seul sur la piste. 5. Cette édition est toute neuve

2.6   Do I use *ce, cette* or *cet*, meaning 'this'?

Which word should be in the blanks below, *ce, cette* or *cet?*

Questions 2.6	Explanations 2.6	Answers 2.6
1. Mais bien sûr que je connais bien ___ ville (INFORMAL). 2. ___ homme est plus grand que vous. 3. Elodie, regarde ___ oiseau, comme il est beau! 4. ___ image terrible m'a complète-ment bouleversé (upset me). 5. Croyez-vous que ___ vieille hache (axe) rouillée couperait bien?	1. *ville* is feminine and begins with a consonant (all the letters except 'a', 'e', 'i', 'o', or 'u'). 2. *homme* is masculine, begins with an 'h' and is written *l'homme.* 3. *oiseau* is masculine, but begins with a vowel ('a', 'e', 'i', 'o', 'u') 4. *image* is feminine; it does not matter whether it begins with a vowel or consonant. 5. *hache* is feminine; it begins with an 'h' but is written *'la hache'.* It works like any other feminine naming word.	1. Mais bien sûr que je connais bien cette ville (INFORMAL). 2. Cet homme est plus grand que vous. 3. Elodie, regarde cet oiseau, comme il est beau! 4. Cette image terrible m'a complètement bouleversé. 5. Croyez-vous que cette vieille hache rouillée couperait bien?

2.7   When do I use *demander* on its own, then *demander à* or *demander de?*

Please insert *demander à, demander de* or *demander* on its own into the gap (in this last case you only need to fill one of the gaps). Use the present tense.

Questions 2.7	Explanations 2.7	Answers 2.7
1. Le samedi Janine ___ ___ sortir. 2. Je n'ose pas lui ___ ___les clés. 3. Il me ___ ___ aller chez lui. 4. Je te ___ ___arrêter de fumer. 5. Il ___ ___ un congé de deux jours (two day's leave). 6. David ne ___ pas ___ chanter.	1. Here *demander* refers to another doing word. 2. Here *demander* refers directly to a thing. 3. Here it is a case of asking a person something. 4. Here too it is a case of asking a person something. 5. Here *demander* refers direct to a thing. 6. Here *demander* refers to another doing word.	1. Le samedi Janine demande à sortir. 2. Je n'ose pas lui demander les clés. 3. Il me demande d'aller chez lui. 4. Je te demande d'arrêter de fumer. 5. Il demande un congé de deux jours (two day's leave). 6. David ne demande pas à chanter.

2.8   When saying 'for' in relation to time in French, do I use *depuis, pendant* or *pour*?

Which is the right word for the gaps below, *depuis, pendant* or *pour*?

Questions 2.8	Explanations 2.8	Answers 2.8
1. J'attends ici ___ une demi-heure. 2. Vous allez partir en Grèce ___ un an! 3. J'habite à Londres ___ trois ans. 4. Ils ont essayé ___ deux heures de sauver la petite fille. 5. Monsieur, vous devez étudier ces questions ___ au moins cinq minutes avant d'y répondre.	1. Here 'for' is found with a present tense and the speaker is still waiting. 2. Here the future is implied. Here you find the starting point of the time period. 3. 'For' is found with the present tense here and the speaker still lives in London. 4. This sentence concerns the past. Here we have an expression of time and the sentence emphasises the full duration of the time period. 5. Here there is a future tense. Here you find the starting points of time periods.	1. J'attends ici depuis une demi-heure. 2. Vous allez partir en Grèce pour un an! 3. J'habite à Londres depuis trois ans. 4. Ils ont essayé pendant deux heures de sauver la petite fille. 5. Monsieur, vous devez étudier ces questions pendant au moins cinq minutes avant d'y répondre.

2.9   How do I say 'to' when referring to towns and cities?

Which is the right choice for the gaps below, *à, au* or *à La*?

Questions 2.9	Explanations 2.9	Answers 2.9
1. Est-ce que ce bus va ___ Lyon? 2. Nous allons ___ Vienne au moins deux fois par an. 3. Aujourd'hui nous devons tous aller ___ Londres. 4. Si vous partez maintenant vous arriverez vers trois heures ___ Havre. 5. Quand nous serons dans la Sarthe nous irons ___ La Flèche.	1. Lyons (in English) . 2. Vienna. 3. London. 4. Le Havre (original meaning 'the harbour'). 5. La Flèche (originally meaning 'the arrow').	1. Est-ce que ce bus va à Lyon? 2. Nous allons à Vienne au moins deux fois par an. 3. Aujourd'hui nous devons tous aller à Londres. 4. Si vous partez maintenant vous arriverez vers trois heures au Havre. 5. Quand nous serons dans la Sarthe nous irons à La Flèche.

2.10   After doing words, do I have *à* or *de* or nothing at all?

Insert the right choice in the gaps below, *à*, *de* or nothing at all?

Questions 2.10	Explanations 2.10	Answers 2.10
1. Et si tu m'aidais ___ faire la vaisselle? (INFORMAL) 2. Ils se sont amusés ___ marcher en se donnant le bras. 3. Je regrette beaucoup ___ avoir arrêté le piano (l'étude du piano). 4. J'adore ___ regarder les couchers de soleil. 5. Nazim a tenté ___ s'expliquer à plusieurs reprises.	1. Positive. 2. Positive. 3. Negative. 4. Positive, but an exception. 5. A doing word concerned with trying.	1. Et si tu m'aidais à faire la vaisselle? (INFORMAL) 2. Ils se sont amusés à marcher en se donnant le bras. 3. Je regrette beaucoup d'avoir arrêté le piano (l'étude du piano). 4. J'adore regarder les couchers de soleil. 5. Nazim a tenté de s'expliquer à plusieurs reprises.

2.11   When do I say *penser* on its own, or *penser à,* or *penser de*?

Insert the present tense of *penser à*, *penser de* or *penser* on its own into the gaps below (if you use the last option you will only have to fill one of the gaps).

Questions 2.11	Explanations 2.11	Answers 2.11
1. ___ ___ moi quand tu seras seule en ville. 2. Je ___ ___il a beaucoup vieilli ces dernières années. 3. Je pense vraiment ___ tout ira mieux dans l'avenir. 4. Alors qu'est-ce qu'ils ___ ___ la nouvelle situation? 5. En rentrant, Michel ___ ___ sa copine Michelle qui est aux Etats-Unis.	1. Here it is a case of contemplating a person. 2. This is general thinking. 3. This is also general thinking. 4. This is deeper thinking where an opinion can be given. 5. This is also a case of contemplation.	1. Pense à moi quand tu seras seule en ville. 2. Je pense qu'il a beaucoup vieilli ces dernières années. 3. Je pense vraiment que tout ira mieux dans l'avenir. 4. Alors qu'est-ce qu'ils pensent de la nouvelle situation? 5. En rentrant, Michel pense à sa copine Michelle qui est aux États-Unis.

2.12   When do I say *manquer* on its own, then *manquer à* or *manquer de*?

Insert the present tense of *manquer à*, *manquer de* or *manquer* on its own into the gaps below (if you use the last option you will only have to fill one of the gaps).

Questions 2.12	Explanations 2.12	Answers 2.12
1. Nos troupes ___ ___ vivres. 2. Mon petit ami me ___ ___. 3. Je ne ___ ___ jamais le bus. 4. Il ___ ___ discrétion. 5. J'ai l'impression qu'il ___ ___ courage.	1. Here the meaning is 'to lack' because *vivres* are foodstuffs, something fundamental. 2. This sentence concerns missing a person, the 'boyfriend from home' comes first. 3. Here the speaker never arrives too late for the bus. The meaning is 'to miss'. 4. Here the meaning is 'to lack'. 5. Here the meaning is 'to lack'.	1. Nos troupes manquent de vivres. 2. Mon petit ami me manque. 3. Je ne manque jamais le bus. 4. Il manque de discrétion. 5. J'ai l'impression qu'il manque de courage.

2.13   When do I use *décider* on its own, then *se décider à* or *décider de*?

Insert the present tense of the doing word into the gaps below. Use either: *se décider à*, (if using this option then fill all three gaps), or *décider de* (if you use this option, you will only have to fill two gaps) or *décider* on its own (if you use the last option you will only have to fill one of the gaps).

Questions 2.13	Explanations 2.13	Answers 2.13
1. Peu à peu le Président ___ ___ ___ revenir sur les réformes. 2. Après un bon moment de réflexion, Janine ___ ___ ___ rentrer à la maison. 3. Le Ministère des Transports ___ ___ ___ que les scooters doivent être immatriculés. 4. Ian arrive chez lui et ___ ___ commencer toute de suite les préparatifs pour le concert de la soirée. 5. Après avoir longtemps réfléchi, le pauvre Brian ___ ___ ___ ne rien faire et il laisse l'incendie embraser tout le bâtiment.	1. Here you have an added element of gradual deliberation, which indicates that the person is making up their mind. 2. Here you have an added element of deliberation, which indicates that the person is making up their mind. 3. Here *décider* is being used in a general way. 4. In this sentence *décider* is used with a specific action. It is not general. It is less stronger that 'to make one's mind up.' 5. Here there is an added element of deliberation: making one's mind up to do nothing can take time.	1. Peu à peu le Président se décide à revenir sur les réformes. 2. Après un bon moment de réflexion, Janine se décide à rentrer à la maison. 3. Le Ministère des Transports décide que les scooters doivent être immatriculés. 4. Ian arrive chez lui et décide de commencer les préparatifs pour le concert de la soirée. 5. Après avoir longtemps réfléchi, le pauvre Brian se décide à ne rien faire et il laisse l'incendie embraser tout le bâtiment.

2.14   When do I use *jouer* on its own, then *jouer* à or *jouer de*?

Fill the gaps below with the present tense of the *jouer à*, *jouer de* or *jouer* on its own (if you use the last option, then one of the blanks will remain unfilled).

Questions 2.14	Explanations 2.14	Answers 2.14
1. Le samedi, ils ___ ___ foot.	1. A named game is being played here.	1. Le samedi, ils jouent au foot.
2. J'aimerais que nos enfants ___ ___ ensemble dans l'équipe.	2. This is general play.	2. J'aimerais que nos enfants jouent ensemble dans l'équipe.
3. Je ___ ___ la guitare chez ma grand-mère.	3. Here a named musical instrument is being played.	3. Je joue de la guitare chez ma grand-mère.
4. Les Smith ___ tous ___ piano le dimanche après-midi.	4. Here too a named musical instrument is being played.	4. Les Smith jouent tous du piano le dimanche après-midi.
5. Monique ___ ___ avec les sœurs Papin.	5. This is general play.	5. Monique joue avec les sœurs Papin.

2.15   How do I say 'worse': *pire, plus mauvais* or *plus mal*?

Insert the appropriate form of *pire, plus mauvais* or *plus mal* into the gaps below. Of course if you choose *pire*, one of the gaps will remain unfilled.

Questions 2.15	Explanations 2.15	Answers 2.15
1. Ces plats sont ___ ___ que ceux qu'on nous a montrés hier.	1. Here the keyword is 'quality'.	1. Ces plats sont plus mauvais que ceux qu'on nous a montrés hier.
2. Est-ce que j'ai vraiment prononcé mon discours ___ ___ que la dernière fois?	2. The reference concerns a doing word here.	2. Est-ce que j'ai vraiment prononcé mon discours plus mal que la dernière fois?
3. Il semble que l'entorse (the sprain) qu'il s'est faite cette fois-ci soit ___ ___ que les précédentes.	3. From the sense of the phrase you expect is going to be bad anyway, now it's worse!	3. Il semble que l'entorse (the sprain) qu'il s'est faite cette fois-ci soit pire que les précédentes.
4. Ne rien dire est ___ ___ que d'essayer de dire quelque chose.	4. From the sense of the phrase you expect is going to be bad anyway, now it's worse!	4. Ne rien dire est pire que d'essayer de dire quelque chose.
5. Après avoir suivi les conseils de cet homme je dessine ___ ___ qu'auparavant!	5. There reference concerns a doing word here.	5. Après avoir suivi les conseils de cet homme je dessine plus mal qu'auparavant!

2.16   How do I say 'the worst': *le pire,* le *plus mauvais* or *le plus mal*?

There are two blanks in each sentence put in either *pire* (leaving the other blank!), *plus mauvais*, *plus mauvaise* or *plus mal*.

Questions 2.16	Explanations 2.16	Answers 2.16
1. Par rapport aux autres catastrophes que j'ai vues, celle-ci est tout simplement la ___ ___.	1. From the sense of the phrase you expect is going to be bad anyway, now it's worse!	1. Par rapport aux autres catastrophes que j'ai vues, celle-ci est tout simplement la pire.
2. C'est la jeune fille la ___ ___ élevée que j'aie jamais vue.	2. There reference concerns a doing word here.	2. C'est la jeune fille la plus mal élevée que j'aie jamais vue.
3. Le ___ c'est qu'il n'a jamais voulu reconnaître ses crimes.	3. From the sense of the phrase you expect is going to be bad anyway, now it's worse!	3. Le pire c'est qu'il n'a jamais voulu reconnaître ses crimes.
4. C'est sans aucun doute la ___ ___ représentation que j'aie jamais vue.	4. Here the keyword is 'quality'.	4. C'est sans aucun doute la plus mauvaise représentation que j'aie jamais vue.
5. Ce soir j'ai bu la boisson la ___ ___ de ma vie: un mélange, il me semble, de beurre et d'alcool.	5. Here the keyword is 'quality'.	5. Ce soir j'ai bu la boisson la plus mauvaise de ma vie: un mélange, il me semble, de beurre et d'alcool.

2.17   How do I say 'would' in French?

Substitute the doing word in the correct tense for the English phrase in brackets.

Questions 2.17	Explanations 2.17	Answers 2.17
1. (Would you) m'aider à faire la vaisselle?	1. This example includes 'you' and is a request, phrased as a question.	1. Voudriez-vous m'aider à faire la vaisselle?
2. Pendant les vacances (they would go) à la piscine tous les matins.	2. This example concerns habit.	2. Pendant les vacances ils allaient à la piscine tous les matins.
3. (Would you) m'accompagner à la gare?	3. This example includes 'you' and is a request, phrased as a question.	3. Voudriez-vous m'accompagner à la gare?
4. (I would like) lui raconter tout ce que j'ai vu.	4. The sentence has two parts arranged around the central hinge of *ce que*.	4. J'aimerais lui raconter tout ce que j'ai vu.
5. Mon oncle (would say) toujours qu'il fallait éviter de se baigner après avoir mangé.	5. This example concerns habit. The uncle said this more than once.	5. Mon oncle disait toujours qu'il fallait éviter de se baigner après avoir mangé.

2.18　How do I say 'number': *nombre, numéro* or *chiffre*?

Choose either *nombre*, *numéro* or *chiffre* to fill the gaps below.

Questions 2.18	Explanations 2.18	Answers 2.18
1. Assez. Montre-moi les ___. 2. Un bon ___ de gens font du sport ici. 3. Est-ce que vous savez à quel ___ ils habitent? 4. Est-ce que tu peux lire ce ___? 5. A partir du mois de septembre les oiseaux sont partis en grand ___ vers des régions plus chaudes.	1. This is a precise request to see the figures in accounts. 2. This is a general term for number, referring to things or people as a whole, to a quantity. 3. This is a precise request to find a house number for identification purposes, distinguished from any other number. 4. This is a highly precise request to see an individual figure. 5. This is a general term for number, referring to things or people as a whole, to a quantity.	1. Assez. Montre-moi les chiffres. 2. Un bon nombre de gens font du sport ici. 3. Est-ce que vous savez à quel numéro ils habitent? 4. Est-ce que tu peux lire ce chiffre? 5. A partir du mois de septembre les oiseaux sont partis en grand nombre vers des régions plus chaudes.

3

There are four ways of saying something in French, where there is only one in English

3.1 What are the different words used to say 'time': *une fois, une époque, l'heure* or *le temps*?

Select either *fois*, *époque*, *heure* or *temps* to fill the gaps below.

Questions 3.1	Explanations 3.1	Answers 3.1
1. A l'___ romaine, on appréciait beaucoup le vin.	1. This is a historical period of time which is large-scale.	1. A l'époque romaine, on appréciait beaucoup le vin.
2. Oui, c'est l'___. Il faut entrer en scène maintenant.	2. Here the reference is to the 'time of day'.	2. Oui, c'est l'heure. Il faut entrer en scène maintenant.
3. Au boulot, je n'ai jamais le ___ de faire une pause à midi. C'est bien malsain. (INFORMAL).	3. Here the period is not defined by numbers and the meaning is general.	3. Au boulot, je n'ai jamais le temps de faire une pause à midi. C'est bien malsain. (INFORMAL).
4. Oui, c'était cette ___où on était en vacances au bord de la mer.	4. This is a specific occasion.	4. Oui, c'était cette fois où on était en vacances au bord de la mer.
5. Quelle ___ est-il?	5. This question relates to the 'time of day' and requires an answer with 'o'clock'.	5. Quelle heure est-il?

3.2 When do I use four of the different ways of saying 'to make': *faire, rendre, fabriquer, confectionner*?

Select either *faire*, *rendre*, *fabriquer* or *confectionner* and fill the gaps below.

Questions 3.2	Explanations 3.2	Answers 3.2
1. Son comportement me ___ fou! 2. Je suis content de ne pas avoir ___ d'erreurs dans mon travail. 3. On ___ des caméscopes (camcorders) dans cette usine. 4. A Londres, je me suis fait ___ un costume. 5. Qu'as-tu ___?	1. Here make is being used with a describing word. 2. Here a general and common meaning of 'make' is intended. 3. Here make concerns something which is constructed in a factory. 4. This time the reference is to an article made by a craftsman or woman. 5. Here a general and common meaning of 'make' is intended.	1. Son comportement me rend fou! 2. Je suis content de ne pas avoir fait d'erreurs dans mon travail. 3. On fabrique des caméscopes (camcorders) dans cette usine. 4. A Londres, je me suis fait confectionner un costume. 5. Qu'as-tu fait?

3.3 What are the four ways of writing the French words for 'old' and when do I use them?

Fill the gaps below with the correct French form of 'old'.

Questions 3.3	Explanations 3.3	Answers 3.3
1. Sur le lit il y avait quelques ___ fleurs couvertes de poussière. 2. Ce ___ ours me fait pitié à cause de son âge. 3. Ils habitent une ___ maison de grand standing (top quality). 4. Je ne comprends rien aux textes en ___ français. 5. Mon ordinateur est malheureusement très ___.	1. Here a feminine plural naming word is being described. 2. Here a masculine singular naming word is being described; it starts with either a, e, i, o, or u. These words are always the shortest form and always ends in the letter 'l'. 3. Here a feminine singular naming word is being described. 4. Here a masculine singular naming word is being described. 5. Here a masculine singular naming words is being described. However although it starts with either a, e, i, o, or u, the describing word is found at the end of the sentence and acts as if a 'normal' masculine singular word was being described.	1. Sur le lit il y avait quelques vieilles fleurs couvertes de poussière. 2. Ce vieil ours me fait pitié à cause de son âge. 3. Ils habitent une vieille maison de grand standing (top quality). 4. Je ne comprends rien aux textes en vieux français. 5. Mon ordinateur est malheureusement très vieux.

3.4   How do I say 'all': *tout, toute, toutes*, or *tous*?

Which is the right word for the gaps below, *tout*, *toute* or *toutes* or *tous*?

Questions 3.4	Explanations 3.4	Answers 3.4
1. Je connais ___ les amis de Robert. 2. Inutile de mentir à la police, elle sait ___. 3. Pour son enterrement, ___ la famille était là. 4. Racine? J'ai lu ___ ses pièces. 5. Maintenant je vais ___ vous dire. 6. ___ ceux qui disent cela se trompent. 7. La vie serait bien monotone si nous étions ___ les mêmes. 8. ___ la presse était là. 9. ___ au travail! 10. Vous êtes ___ des génies!	1. Here the reference is to a masculine singular naming word. 2. Here the reference is general in nature and does not concern a specific naming word. 3. Here the reference is to a feminine singular naming word. 4. Here the reference is to a feminine plural naming word. 5. Here the reference is general in nature and does not concern a specific naming word. 6. Here the reference is to a general mixed plural for which the masculine is used. 7. Here the reference is to a mixed plural for which the masculine is used. 8. The reference here is to a feminine singular naming word. 9. Here the reference is to a general mixed plural for which the masculine is used. 10. Here the reference is to a mixed plural for which the masculine is used.	1. Je connais tous les amis de Robert. Pronounced 'TOU' i.e. without the 's'. 2. Inutile de mentir à la police, elle sait tout. Pronounced 'TOU' i.e. without the 's'. 3. Pour son enterrement, toute la famille était là. Pronounced 'TUTE'. 4. Racine? J'ai lu toutes ses pièces. Pronounced 'TUTE'. 5. Maintenant je vais tout vous dire. Pronounced 'TOU' i.e. without the 's'. 6. Tous ceux qui disent cela se trompent. Pronounced 'TOU' i.e. without the 's'. 7. La vie serait bien monotone si nous étions tous les mêmes. Pronounced 'TUS' with the 's'. 8. Toute la presse était là. Pronounced 'TUTE'. 9. Tous au travail! Pronounced 'TUS' with the 's'. 10. Vous êtes tous des génies! Pronounced 'TUS' with the 's'.

3.5 Do I say *de, d', du* or *des* when I mean 'from' when speaking about towns and cities?

Which is the right word for the gaps below, *de, d'* or *du* or *des*?

Questions 3.5	Explanations 3.5	Answers 3.5
1. Il est originaire ___ Havre. 2. Quand reviens-tu ___ Nîmes? 3. Ils sont tout de suite rentrés ___Avignon. 4. Je crois qu'ils seront déjà partis ___ Caire. 5. Il n'est pas encore rentré ___ Arcs.	1. The name of this town includes the masculine word for 'the'. 2. This is the form used in the majority of cases. 3. The name of this town begins with 'a', 'e', 'i', 'o', or 'u'. 4. The name of this town includes the masculine word for 'the'. 5. The name of this town includes the plural word for 'the'.	1. Il est originaire du Havre. 2. Quand reviens-tu de Nîmes? 3. Ils sont tout de suite rentrés d'Avignon. 4. Je crois qu'ils seront déjà partis du Caire. 5. Il n'est pas encore rentré des Arcs.

3.6 Do I say *à, au, aux* or *dans* when I mean 'in' when speaking about towns and cities?

Which is the right word for the gaps below, *à, au* or *aux* or *dans*?

Questions 3.6	Explanations 3.6	Answers 3.6
1. Je suis né __ Meols. 2. La circulation est toujours très dense __ Paris. 3. Notre plus grand magasin se trouve __ Havre. 4. Ce monsieur possède également un restaurant __ Arcs. 5. Je ne suis jamais allé __ La Rochelle.	1. The name of the town may sound strange, but it uses the same form as in the vast majority of cases. 2. Here 'in' means within the city limits. 3. The name of this town includes the masculine word for 'the'. 4. The name of this town includes the plural word for 'the'. 5. The name of the town may include the feminine word for 'the', but it uses same form as in the vast majority of cases.	1. Je suis né à Meols. 2. La circulation est toujours très dense dans Paris. 3. Notre plus grand magasin se trouve au Havre. 4. Ce monsieur possède également un restaurant aux Arcs. 5. Je ne suis jamais allé à La Rochelle.

3.7 *Il s'est lavé*, the base form of *se laver* in the 'have' tense (the perfect), frequently changes, adding 'e', 's' or 'es', but when?

Please add 'e', 's' or 'es' or nothing at the point marked by the dash (___).

Questions 3.7	Explanations 3.7	Answers 3.7
1. Ma mère s'est rendu___ compte qu'elle avait tort.	1. You are dealing with a feminine here.	1. Ma mère s'est rendue compte qu'elle avait tort.
2. Mon ami Milton s'est levé___ le premier.	2. Here the sentence has the masculine base form.	2. Mon ami Milton s'est levé le premier.
3. Les deux prisonniers se sont évadé___ hier soir.	3. The *se sont* trigger indicates that there will be something added. Now you have to check whether the addition will be masculine or feminine.	3. Les deux prisonniers se sont évadés hier soir.
4. Les jeunes filles se sont blotti___ l'une contre l'autre.	4. The *se sont* trigger indicates that there will be something added. Now you have to check whether the addition will be masculine or feminine.	4. Les jeunes filles se sont blotties l'une contre l'autre.
5. Le Président s'est évanoui___ pendant qu'il était à table.	5. Here the sentence has the masculine base form.	5. Le Président s'est évanoui pendant qu'il était à table.

3.8 How do I say 'some': *de la*, *du*, *de l'* or *des*?

Please insert *de la*, *du*, *de l'* or *des* in the single gap provided.

Questions 3.8	Explanations 3.8	Answers 3.8
1. Quoi? Tu bois ___alcool au petit déjeuner.	1. The naming word here *l'alcool* is masculine and starts with 'a', 'e', 'i', 'o', or 'u'.	1. Quoi? Tu bois de l'alcool au petit déjeuner.
2. Veux-tu que je rajoute ____ farine à la pâte?	2. Here the naming word *farine* is feminine.	2. Veux-tu que je rajoute de la farine à la pâte?
3. Je crois qu'il y a ___ papier à lettres dans le tiroir.	3. Here the naming word *papier* is masculine.	3. Je crois qu'il y a du papier à lettres dans le tiroir.
4. Madame, vous désirez? Je vais prendre ___ roses, s'il vous plaît.	4. The naming word is here is plural.	4. Madame, vous désirez? Je vais prendre des roses, s'il vous plaît.
5. Est-ce qu'il reste ___argent sur ton compte?	5. The naming word here *l'argent* is masculine and starts with 'a', 'e', 'i', 'o', or 'u'.	5. Est-ce qu'il reste de l'argent sur ton compte?

3.9 Usually words like *joué*, *fini* and *rendu* (and other simple past participles) don't change, but sometimes they take 'e' 's' or 'es'? When?

In the gaps provided add either nothing, 'e' 's' or 'es'

Questions 3.9	Explanations 3.9	Answers 3.9
1. Voilà les lettres que vous avez écrit___. 2. Gérard a parlé___ pendant deux heures. 3. Quelle histoire aurais-tu écouté___? 4. Combien de matchs de football avez-vous vu___? 5. Je t'ai bien rendu___ la monnaie, non?	1. Here the reversal in the word order includes a word in the feminine plural. 2. The word order does not depart from the norm. 3. Note that there is a hyphen in this reversal of usual word order. 4. There is also a hyphen in this reversal or usual word order. 5. The word order does not depart from the norm.	1. Voilà les lettres que vous avez écrites. 2. Gérard a parlé pendant deux heures. 3. Quelle histoire aurais-tu écoutée? 4. Combien de matchs de football avez-vous vus? 5. Je t'ai bien rendu la monnaie, non?

4

There are five ways of saying something in French, where there is only one in English

4.1 What are the five ways of writing the French words for 'soft', 'new', 'mad', 'beautiful' and when do I use them?

Fill the correct form of the appropriate describing word in the space provided.

Questions 4.1	Explanations 4.1	Answers 4.1
1. Vous avez un très ___ (beautiful) fils, Madame Gobain. 2. Alice a également acheté un ___ (new) tailleur (suit). 3. Gaby regarde ses sœurs: 'Mais vous êtes ___ (mad)!' 4. Un Camembert mûr est un fromage à pâte ___ (soft). 5. La ville de Chartres possède une ___ (beautiful) cathédrale.	1. Here a masculine singular naming word is being described. It begins with the letter 'f'. 2. Here a masculine singular naming word is being described. It begins with the letter 't'. 3. Here a feminine plural naming word is being described. 4. Here a masculine singular naming word is being described. 5. Here a feminine singular naming word is being described.	1. Vous avez un très beau fils, Madame Gobain. 2. Alice a également acheté un nouveau tailleur. 3. Gaby regarde ses sœurs: 'Mais vous êtes folles!' 4. Un Camembert mûr est un fromage à pâte molle. 5. La ville de Chartres possède une belle cathédrale.

5

There are seven ways of saying something in French, where there is only one in English

5.1 What are the seven words meaning 'what' in French?

Put the correct word or words for 'what' into the gaps below.

Questions 5.1	Explanations 5.1	Answers 5.1
1. Oui, je vois que ___ tu me dis est correct.	1. Here an unnamed thing is receiving the action of telling.	1. Oui, je vois que ce que tu me dis est correct.
2. ___ corvée (awful chore)!	2. Here the reference is to something which is named.	2. Quelle corvée (awful chore)!
3. ___ fait un bruit comme ça?	3. Here 'what' comes at the start of a phrase and you are describing a doing word. However, the meaning here is strong and resembles: 'what on earth.'	3. Qu'est-ce qui fait un bruit comme ça?
4. ___ dire face à une tragédie pareille?	4. Here 'what' comes at the start of a phrase and you are describing a doing word.	4. Que dire face à une tragédie pareille?
5. Sans blague, il a fait ___ (VERY INFORMAL)?	5. Here 'what' indicates extreme surprise and can be considered impolite when used on its own.	5. Sans blague, il a fait quoi (VERY INFORMAL)?
6. ___? Je ne suis pas sûr d'avoir très bien entendu.	6. This is the polite way of letting a person know that you haven't heard or understood what they have said.	6. Comment? Je ne suis pas sûr d'avoir très bien entendu.
7. ___ peuvent-ils bien faire là à cette heure-ci?	7. Here 'what' comes at the start of a phrase and you are describing a doing word.	7. Que peuvent-ils bien faire là à cette heure-ci?
8. Ce vendeur sait exactement ___ vous avez besoin.	8. Here, 'what' is being used in the same way as in the first sentence but the doing word is followed by de i.e. avoir besoin de.	8. Ce vendeur sait exactement ce dont vous avez besoin.
9. Tu as posé la sculpture sur ___?	9. Here 'what' refers to a thing not named and accompanies words like à, de, autour de, sur.	9. Tu as posé la sculpture sur quoi?
10. Malheureusement, ___ s'est passé hier soir est gênant pour nous.	10. Here the person or thing did the unnamed action.	10. Malheureusement, ce qui s'est passé hier soir est gênant pour nous.

6

There are eight ways of saying something in French, where there is only one in English

6.1   What are the eight different ways to say 'half' in French?

Find the right word for the gaps below.

Questions 6.1	Explanations 6.1	Answers 6.1
1. Il est midi et ___ et les enfants n'ont pas encore faim. 2. Une ___-bouteille de vin rouge s'il vous plaît. 3. Mon père était ___-hongrois ___-libanais. 4. Mais permettez-moi de vous resservir, je ne vous ai servi qu'un ___-verre de vin. 5. il y a une ___-tasse de sucre en poudre (icing sugar) dans le placard. 6. Sers-toi, mais ne prends pas plus que la ___, s'il te plaît. 7. Mon fils a deux ans et ___. 8. Je suis debout depuis six heures et ___. 9. Garçon, un ___ pression s'il vous plait. 10. Il n'a accompli que la ___ de la tâche qu'on lui avait demandé de faire.	1. Here the focus is on a half as a quantity in itself and *midi* takes *le*. 2. Here the focus is on a half as a quantity in itself and here the person is referring to half a bottle. 3. These two words for half are normally found together and they stress the harmoniousness of the combination of the two halves, rather than the individuality of each fifty percent. 4. Here you are focusing on a half as a quantity in itself and is joined to the front of the word to which it refers; that word is *le verre*. 5. Here you are focusing on a half as a quantity in itself and is joined to the front of the word to which it refers; that word is *la tasse*. 6. Here there is some understanding of the whole object, idea or group from which the half was taken or to which the half belongs. 7. Here the focus is on a half as a quantity in itself and an takes *le*. 8. Here the focus is on a half as a quantity in itself and *heure* takes *la*. 9. Here the focus is on a half as a quantity in itself and here the person is referring to half a draught beer. 10. Here there is some understanding of the whole object, idea or group from which the half was taken or to which the half belongs.	1. Il est midi et demi et les enfants n'ont pas encore faim. 2. Une demi-bouteille de vin rouge s'il vous plaît. 3. Mon père était mi-hongrois mi-libanais. 4. Mais permettez-moi de vous resservir, je ne vous ai servi qu'un demi-verre de vin. 5. il y a une demi-tasse de sucre en poudre dans le placard. 6. Sers-toi, mais ne prends pas plus que la moitié, s'il te plaît. 7. Mon fils a deux ans et demi. 8. Je suis debout depuis six heures et demie. 9. Garçon, un demi pression s'il vous plaît. 10. Il n'a accompli que la moitié de la tâche qu'on lui avait demandé de faire.

7

French is the exact opposite of English

7.1 When do I use a capital letter when writing the names of months in French?

Translate the following sentences into French, paying special attention to how the month is written in French.

Questions 7.1	Explanation 7.1	Answers 7.1
1. My birthday is on the second (*est le deux*) of May.	French is the opposite of English in all of these case and takes a simple letter when English has a capital.	1. Mon anniversaire est le deux mai.
2. The match will take place (*aura lieu*) on the seventeenth of April.		2. Le match aura lieu le dix-sept avril.
3. He said that he would (*serait*) be with (*parmi*) us on the fourteenth of March. (FORMAL).		3. Il a dit qu'il sera parmi nous le quatorze mars.

7.2   When do I use a capital letter when writing the names of days of the week in French?

Exercises in correction. Choose whether or not to correct the capital or simple letter at the start of all of the words in the question sentences.

Questions 7.2	Explanation 7.2	Answers 7.2
1. Viens-tu me voir Mardi soir? 2. On Dit que le professeur Pargeter va annoncer son départ en retraite vendredi lors de la réunion. 3. depuis Mercredi soir marie sort avec christelle.	The days of the week take a capital in English and a simple letter in French. That is the same pattern as with the months.	1. Viens-tu me voir mardi soir? 2. On dit que le professeur Pargeter va annoncer son départ en retraite vendredi lors de la réunion. 3. Depuis mercredi soir Marie sort avec Christelle.

7.3   When do I use a capital letter when writing the names of languages in French?

Exercises in correction. Choose whether or not to correct the capital or simple letter at the start of all of the words in the question sentences.

Questions 7.3	Explanation 7.3	Answers 7.3
1. Tous les français sont censés parler Le Français. 2. Je crois qu'il parle chinois. 3. Etes-vous espagnole, Madame? 4. Voici ce que ce Monsieur m'a dit : 'je parle couramment L'Italien et l'Espagnol.' 5. J'ai écouté le Belge parler flamand hier.	Languages have a capital letter in English and a simple letter in French. Words for people who come from a given country begin with upper case letters as in English.	1. Tous les Français sont censés parler le français. 2. Je crois qu'il parle chinois. 3. Etes-vous Espagnole, madame? 4. Voici ce que ce monsieur m'a dit: 'je parle couramment l'italien et l'espagnol.' 5. J'ai écouté le Belge parler flamand hier.

7.4   Do I use a capital letter for describing words which refer to a particular town or city?

Exercises in correction. Choose whether or not to correct the capital or simple letter at the start of all of the words in the question sentences.

Questions 7.4	Explanation 7.4	Answers 7.4
1. Ce toit est typique des immeubles de londres. 2. C'est une Parisienne qui ne peut pas se passer de la vie parisienne. 3. Je suis heureuse d'avoir quitté la pollution new-yorkaise.	When using describing words which refer to a particular town or city French is the opposite of English which uses capital letters. However, when referring to a person, French uses a capital in the same way as English.	1. Ce toit est typique des immeubles de Londres. 2. C'est une Parisienne qui ne peut pas se passer de la vie parisienne. 3. Je suis heureuse d'avoir quitté la pollution new-yorkaise.

7.5   When some words are singular in French, how are they written in English?

Translate the following sentences into English or French, paying particular attention to whether naming words are singular or plural.

Questions 7.5	Explanations 7.5	Answers 7.5
1. I have been teaching physics for three years now (use *j'ensei-gne... depuis*). 2. Les politiciens ne peuvent pas se passer des données fournies par la statistique. 3. In South Africa the police have undergone (*subi*) reforms (*des réformes*).	1. Physics takes *la* in French. 2. French is the opposite of English with reference to *la statistique*. 3. Police takes *la* in French.	1. *J'enseigne la physique depuis trois ans.* 2. Politicians cannot do without the data provided by statistics. 3. *En Afrique du Sud la police a subi des réformes.*

7.6   When some words are plural in French, how are they written in English?

Translate the following sentences into English or French, paying particular attention to whether naming words are singular or plural.

Questions 7.6	Explanation 7.6	Answers 7.6
1. Le nom des services secrets de l'État hébreu (Israel) est 'le Mossad'. 2. When are you (tu) going on holiday? 3. One can buy almost anything at auction. 4. He has a vast knowledge of (sur) all sort of subjects.	Here the naming words in French are the opposite of their English counterparts as far as singular and plural are concerned.	1. Israel's secret service is called Mossad. 2. Quand est-ce que tu pars en vacances? 3. On peut presque tout acheter dans les ventes aux enchères. 4. Il a de vastes connaissances sur toutes sortes de sujets.

7.7   How do I write family names in the plural in French?

Translate the following sentences into French.

Questions 7.7	Explanation 7.7	Answers 7.7
1. I do not want to invite the Fowlers. 2. Oh, the Burgesses always arrive late. 3. The Houdard-Kochs, they are (voilà) a family who have been living in this village for more than a hundred years (depuis plus de cent ans).	Unlike English, family names in French do not add an 's'.	1. Je ne veux pas inviter les Fowler. 2. Ah les Burgess arrivent toujours en retard. 3. Les Houdard-Koch, voilà une famille qui habite dans ce village depuis plus de cent ans.

7.8   Do I use le, la and l', when writing job titles and names?

Translate the following sentences into French.

Questions 7.8	Explanation 7.8	Answers 7.8
1. Major Dulardon has arrived. 2. President Jones was a pilot in the airforce (dans l'armée de l'air). 3. Sorry, father Brock has already left.	In French, the titles of jobs take le, la or l'; to English-speaking people it makes the French job holder sound very grand!	4. Le majeur Dulardon est arrivé. 5. Le Président Jones était pilote dans l'armée de l'air. 6. Désolé, le père Brock est déjà parti.

7.9   Do I use *le, la* and *l'*, when writing the names of countries in French?

Translate the following sentences into French.

Questions 7.9	Explanation 7.9	Answers 7.9
1. I will never forget Canada. 2. Have you (*vous*) ever seen Scotland on a map? 3. Do you know Paraguay?	When writing the names of countries in French, you need to put in a *le, la* or *l'* and of course a capital letter as in English.	1. Je n'oublierai jamais le Canada. 2. Avez-vous jamais vu l'Ecosse sur une carte? 3. Connaissez-vous le Paraguay?

7.10   Must I repeat *à, de, en* and other position words in lists?

Add *à, de* or *en* as required in the blanks; note that not all the blanks must be filled).

Questions 7.10	Explanations 7.10	Answers 7.10
1. J'ai été en poste dans plusieurs pays comme ambassadeur: ____ France, ____ Japon, _____ Canada et ____ Etats-Unis. 2. En 1988 le Tour de France est passé par ___ Chartres, ___ Angers, ___ La Rochelle, ___ Bordeaux, ___ Toulouse et ___ Nîmes pour se terminer à Paris. 3. Martin Dumont est très doué, il joue ___ violon, ___ piano, ___ flûte, ___ harpe et même ___ violoncelle. 4. En Chine autrefois le paquetage des soldats consistait en un sac à dos, ___ une tente et ___ une petite provision de riz. 5. Devant une situation de crise et ___ une heureuse occasion notre chef n'a pas réagi d'une manière raisonnable.	1. There is more than one position word used in this example. Here are the genders: *la France, le Japon, le Canada, les Etats-Unis* (masculine plural). 2. Only one position word to be used here. Check whether it belongs to the group that is repeated. 3. Different combinations of the same position word are required here. Here are the genders of the instruments: *le violon, le piano, la flûte, la harpe, le violoncelle*. 4. These elements are considered together. 5. The writer is stressing the individuality of the items here.	1. J'ai été en poste dans plusieurs pays comme ambassadeur: en France, au Japon, au Canada et aux Etats-Unis. 2. En 1988 le Tour de France est passé par Chartres, Angers, La Rochelle, Bordeaux, Toulouse et Nîmes pour se terminer à Paris. 3. Martin Dumont est très doué, il joue du violon, du piano, de la flûte, de la harpe et même du violoncelle. 4. En Chine autrefois le paquetage des soldats consistait en un sac à dos, une tente et une petite provision de riz. Voilà tout ce dont on avait besoin à cette époque-là. 5. Devant une situation de crise et devant une heureuse occasion notre chef n'a pas réagi d'une manière raisonnable.

7.11 Do I use *le*, *la* and *l'*, when writing general, non-specific statements?

Translate the following sentences into French.

Questions 7.11	Explanation 7.11	Answers 7.11
1. If we draw a conclusion from this case (*suivant ce cas*) we can say that courage is frequently rewarded (*est souvent récompensé*). 2. It is not too early (*tôt*) to (*pour*) assess the value (*estimer la valeur*) of surrealism. 3. 'Money is not everything in life' said the guru (*le gourou*).	General statements which are intended to have value outside the specific context in which they appear, just have a naming word in English. In French, they also have a *le, la* or *l'*.	1. Si l'on tire une conclusion suivant ce cas nous pouvons dire que le courage est souvent récompensé. 2. Il n'est pas trop tôt pour estimer la valeur du surréalisme. 3. 'L'argent n'est pas tout dans la vie' a dit le gourou.

7.12 With the names of jobs and professions in French, should I translate the English 'a' or 'the'?

Translate the following sentences into French.

Questions 7.12	Explanation 7.12	Answers 7.12
1. She is a taxi driver. 2. She has been a Liverpool taxi driver for twenty years. 3. Mr Ninsen is a famous surgeon. 4. Mrs Ali is an architect. She works in London. 5. Janice wants (*voudrait*) to be a football coach (*entraîneur d'une équipe de football*).	When the name of a job or profession has an 'a' or a 'the' in English it has nothing in French.	1. Elle est chauffeur de taxi. 2. Elle est chauffeur de taxi à Liverpool depuis vingt ans. 3. Monsieur Ninsen est un chirugien célèbre. 4. Mme Ali est architecte. Elle travaille à Londres. 5. Janice voudrait être entraîneur d'une équipe de football.

7.13 With persons belonging to religions in French, should I translate the English 'a'?

Translate the following sentences into French using the material in brackets to guide you.

Questions 7.13	Explanation 7.13	Answers 7.13
1. 'Is he a Catholic?' wondered (*se demanda*) Jean-Paul. 2. 'I am a protestant' Frederike told us proudly (*avec fierté*). 3. Prambodh is a Sikh.	When describing a person belonging to a specific religion in French, just use the describing word beginning with a simple letter and don't use 'a'.	1. 'Est-ce qu'il est catholique?', se demanda Jean-Paul. 2. 'Je suis protestante', nous dit Frederike avec fierté. 3. Prambodh est sikh.

7.14 With the names of monarchs and popes with a number in French, should I say 'the' as in English?

Translate the following sentences into French.

Questions 7.14	Explanation 7.14	Answers 7.14
1. 'Francis the Ninth also had mental problems' said John suddenly. 2. Was there a pope named John the First? 3. Louis the Fourteenth is probably one of the most famous French kings (l'un des rois de France les plus célèbres).	The names of kings, queens and popes are written as just a simple number in French. When writing these names use Roman numbers, and when speaking just say the number. The exception is 'the First' which is written Ier and spoken 'premier'.	1. 'François IX avait, lui aussi, des troubles mentaux' a dit John soudainement. 2. Y a-t-il eu un pape nommé Jean Ier? 3. Louis XIV est probablement l'un des rois de France les plus célèbres.

7.15 How do I translate the words for decades such as: 'the fifties', 'the nineties', 'the sixties' into French?

Translate the following sentences into French.

Questions 7.15	Explanation 7.15	Answers 7.15
1. I do not understand this nostalgia for the fifties. 2. Do you like the music of the eighties? 3. On (dans) that street, there is a shop which sells clothing which was fashionable in the seventies.	In these sentences the number remains 'pure' and does not have an 's' added to it.	1. Je ne comprends pas cette nostalgie pour les années cinquante. 2. Aimez-vous la musique des années quatre-vingt? 3. Dans cette rue, il y a un magasin qui vend des vêtements qui étaient à la mode dans les années soixante-dix.

8

French has unique forms which are not found in English

8.1 How do I say 'on Mondays' and 'on Tuesdays'?

Translate the following sentences into French (using the information in brackets to help you).

Questions 8.1	Explanation 8.1	Answers 8.1
1. We can no longer meet each other on Saturdays. 2. It is very difficult to drive around (*circuler*) in this town on Friday evenings. 3. Do you remember? On Sundays we would go and have (*allait boire*) tea together. 4. I always meet them on Sundays in the park (*au jardin public*). 5. I am never tired on Mondays.	When saying 'on' with a day of the week, French uses the singular with the word *le*.	1. Nous ne pouvons plus nous rencontrer le samedi. 2. Il est très difficile de circuler dans cette ville le vendredi soir. 3. Tu t'en souviens? Le dimanche on allait boire un thé ensemble. 4. Je les rencontre toujours au jardin public le dimanche. 5. Je ne suis jamais fatigué le lundi.

8.2   How is it possible to say whether some words take *la* or *le* or *un* or *une*?

Put the *le* or *la* or *un* or *une* in the gaps in the sentences below.

Questions 8.2	Explanation 8.2	Answers 8.2
1. Je prendrais bien ___ limon**ade**.	Feminine endings: -*ade*, -*eine*, -*anse* and -*erie*. Masculine endings: -*ai*, -*acle*, -*ème*, -*er*, -*c* and -*ing*.	1. Je prendrais bien **une** limon**ade**.
2. Il faut terminer ce projet dans ___ dél**ai** de trois semaines.		2. Il faut terminer ce projet dans **un** dél**ai** de trois semaines.
3. On associe toujours Jonas avec ___ bal**eine** qui l'avait avalé.		3. On associe toujours Jonas avec **la** bal**eine** qui l'avait avalé.
4. Ce que j'ai vécu c'était un peu comme ___ tr**anse**.		4. Ce que j'ai vécu c'était un peu comme **une** tr**anse**.
5. Ah zut! J'ai oublié les saucisses à ___ bouch**erie**.		5. Ah zut! J'ai oublié les saucisses à **la** bouch**erie**.
6. Vous êtes vraiment ___ or**acle**.		6. Vous êtes vraiment **un** or**acle**.
7. Quand j'ai fait mes études nous devions faire ___ th**ème** tous les deux jours.		7. Quand j'ai fait mes études nous devions faire **un** th**ème** tous les deux jours.
8. Va chercher quelques betteraves dans ___ potag**er**.		8. Va chercher quelques betteraves dans **le** potag**er**.
9. Il y a ___ superbe viadu**c** au Sud de la ville.		9. Il y a **un** superbe viadu**c** au Sud de la ville.
10. Tu as ___ smok**ing**?		10. Tu as **un** smok**ing**?

8.3   Which naming words take -*aux* in the plural?

Replace the English word in **bold** with the correct plural form of its French translation.

Questions 8.3	Explanations 8.3	Answers 8.3
1. Il va falloir que tu achètes deux **cakes** pour les amis de Pauline.	1. Un gâteau.	1. Il va falloir que tu achètes deux gâteaux pour les amis de Pauline.
2. Cela ne me gêne pas du tout de voir les **animals** sauvages dans un cirque.	2. Un animal.	2. Cela ne me gêne pas du tout de voir les animaux sauvages dans un cirque.
3. Oui j'admire beaucoup les **paintings** de Clara Peeters.	3. Un tableau	3. Oui j'admire beaucoup les tableaux de Clara Peeters.
4. Heureusement les **jackals** (*chacal*) ne viennent jamais rôder autour de la maison.	4. *Un chacal*, does not follow the expected pattern.	4. Heureusement les chacals ne viennent jamais rôder autour de la maison.
5. Les **interest rates** sont actuellement intéressants.	5. *Les taux d'intérêt*.	5. Les taux d'intérêt sont actuellement intéressants.

8.4   What are the two ways to say and write words beginning with a letter 'h' in French?

Replace the English word in bold with the correct form of its French translation.

Questions 8.4	Explanations 8.4	Answers 8.4
1. **I hate** ce genre de spectacle.	1. The 'to' form of this doing word is written: *haïr* – the dieresis marks a separation between 'a' and 'i' when you say the word.	2. Il avait la hardiesse de s'adresser à la princesse.
2. Il avait **the boldness** (hardiesse) de s'adresser à la princesse.		3. On a tendance à sous-estimer les effets du hasard dans la vie.
3. On a tendance à sous-estimer les effets du **chance** dans la vie.	2. Pronounce and write this as two words: hardiesse and the right word for 'the'.	4. J'habite dans cette ville depuis plus de vingt ans.
4. **I live** dans cette ville depuis plus de vingt ans.	3. The French word is *hasard*.	5. A midi, le hibou était encore dans l'arbre.
5. A midi, **the owl** (hibou) était encore dans l'arbre.	4. The 'normal' one-word form is used here.	
	5. Pronounce and write this as two words.	
	1. Je hais ce genre de spectacle.	

8.5   When is there an *é* at the start of a word and when not?

This is a correction exercise. Choose whether or not to put in an *é* at the start of the words below.

Questions 8.5	Explanation 8.5	Answers 8.5
1. Je crois que ces bâtiments étaient des **et**ables autrefois.	The following pairs of letters never have an 'é' when they begin words: ef-, emb-, es-, ex- and eu-. The following pairs of letters always have an 'é' when they begin words: éb-, éc-, éd-, ég-, éj-, él-, éma-, ép-, éra-, ét-, and év-.	1. Je crois que ces bâtiments étaient des **ét**ables autrefois.
2. Il risque d'être **ex**clu par ses collègues.		2. Il risque d'être **ex**clu par ses collègues.
3. 'Ma fantasque **es**crime', c'est ainsi que Baudelaire a appelé la poésie.		3. 'Ma fantasque **es**crime', c'est ainsi que Baudelaire a appelé la poésie.
4. Je me vois obligée de terminer mes **et**udes aussi vite que possible.		4. Je me vois obligée de terminer mes **ét**udes aussi vite que possible.
5. Le chevalier fut tué par un coup d'ep̄ée.		5. Le chevalier fut tué par un coup d'**ép**ée.

8.6   What is the unique pattern of describing words with *gens*?

In the following sentences, make the describing word agree appropriately and insert it either before or after the word *gens*.

Questions 8.6	Explanations 8.6	Answers 8.6
1. Ces gens me font pitié (malheureux). 2. Evitez de passer du temps chez ces gens (méchant). 3. Mes parents sont en effet des gens (aisé). 4. Regardez ces maisons, ce sont les demeures des gens (fortuné). 5. Les gens ont souvent une existence difficile dans cette société (vieux).	1. *Malheureux* follows the normal pattern of a describing word in French. 2. *Méchant* displays a highly unusual pattern and is temporarily transformed into a word with 'la'. 3. *Aisé* follows the normal pattern of a describing word in French. 4. *Fortuné* follows the normal pattern of a describing word in French. 5. *Vieux* displays a highly unusual pattern and is temporarily transformed into a word with 'la'.	1. Ces gens malheureux me font pitié. 2. Evitez de passer du temps chez ces méchantes gens. 3. Mes parents sont en effet des gens aisés. 4. Regardez ces maisons, ce sont les demeures des gens fortunés. 5. Les vieilles gens ont souvent une existence difficile dans cette société.

8.7   On occasions the *vous* and *tu* form are mixed, in a form which is neutral.

Insert the unique fixed expression in the *vous* form which can be inserted beside the *tu* expressions below.

Questions 8.7	Explanation 8.7	Answers 8.7
1. ___, viens avec moi. 2. ___, ne dis pas ça. 3. Non, non, ___, je te le jures, tu ne risques absolument rien.	Rearrange the following letters and you will find the unique fixed expression: e, l, a, z and l.	1. Allez, viens avec moi. 2. Allez, ne dis pas ça. 3. Non, non, allez, tu ne risques absolument rien.

8.8 Which French doing words have 'ç', an extra 'e', an 'è', a double letter, or a change from 'y' to 'i' and when?

Translate the phrases below into French using the doing words, vocabulary and the *je*, *tu*, *il*, *nous*, *vous*, *ils* or *elles* given.

Questions 8.8	Explanations 8.8	Answers 8.8
1. You are bored! Use *tu*.	1. Use *s'ennuyer*.	1. Tu t'ennuies.
2. He began to laugh. Use the 'have' tense.	2. Use *commencer*.	2. Il a commencé à rire (you can also use *de* after *commencé*, but only with *il* or *elle*).
3. We eat the chocolate cakes.	3. Use *manger*.	
4. You get up early. Use *tu*.	4. Use *se lever*.	3. Nous mangeons les gâteaux au chocolat.
5. We call him back.	5. Use *rappeler*.	
6. Valérie never cleans her car.	6. Use *nettoyer*.	4. Tu te lèves tôt.
7. My name is Leopold.	7. Use *s'appeler*.	5. Nous le rappelons.
8. We always get up late.	8. Use *se lever*.	6. Valérie ne nettoie jamais sa voiture.
9. They were beginning to smile. Use *commencer*.	9. Use the *aient* ending.	7. Je m'appelle Léopold.
10. We are not wiping this.	10. Use *essuyer*.	8. Nous nous levons toujours tard.
		9. Ils commençaient à sourire.
		10. Nous n'essuyons pas ceci.

8.9 Am I sure about the tenses which follow *venir de*?

Translate the following sentences into English or French.

Questions 8.9	Explanations 8.9	Answers 8.9
1. That is what I have just said.	1. When you have a 'have just' in English, in French there is a present tense.	1. *C'est ce que je viens de dire.*
2. I had just come in.		2. *Je venais de rentrer.*
3. *Je venais de la salle de sports quand j'ai vu l'accident.*	2. When you have a 'had just' in English, in French you have a 'was' tense.	3. I was coming from the sports hall when I saw the accident.
4. *Je venais de tomber par terre.*		4. I had just fallen to the ground.
5. *Michel vient de s'acheter un appartement.*	3. When *venir de* is used with a place it is translated word for word.	5. Michel has just bought himself an apartment.
	4. When you have a 'had just' in English, in French you have a 'was' tense.	
	5. When you have a 'have just' in English, in French there is a present tense.	

8.10   Am I sure about the tenses which follow *depuis*?

Translate the following sentences into English or French.

Questions 8.10	Explanations 8.10	Answers 8.10
1. He had been cycling (*faire du cyclisme*) for fifteen years when he won the tour.	1. When you have a 'had' in English, in French you have a 'was' tense.	1. *Il faisait du cyclisme depuis quinze ans quand il a gagné le tour.*
2. *Je vis à Barcelone depuis dix ans et demi.*	2. When you have a present tense in French you have a 'have' in English.	2. I have been living in Barcelona for ten and a half years.
3. The party has been going (*se déroule*) since three.	3. When you have a 'have' in English, in French there is a present tense.	3. *La fête se déroule depuis trois heures.*
4. *Samuel montait la pente depuis plus d'une demi-journée quand il a vu les autres descendre.*	4. When you have a 'was' tense in French you have a 'had' tense in English.	4. Samuel had been climbing the slope for more than half a day when he saw the others coming down.
5. Emily and Barbara have been living together for three years.	5. When you have a 'have' tense in English you have a have a present tense in French.	5. Emily et Barbara vivent ensemble depuis trois ans.

8.11   Which tenses accompany both parts of sentences with *si* meaning 'if'?

Translate the following sentences into English or French.

Questions 8.11	Explanations 8.11	Answers 8.11
1. Si tu le vois, tu lui diras la même chose que moi.	1. In the part of the sentence with *si*: present tense and in the part of the sentence without *si*, complementing it: future tense.	1. If you see him, you will tell him the same thing as me.
2. If she was more attentive in class, she would get better marks.	2. In the part of the sentence with *si*: 'was' tense and in the part of the sentence without *si*, complementing it: 'would' tense.	2. Si elle était plus attentive en classe, elle aurait de meilleures notes.
3. If you (*vous*) want to come you'll have to bring a bottle of wine.	3. In the part of the sentence with *si*: present tense and in the part of the sentence without *si*, complementing it: future tense.	3. Si vous voulez venir, il vous faudra apporter une bouteille de vin.
4. Si Jules et Jim partaient en vacances ensemble, ils resteraient amis à vie.	4. In the part of the sentence with *si*: 'was' tense and in the part of the sentence without *si*, complementing it: 'would' tense.	4. If Jules and Jim were to go on holiday together, they would stay friends for life.
5. If I'd known, I'd've warned him.	5. In the part of the sentence with si: 'had' tense and in the part of the sentence without *si*, complementing it: 'would have' tense.	5. Si je l'avais su, je l'aurais prévenu.

8.12 When is *aurait dit* not translated by 'would have said'?

Translate the following sentences into French.

Questions 8.12	Explanations 8.12	Answers 8.12
1. Apparently Maurice has said something intelligent for once. 2. Apparently, he lied to her continuously. 3. There may well be some truth (*un peu de vrai*) in his story. 4. We believe we know that the train seems to have been hijacked half-way between Dreux and Caen. 5. Apparently, it seems that he killed himself by jumping from a sixth floor window.	1. Use the 'would have' tense of *dire*. 2. Use the 'would have' tense of *mentir*. 3. Use the 'would have' tense of *il y a*. 4. Use the 'would have' tense of *être détourné*. 5. Use the 'would have' tense of *se donner la mort*.	1. Apparemment, Maurice aurait dit quelque chose d'intelligent pour une fois. 2. Apparemment, il lui aurait menti sans cesse. 3. Il y aurait un peu de vrai dans son histoire. 4. Nous croyons savoir que le train aurait été détourné à mi-chemin entre Dreux et Caen. 5. Apparemment il se serait donné la mort en sautant d'une fenêtre du sixième étage.

9

French uses this form frequently, where English hardly uses it at all

9.1   The use of the subjunctive after certain types of expression.

Some of these sentences do not require the subjunctive. To help you, the full forms of the doing words (the forms listed first in dictionaries) are found at the end of each sentence and the answers we provided in random order at the end of the exercise.

Questions 9.1	Explanations 9.1	Answers 9.1
1. Jacques, elle veut que tu lui ___ la vérité maintenant (*dire*).	1. An expression of wish and desire.	1. Jacques, elle veut que tu lui dises la vérité maintenant.
2. Elle était contente que Thomas ___ amené Jacques (*avoir*).	2. An expression of happiness.	2. Elle était contente que Thomas eût amené Jacques.
3. Thomas ne s'est pas fâché que son ami Jacques lui ___ menti (*avoir*).	3. An expression of anger; it does not matter that the sentence is in the negative.	3. Thomas ne s'est pas fâché que son ami Jacques lui ait menti.
4. Il était essentiel qu'ils ___ le problème aussitôt que possible (*résoudre*) (FORMAL).	4. An expression of necessity.	4. Il était essentiel qu'ils résolvent le problème aussitôt que possible (FORMAL).
5. Thomas pensait: 'Il se peut que Jacques se ___ à pleurer et Tina à crier' (*mettre*).	5. An expression of possibility.	5. Thomas pensait: 'Il se peut que Jacques se mette à pleurer et Tina à crier'.
6. 'J'ai pensé que tu me ___ Tina' dit Jacques (*pardonner*).	6. A positive expression of thought or belief.	6. 'J'ai pensé que tu me pardonnerais, Tina' dit Jacques.
7. 'Je ne peux pas croire que tu ___ dire une chose aussi stupide', répondit Tina (*pouvoir*).	7. An expression of thought or belief in the negative.	7. 'Je ne peux pas croire que tu puisses dire une chose aussi stupide', répondit Tina.
8. Il paraît qu'elle ___ eu le coup de foudre (*avoir*).	8. An expression of doubt/probability **not** linked to a specific person.	8. Il paraît qu'elle ait eu le coup de foudre.
9. Il me semblait que même les parents de David me ___ confiance (*faire*).	9. An expression of doubt/probability linked to a specific person.	9. Il me semblait que même les parents de David me faisaient confiance.
10. Je préfère ___ me coucher maintenant (*aller*).	10. An expression of wanting, but there is the same person in both parts of the sentence.	10. Je préfère aller me coucher maintenant.
11. Il serait bon que vous ___ un peu de repos (*prendre*).	11. An expression which is related to happiness.	11. Il serait bon que vous preniez un peu de repos.
2. Je ne pense pas qu'il ___ (*mentir*).	12. Not thinking something is equivalent to doubt in French.	12. Je ne pense pas qu'il mente.
3. J'aimerais bien qu'ils ___ (*faire*) plus attention à ce qu'ils disent.	13. An expression of wanting, wishing or desire.	13. J'aimerais bien qu'ils fassent plus attention à ce qu'ils disent.
4. La patronne souhaiterait qu'ils ___ (*venir*) la voir tout de suite.	14. An expression of wanting, wishing or desire.	14. La patronne souhaiterait qu'ils viennent la voir tout de suite.
5. Je ne voudrais pas qu'il me ___ (*dire*) demain qu'il ne peut pas me rendre l'argent.	15. An expression of wanting, wishing or desire; it does not matter that it is in the negative.	15. Je ne voudrais pas qu'il me dise demain qu'il ne peut pas me rendre l'argent.
Answers in random order *ait menti • dise • eût • viennent • puisse • préfère aller • dises • mente • fassent • ait • preniez • pardonnerais • se mette faisaient • résolvent*		

9.2   Use of the subjunctive after certain words and phrases

Translated the sentences below into French (using the information in brackets to help you).

Questions 9.2	Explanations 9.2	Answers 9.2
1. Although my father is seventy five he walks three kilometres each day (*il fait ses 3 km à pied tous les jours*). 2. As far as I know, his brother is a university teacher. 3. Please put away these dangerous tools (*ranger ces outils dangereux*) before little Sandrine comes back. 4. Let's suppose that I were to go and see him tomorrow... (*aller le voir*). 5. It's not that I am afraid, on the contrary, I like going to the dentist (*aller chez le dentiste*). 6. Provided that our equipment (*équipement*) is reliable (*fiable*), we can reach Gora. 7. The fact that he always says the same thing makes me smile (*me fait sourire*). 8. The children speak slowly so that he can understand them. 9. He left for town, whereas the others stayed at home. 10. I spoke to them without thinking that their family situation was difficult (*penser que leur situation familiale était difficile*).	1. An expression of contrast with 'although'; there are two possible answers. 2. This is a near negative because it refers to the limits of knowledge. It is a very formal expression. 3. Here there is a time distinction. 4. This is a 'just imagine...' expression. 5. Here a negative is imagined. 6. This is a reason for a result. 7. This is a reason for a result. 8. This is a reason for a result. 9. There is a contrast here, but no 'although.' 10. Here the negative is factual and there is the same person in both parts of the sentence.	1. Bien que/ Quoique mon père ait soixante-quinze ans il fait ses trois kilomètres à pied tous les jours. 2. Autant que je sache, son frère est professeur de fac. 3. S'il te plaît, range les outils dangereux avant que la petite Sandrine ne revienne. 4. Supposons que j'aille le voir demain... 5. Ce n'est pas que j'aie peur, au contraire, j'aime aller chez le dentiste. 6. A condition que notre équipement soit fiable, nous pouvons atteindre Gora. 7. Le fait qu'il dise toujours la même chose me fait sourire. 8. Les enfants parlent lentement pour qu'il puisse les comprendre. 9. Il est parti en ville, alors que les autres sont restés à la maison. 10. Je leur ai parlé sans penser que leur situation familiale était difficile.

9.3   The historic present

Would you use the historic present in these cases? If so, which tense would you use when translating the underlined doing words into English?

Questions 9.3	Explanations 9.3	Answers 9.3
1. *Il* <u>*est*</u> *trois heures et demie du matin et Aimé ne* <u>*peut*</u> *pas dormir. Il* <u>*va*</u> *à la cuisine chercher un verre d'eau, puis il* <u>*revient*</u> *se coucher (revenir se coucher – to come back to bed) avec son livre préféré, une biographie de Rembrandt.*	1. There is an expression of time, but it does not necessarily situate these events in the past. In addition, the type of the events in the story do not situate it outside the contemporary period. Finally the events are not particularly dramatic.	1. NO historic present, therefore translate into English using the present tense: 'it is three o'clock', 'cannot sleep', 'he goes', 'he comes back to bed'.
2. *Les canons des Français* <u>*se trouvent*</u> *sur la colline* (the hill) *qui* <u>*domine*</u> *la plaine. Napoléon* <u>*est*</u> *encore dans sa tente, il* <u>*consulte*</u> *les cartes. Nous* <u>*sommes*</u> *à la veille* (the day before) *de la grande bataille de Monte Bello en 1800.*	2. This is a dramatic situation with an identifiable historical figure, a date is also mentioned.	2. Historic present, therefore translate into English using the past tense: 'were on the hill', 'overlooked', 'was still in his tent', 'was looking at', 'it was the day before'.
3. *Le prochain patient a une crise cardiaque. Le docteur Rivière* <u>*prend*</u> *la situation en main, il* <u>*écarte*</u> *tous les passants* (passers-by) *et* <u>*fait venir*</u> *ses collègues Bondin et Gounart. Les trois médecins* <u>*se mettent*</u> *à l'œuvre (se mettre à l'œuvre – to get to work). D'abord il* <u>*faut*</u> *s'assurer que la victime peut respirer* (be sure that).	3. This is a dramatic life-and-death situation.	3. Historic present, therefore translate into English using the past tense: 'was having', 'took charge of the situation', 'moved the passers-by aside', 'sent for his colleagues', 'got to work', 'they had to be sure'.
4. *Le vol en provenance de* (from) *Boston* <u>*arrive*</u> *à Paris Charles de Gaulle à dix-sept heures trente-cinq tous les jours. Ensuite les passagers* <u>*débarquent*</u> (disembark), *les uns* <u>*prennent*</u> *un car* (bus) *qui les amène à Paris, les autres* <u>*prennent*</u> *le train. Les touristes* <u>*restent*</u> *d'habitude en groupes de dix ou de vingt pendant leur séjour dans la capitale.*	4. The expression of time does not situate the events in the past, the events are contemporary and are not especially dramatic.	4. NO historic present, therefore translate into English using the present tense: 'arrives', 'disembark', 'some take', 'which takes them', 'others take the train', 'remain in groups'.
5. *Depuis trois heures le commando* (commando unit) *se tenait prêt pour assassiner le général mais à la dernière minute* <u>*il y a*</u> *une surprise: au lieu de prendre le chemin qui longe la fleuve* (the road beside the river), *la voiture du général* <u>*s'arrête*</u> *aux feux* (traffic lights) *pour tourner ensuite à gauche. Ils* <u>*ont*</u> *sans doute l'intention d'éviter les rues étroites* (narrow) *du centre ville et d'atteindre la place principale en traversant la cour du Palais de Justice* (the courtyard of the Law Courts). *Le général* <u>*a*</u> *sûrement quelque chose de très important à y régler avant d'assister à* (attending) *la cérémonie. Donc pour le moment il* <u>*est*</u> *hors de portée.*	5. Although no dates are mentioned, this is the build-up to a dramatic situation, which begins with the phrase *à la dernière minute.*	5. Historic present, therefore translate into English using the past tense: 'there was', 'stopped at traffic lights', 'they probably intended', 'the general had', 'he was out of range'.

9.4   Different word order in French

Arrange the translated French parts of the sentences below in the frequently used order.

Questions 9.4	Explanations 9.4	Answers 9.4
1. He stood (*il resta*) open-mouthed (*bouche bée*) in astonishment (*étonné,*). 2. Abraham Lincoln (*Abraham Lincoln*), the first president of the United States (*le premier président des Etats-Unis*), was a man of courage (*était un homme courageux*). 3. This man possessed the necessary qualities (*les qualités requises*) to become an astronaut: he was tall, intelligent and sporty (*grand, intelligent et sportif*). 4. She had had (*avait eu*) two children and had invested hundred thousand dollars in the stock market for them (*avait investi cent mille dollars à la bourse*) when she was twenty years old (*à vingt ans*). 5. Each Summer we used to hear the cart of the Roma gypsy family approaching (*nous entendions s'approcher la charette de la famille Roma*), followed by at least ten of the village dogs (*suivie par au moins dix chiens du village*) and with its wheels squeaking (*avec ses roues qui grinçaient*).	1. 'He' is the person and comes first in English, stood is the doing word and comes second. Next comes 'open-mouthed', a direct description of how he was standing and 'in astonishment' is the general context. 2. 'Abraham Lincoln' comes first in English as the person, the first president is between commas so it can be inserted next; finally, 'was a man of courage' contains the doing word and the main description. 3. This man is the person and comes first in English, next is the doing word 'possessed'. English includes 'was' before the three qualities, but French would only need the words for the qualities themselves. 4. English begins with the person, immediately followed by the action and the person to whom it is directed. Only at the end are there are further details about the person who acted. 5. The phrases describing the cart come at the end of the sentence in English, which begins with the doing word 'followed'.	1. Etonné, il resta bouche bée. 2. Le premier président des Etats-Unis, Abraham Lincoln, était un homme courageux. 3. Grand, intelligent et sportif, cet homme possédait les qualités requises pour devenir astro-naute. 4. A vingt ans, elle avait eu deux enfants et avait investi cent mille dollars à la bourse pour eux. 5. Suivie par au moins dix chiens du village et avec ses roues qui grinçaient, nous entendions s'approcher chaque été la charette de la famille Roma.

10

English uses this form frequently, where French uses it hardly at all

10.1 What are the ways of avoiding the frequently-occurring English passives? and what is their effect on tense in French?

In the first three examples, identify the parts of the sentences in first and second positions and reverse them to make passive sentences or, if they are already in the passive, make sentences with normal word order. There is no need to translate these sentences.

In examples 4 to 6 translate the English sentences into French avoiding the passive in the most appropriate way.

In examples 7 to 10 translate the English sentences into French using the passive and stating whether each one refers to an action or to a state.

Questions 10.1	Explanations 10.1	Answers 10.1
1. He opened a new shop.	1. Normal word order where 'opened' is in first position and 'a new shop' is in second position.	1. A new shop was opened by him.
2. He was told by them to pay back the money.		2. They told him to pay back the money.
3. You were requested to leave by the doorman.	2. Passive word order: 'he' is in first position and 'they' is in second position.	3. The doorman requested you to leave.
4. He was approached (s'approcher de) in the street.	3. Passive word order: 'you' is in first position and 'the doorman' is in second position.	4. On s'approcha de lui dans la rue.
5. Thousands of copies (des milliers d'exemplaires) of this record will be sold.		5. Ce disque va se vendre à des milliers d'exemplaires.
6. Were you well advised?	4. You have a choice between using on or the doing word with se.	6. Est-ce qu'on vous a bien conseillé?
7. Jacques was bitten (mordu) by a snake (un serpent).	5. You have a choice between using on or the doing word with se.	7. Jacques a été mordu par un serpent. ACTION
8. Fresh (frais) milk is never kept in the fridge at our house.	6. Here, you can only use one of the options: on or the doing word with se.	8. Chez nous le lait frais n'est jamais rangé dans le frigo. STATE
9. The sculpture was suspended by a metal wire (fil métallique) at the end of the gallery (au fond de la galerie).	7. Being bitten by a snake involves movement.	9. La sculpture était suspendue par un fil métallique au fond de la galerie. STATE
10. The baby was lifted up (relevé) by her father	8. Being kept in one place is a stationary situation.	10. Le bébé a été relevé par son père. ACTION.
	9. Being suspended is a stationary situation!	
	10. Being lifted up involves movement.	

10.2　How to I translate English doing words ending in '-ing'?

Write the following sentences in French using a series of different translations of the word '-ing'.

Questions 10.2	Explanations 10.2	Answers 10.2
1. Martin is getting older and older. 2. I am still wondering how he got up the stairs. 3. Translating literature is an art. 4. I'll be waiting for you on the bridge at two o'clock. 5. No (défense de) smoking.	1. Try to translate 'is getting' with one doing word in French. 2. Here the doing word in both French and English has two parts, but they are different: in French one of the parts is *me*. 3. Here the word ending in '-ing' is translated by the form of the French doing word which is listed first in dictionaries. 4. 'I'll be waiting' is translated by two words in French and one of those is *je*. 5. Here the word ending in '-ing' is translated by the form of the French doing word which is listed first in dictionaries.	1. Martin vieillit de plus en plus. 2. Je me demande encore comment il a pu monter l'escalier. 3. C'est un art de traduire les textes littéraires. 4. Je vous attendrai sur le pont à deux heures. 5. Défense de fumer.

10.3　Do the colours in French change to follow *le*, *la* and *les*, when I add *clair* and *sombre*, the words for 'light' and 'dark'?

Translate the following sentences into English.

Questions 10.3	Explanations 10.3	Answers 10.3
1. She has light blue eyes. 2. The lawn was dark green. 3. The wood was a very light brown. 4. However, the bricks were dark brown. 5. The plastic parts (*les pièces en plastique*) in the machine was light yellow.	The names of colours (*brun*, *vert*) do not change (adding, e, es or s) when they are written with words *clair* and *foncé*, meaning light' and 'dark'.	1. Elle a les yeux bleu clair. 2. La pelouse était vert foncé. 3. Le bois était brun très clair. 4. Pourtant les briques étaient marron foncé. 5. Les pièces en plastique dans la machine étaient jaune clair.

11

There are two words, or ways of saying something in English, where there is only one in French

11.1 How do I translate 'it' and 'them' with doing words with *à*?

Translate the following sentences into English, deciding whether to use 'it' or 'them'. You can find other sentences with similar doing words in section 2.10.

Questions 11.1	Explanations 11.1	Answers 11.1
1. Le vieux lit en bois? Oui, j'y tiens beaucoup.	1. *Tenir à* refers to 'the old wooden bed'.	1. The old wooden bed? Yes, I am very fond of it.
2. Quel défi (challenge)! j'ai essayé tant de fois de résoudre ce puzzle, mais je n'y parviens pas.	2. *Parvenir à* refers to 'this puzzle'.	2. What a challenge! I tried so many times to solve this puzzle, but I cannot manage it.
3. Les modèles de navires en bois que vous m'avez offerts (gave) à Noël? Alors je ne les ai pas oublié, j'y travaille tous les soirs.	3. *Travailler à* refers to the 'models'.	3. The wooden model ships that you gave me for Christmas? Well, I haven't forgotten them. I work on them every evening.
4. Le départ de Jacques? En fin de compte, je m'y attendais.	4. *S'attendre à* refers to 'the departure'.	4. Jack's departure? At the end of the day, I was expecting it.
5. Le parti conservateur en l'an deux mille? Je n'éprouve aucune difficulté à y appartenir.	5. *Appartenir à* refers to the 'Conservative Party'.	5. The Conservative Party in the year 2000? I don't experience any difficulty at all in belonging to it.

260   PART TWO • THE GRAMMAR WORKBOOK

11.2 How do I translate 'it' and 'them' with doing words with *de*?

Translate the following sentences into English, deciding whether to use 'it' or 'them'. You can find other sentences with similar doing words in section 2.10.

Questions 11.2	Explanations 11.2	Answers 11.2
1. Tu te sauves quand tu vois des formes dans l'obscurité, mais moi, je n'en ai pas peur. (INFORMAL) 2. La musique classique? J'en raffole. 3. Oui je sais que le projet a été retenu par le jury l'année dernière. Néanmoins je ne m'en souviens pas. 4. C'est la mini-chaîne là-bas qui t'intéresse? Je pense quand même que nous pouvons nous en passer pour le moment. 5. Les promesses que tu m'as faites, franchement, je m'en moque.	1. *Avoir peur de* refers to 'the dark shapes'. 2. *Raffoler de* refers to 'classical music'. 3. *Se souvenir de* refers to 'my project'. 4. *Se passer de* refers to 'the hi-fi'. 5. *Se moquer de* refers to 'the promises'.	1. You run for it when you see in the dark, but I am not afraid of them. (INFORMAL). 2. Classical music? I am mad about it. 3. Yes I know that the project was chosen by the jury last year. Nevertheless I do not remember it? 4. Is it the mini hi-fi over there which interests you? All the same, I think that we can do without it for the moment. 5. The promises that you made me, frankly, I couldn't give a damn about them.

11.3 When does *même* mean 'same' and when does it mean 'even'?

Translate the following sentences into English using 'same' or 'even' as appropriate.

Questions 11.3	Explanations 11.3	Answers 11.3
1. Il y en a des bleus et des noirs, mais en fin de compte il s'agit du même format. 2. Écoute, je commence à en avoir assez, tu n'as même pas fait la vaisselle. 3. Même moi, je comprends la différence entre ces deux choses-là. 4. Julie et Juliette ont exactement la même taille. 5. Nous reconnaissons que nous avons fait la même erreur que la dernière fois.	1. Here *même* is written with a naming word. 2. Here *même* is not written with a naming word. 3. Here *même* is not written with a naming word. 4. Here *même* is written with a naming word. 5. Here *même* is written with a naming word.	1. There are blue and black ones, but at the end of the day, they are in the same format. 2. Listen, I am starting to get tired of this, you haven't even done the washing up. 3. Even I understand the difference between both of these things. 4. Julie and Juliette are exactly the same size. 5. We recognise that we have made the same mistake as last time.

11.4   When does *son* mean 'his' and when 'her'?

Translate the following sentences into English, using 'his' or 'her' as appropriate.

Questions 11.4	Explanations 11.4	Answers 11.4
1. Natalie a beaucoup aidé Simone dans l'affaire de son argent perdu.	1. *Argent* takes *le*, it is not important whether the owner of the money was a man or a woman.	1. Natalie helped Simone a lot in the business of her missing money.
2. Voici Bernard, rappelles-toi l'année dernière quand on avait oublié la date de son anniversaire?	2. *Anniversaire* takes *le* and it is not important whether the person who has the birthday is a man or a woman.	2. Here is Bernard, do you remember last year when we forgot his birthday?
3. Voilà Ginette, son cousin joue dans l'équipe de France de volley-ball.	3. *Cousin* takes *le*.	3. There is Ginette, her cousin plays in the French volleyball team.
4. Robert: Tu as vu son canif? Reza: Le canif de qui? Robert: Eh bien, le canif de Mateo Falcone bien sûr!	4. In the question it is impossible to know how to translate *son* into English until we see that the name of its owner indicates a man.	4. Robert: Have you seen his penknife? Reza: Whose penknife? Robert: Well, Mateo Falcone's penknife of course!
5. Ma mère a perdu son alliance.	5. *Alliance* takes *la*, is written *l'alliance* because it begins with 'a', 'e', 'i', 'o', or 'u' and therefore takes *son*.	5. My mother has lost her wedding ring.

11.5   When does *sa* mean 'his' and when 'her'?

Translate the following sentences into English, using the 'his' or 'her' as appropriate

Questions 11.5	Explanations 11.5	Answers 11.5
1. Mon oncle vient de perdre sa montre.	1. *Montre* takes *la* regardless of whether the owner is a man or a woman.	1. My uncle has just lost his watch.
2. Mireille nous a dit que sa tante viendrait la prendre à minuit.	2. *Tante* takes *la*, regardless of whether the person whose aunt it is, is a man or a woman.	2. Mireille told us that her aunt would come and pick her up at midnight.
3. Gérald nous a dit que sa cousine fait beaucoup de sport.	3. *Cousine* takes *la*, regardless of whether the person whose female cousin it is a man or a woman.	3. Gerald told us that his female cousin does a lot of sport.
4. Audrée nous a montré le grenier du château de sa grand-mère.	4. *Grand-mère* takes *la*, regardless of whether the person whose grandmother it is, is a man or a woman.	4. Audrée showed us the attic of her grandmother's castle.
5. John: oui, c'est sa copine qui me l'a dit. Mustapha: la copine de qui? John: Bon, la copine de Jerry bien sûr! (INFORMAL).	5. *Copine* takes *la*, regardless of whether the person whose female friend it is, is a man or a woman.	5. John: yes, it was his (woman) friend who told me that. Mustapha: whose friend? John: well, Jerry's friend of course! (INFORMAL)

11.6   When does *aussi* mean 'also' and when does it mean 'therefore'?

Translate the following sentences into English using 'also' or 'therefore' as appropriate.

Questions 11.6	Explanations 11.6	Answers 11.6
1. 'Elle aussi, elle a du travail à faire', lui a-t-il répondu. 2. Veux-tu que je remonte les bouteilles vides aussi? 3. Puisqu'il ne pèse que 40 kilos. Aussi dit-il que Manuel est trop jeune pour travailler comme maçon. 4. Ils sont partis après le petit-déjeuner. Aussi arriveront-ils plus en retard que nous. 5. Là aussi il y a un couvre-feu.	1. The normal order of the person and the doing word is not reversed in the sentence with *aussi*. However, it is of course reversed in the phrase which follows the speech marks. 2. The normal order of the person and the doing word is not reversed in the sentence with *aussi*. 3. Here the normal order of the person and the doing word is reversed. 4. Here the normal order of the person and the doing word is reversed. 5. The normal order of the person and the doing word is not reversed in the sentence with *aussi*.	1. 'She also has work to do', he replied to her. 2. Do you want me to also bring up the empty bottles? 3. Since he only weighs 40 kg. Therefore he says that Manuel is too young to work as a builder. 4. They left after breakfast. Therefore they will arrive later than us. 5. There is also a curfew there.

11.7   How does a change in position affect the words *ancien*, *anciens*, *ancienne* and *anciennes*?

Translate these sentences into English using 'former' or 'ancient' as appropriate.

Questions 11.7	Explanations 11.7	Answers 11.7
1. Là vous pouvez voir les ruines de l'ancienne abbaye. 2. A Athènes j'ai visité les ruines les plus anciennes. 3. Au coin de la rue vous verrez un temple ancien qui sert toujours. 4. Tu vois cette femme là-bas? C'est mon ancienne dentiste. 5. On a construit le nouveau centre culturel de Seeheim dans les anciens abattoirs de la ville.	1. Here *ancienne* comes before the naming word *abbaye*. 2. Here *anciennes* comes after the naming word *ruines*. 3. Here *ancien* comes after the naming word *moulin*. 4. Here *ancienne* comes before the naming word *dentiste*. 5. Here *anciens* comes before the naming word *abattoirs*.	1. There you can see the ruins of the former abbey. 2. In Athens I visited the most ancient ruins. 3. At corner of the street you will see an ancient temple which is still in use. 4. You see that woman over there? She is my former dentist. 5. Seeheim's new arts centre was built in the town's former abattoirs.

11.8   When does *faire* mean to 'make', to 'do' and when does it mean to 'have something done'?

Translate the following sentences into English using to 'make', to 'do' or to 'have something done' as appropriate.

Questions 11.8	Explanations 11.8	Answers 11.8
1. Madame Dira, est-ce que vous avez déjà fait les calculs nécessaires?	1. This is the standard meaning of *faire*.	1. Madame Dira, have you already done the necessary calculations?
2. J'ai fait savoir à M. Perlman que sa commande était prête.	2. Here the person doesn't tell Mr. Pearlman directly.	2. I have let Mr Perlman know that his order was ready.
3. Voilà, c'est fait.	3. This is the standard meaning of *faire*.	3. There, it's done.
4. Monsieur je suis au regret de vous dire que vous avez fait une erreur. (FORMAL).	4. Here you have to think about which doing word fits better with 'mistake'.	4. Sir I am sorry to say that you have made a mistake. (FORMAL)
5. J'ai fait construire une nouvelle piscine à côté de notre résidence secondaire en Corse.	5. Here the meaning of *faire* refers to something that is not done directly. The homeowners cannot construct the pool themselves.	5. I have had a new swimming pool built beside our second home in Corsica.

11.9   When is there one form of the present tense in French and two forms in English?

When translating the sentences below into English, use the correct form of the present tense.

Questions 11.9	Explanations 11.9	Answers 11.9
1. La chose à laquelle nous avons à faire ici, n'est qu'un simple cas de tromperie sur la marchandise.	1. There is a sense here of an action – the 'dealing with' which has been going on for some time.	1. What we are dealing with here is a simple case of cheating with merchandise.
2. Je refuse d'y croire, c'est tout.	2. This is a straightforward present tense in English.	2. I refuse to believe it, that's all.
3. On voit toujours des images terribles de guerre à la télévision.	3. Translate *on* by 'we' here. There is a sense of an action which has been going on for some time.	3. We are still seeing terrible war pictures on television.
4. Je suis certain qu'on me suit.	4. Change this passive phrase in French into one which begins with 'I' in English. Here there is the impression that the action has been going on for some time.	4. I am sure that I am being followed.
5. J'ai le manuel de l'utilisateur en main et je le suis.	5. There is a sense here of the action not being isolated and going on for some time.	5. I have the instruction manual in my hands and I am following them.

11.10 What is the one word in French which means both 'thank you' and 'no thank you'?

Translate *merci* in the correct way within the sentences below.

Questions 11.10	Explanations 11.10	Answers 11.10
1. Hannah: Tiens, je t'ai apporté un chocolat chaud. Helga: Merci. 2. Max: Marie, si tu veux encore du curry, n'hésite pas? Marie: Merci Max, je cale. (INFORMAL) 3. Simon: Tu veux une cigarette? Brigitte: Merci, ça fait une année que je ne fume plus. 4. Anatole: Je crois que c'est du cheval. Tu vas quand même en prendre? Malcolm: Euh, merci, j'ai déjà mangé. 5. Merci de m'avoir tout raconté.	1. This is a simple 'thank you'. 2. There is a clear choice here and *merci* thanks the person for the offer and also refuses it. 3. There is a clear choice here and *merci* thanks the person for the offer and also refuses it. 4. There is a clear choice here and *merci* thanks the person for the offer and also refuses it. 5. This is a simple 'thank you'.	1. Hannah: Here you are, I have brought you a hot chocolate. Helga: Thanks. 2. Max: Marie, if you want more curry, just serve yourself? Marie: No thanks Max, I'm full. 3. Simon: Do you want a cigarette? Brigitte: No thanks, I gave up smoking a year ago. 4. Anatole: I think it is horsemeat. Are you going to have some all the same? Malcolm: Erm, no thanks, I've already eaten. 5. Thanks for telling me everything.

11.11 What is the one word in French which means both 'expensive' for someone and 'dear' to a person?

Translate the following sentences into English using 'expensive' or something 'dear' to a person.

Questions 11.11	Explanations 11.11	Explanations 11.11
1. On dit que le Japon est un pays cher. 2. Ah, c'est toi, mon cher Jean. Viens t'installer près de moi. 3. Ma très chère nièce. 4. Dans ce magasin on ne vend que des produits très chers. 5. Cette table de nuit m'est très chère puisqu'elle appartenait à ma mère.	1. Here *cher* follows the naming word *pays*. 2. Here *cher* comes before the naming word Jean. 3. *Chère* precedes the naming word *nièce*. A person is involved 4. When translating *on* use a passive in English and here *chers* follow the naming word *produits*. 5. This is special case a set form, where something is dear to a person that person is referred to by *me, te, lui, nous, vous* or *leur*. Here *chère* follows the naming word, which is a thing.	1. It is said that Japan is an expensive country. 2. Oh it's you my dear John, come and sit down by me. 3. My dearest niece. 4. In this shop they only sell very expensive products. 5. This bedside table is very dear to me because it belonged to my mother.

11.12 What is the one word in French, which means both 'poor, pitiable' and 'poor, with no money'?

Use 'poor' meaning pitiable or 'poor' meaning penniless as appropriate when translating the following sentences from French into English.

Questions 11.12	Explanations 11.12	Answers 11.12
1. La plupart des quartiers pauvres se trouvent à l'est de la capitale. 2. Ces pauvres réfugiés qui sont contraints de vivre dans des conditions bien pénibles. 3. Perché au haut de la colline se trouve un village pauvre, très peu de gens y vivent. 4. Elle l'a traité de 'pauvre type' et est partie en claquant la porte. 5. Près du port on distinguait deux pauvres formes humaines (figures) blottis contre (crouching against) un hangar.	1. Here *pauvres* follows the naming word *quartiers*. 2. *Pauvres* follows the naming word *réfugiés* here. 3. Here *pauvre* also follows the naming word *village*. 4. Here *pauvre* comes before the naming word *type*. This insult is somewhat of a fixed expression. 5. *Pauvres* here precedes the naming word *formes humaines*.	1. Most of the poor districts are to be found to the East of the capital. 2. These poor refugees who are forced to live in very straightened circumstances. 3. Perched on the top of the hill there is a poor village, very few people live there. 4. She called him a 'real pig' and left slamming the door. 5. Near the port we could make out two miserable figures crouching against a hangar.

11.13 What is the one word in French which means both 'clean' and 'own'?

Translate the following sentences into in English using 'clean' or 'own' as appropriate.

Questions 11.13	Explanations 11.13	Answers 11.13
1. Je ne crois pas que Laurence ait sa propre voiture. 2. Où y a-t-il une serviette propre? 3. C'est inouï, insulter ses propres parents de cette manière... 4. L'affaire Duval de mai 1999 n'était pas des plus propres. 5. Vous voyez là des notes écrites de sa propre main.	1. Here *propre* comes before the naming word *voiture*. 2. *Propre* here comes after the naming word *serviette*. 3. *Propres* precedes the naming word *parents*. 4. *Propres* follows the implied naming word *affaires*. 5. Here *propre* comes before the naming word *main*.	1. I do not believe that Laurence has her own car. 2. Where is there a clean towel? 3. It's unheard of, insulting one's own parents in that way... 4. The Duval affair of May 1999 was not one of the cleanest. 5. There you can see note written in his own hand.

11.14 What is the one word in French, which means 'look at' in English?

Translate the following sentences into English, paying particular attention to *regarder*.

Questions 11.14	Explanation 11.14	Answers 11.14
1. Regarde-le! Comme il a l'air ridicule. 2. Oh! regardez donc cet oiseau de proie sur le poteau. 3. Regardez moi très attentivement, je vais vous surprendre. 4. Regarde, les voilà. 5. Regardez, le vase avec les fleurs est tombé par terre.	The following explanation applies to all sentences: English needs an 'at' when there is a specific object or individual to be observed and when it is implied that the observation takes place for certain duration of time. In the case of questions 4 and 5, *regarder* is being used in a general sense of notice and not as observation.	1. Look at him! How ridiculous he seems. 2. There, look at that bird of prey on the post. 3. Look at me carefully, I am going to surprise you. 4. Look, here they are. 5. Look, the vase with the flowers has fallen onto the floor.

11.15 What is the one word in French, which means 'pay for' in English?

Translate the following sentences into English, paying special attention to *payer*.

Questions 11.15	Explanations 11.15	Answers 11.15
1. C'est qui qui va payer les boissons cette fois? 2. Il faut payer la somme qu'on vous demande. 3. Oh zut! j'ai oublié mon porte-monnaie chez moi, qui peut payer mes consommations? 4. Je vous ai déjà payé, il me semble. 5. Mes parents n'ont pas les moyens de payer des vacances à l'étranger à leurs enfants tous les ans.	1. There is a specific object to pay for in this sentence. 2. In this sentence the thing that has to be paid for is indefinite; it is not a specific object and therefore this sentence is different from the one which precedes it. 3. There is a specific object to pay for in this sentence. 4. In this sentence the thing that has to be paid for is indefinite; it is not a specific object and therefore this sentence is different from the one which precedes it. 5. There is a specific object to pay for in this sentence.	1. Who's going to pay for the drinks this time? 2. You have to pay the sum that you are asked for. 3. Oh no! I left my wallet at home, who can pay for my drinks? 4. I have already paid you, I believe. 5. My parents cannot afford to pay for foreign holidays for their children every year.

11.16 What is the one word in French, which means to 'wait for' in English?

The following sentences are for translation into English; pay special attention to the way in which you translate *attendre*.

Questions 11.16	Explanations 11.16	Answers 11.16
1. Si vous attendez un peu vous verrez l'aigle s'envoler.	1. Here wait doesn't refer to a specific time or waiting for a specific person: *un peu*.	1. If you wait a little you will see the eagle take flight.
2. Attendez-moi sous le pont à midi, j'aurai tout l'argent avec moi.	2. Here wait refers to a specific time and to a specific person...*moi sous le pont*.	2. Wait for me under the bridge at midday, I will have all the money with me.
3. Tu peux pas attendre que le feu passe au vert avant de démarrer? (INFORMAL)	3. Here wait refers to a phrase with is own doing word: *le feu passe au vert*.	3. Can't you wait for the lights to change before starting? (INFORMAL)
4. Madame je suis désolé mais il faut attendre la fin du premier acte avant d'entrer dans la salle.	4. Here wait refers to a specific thing: *la pause*.	4. Madam I am sorry, but you will have to wait for the end of the first act before going into the auditorium.
5. Je suis persuadé que la pièce s'appelle *En Attendant Godot*.	5. Here the name of the play with wait refers to a specific entity: Godot.	5. I am convinced that the play is called *Waiting for Godot*.

11.17 What is the one word in French, which means 'listen to'?

Translate these sentences into English, paying special attention to the doing word *écouter*.

Questions 11.17	Explanations 11.17	Answers 11.17
1. J'écoute souvent les informations à la radio le matin en prenant mon petit déjeuner.	1. English has two words, where French has one.	1. I often listen to the radio news in the mornings while having my breakfast.
2. Écoute, il faut que tu comprennes que ça suffit maintenant.	2. This is a general appeal for attention and is not directly linked to listening.	2. Listen, you have to understand that that's enough now.
3. Janine s'il te plaît, écoute bien ce que je vais te dire.	3. English has two words, where French has one.	3. Please Janine, listen to what I am going to tell you.
4. Je suis persuadée que on entend des bruits bizarres dans le grenier. Écoute-bien!	4. This is a direct appeal to hearing as a sense.	4. I am convinced that you can hear strange noises in the attic. Listen carefully!
5. Nous sommes sortis sur le balcon de l'hôtel pour écouter la musique qui venait de la place.	5. English has two words, where French has one.	5. We went out on to the hotel balcony to listen to the music coming from the square.

11.18 What is the one word in French, which means 'ask for'?

Translate the sentences below into English; the most important thing here is how to translate *demander*.

Questions 11.18	Explanations 11.18	Answers 11.18
1. T'inquiètes pas, j'ai déjà demandé l'addition et dès qu'on l'aura réglée on pourra partir. (INFORMAL) 2. Es-tu sûr que tu vas demander un rabais? 3. Si tu as besoin de quelque chose, tu n'as qu'à me demander. 4. Aussitôt que vous arrivez chez eux demandez à voir les bijoux. 5. Dans cet hôtel-là, il ne faudrait surtout pas demander la chambre 101.	1. Here a person is asking for something specific, which is mentioned in the sentence. English has two words, where French has one. 2. Here a person is asking for something specific, which is mentioned in the sentence. English has two words, where French has one. 3. Here *demander* does not refer to something specific. It is a single word which ends the sentence. 4. Here the thing being asked for is a phrase with a doing word. Both French and English use two words here. 5. Here a person is asking for something specific, which is mentioned in the sentence. English has two words, where French has one.	1. No worries, I have already asked for the bill and as soon as we have paid it we will leave. (INFORMAL) 2. Are you sure that you are going to ask for a reduction. 3. If you need anything you only have to ask me. 4. As soon as you arrive at their place ask to see the jewels. 5. In that hotel, you shouldn't ask for room 101 under any circumstances.

12

There are three ways of saying something in English, where there is only one in French

12.1   How do I translate *il y a*?

Translate the following sentences into English using: 'ago', 'there is' or 'there are'.

Questions 12.1	Explanations 12.1	Answers 12.1
1. Regarde! Il y a des carottes dans le frigo.	1. The naming word which *il y a* refers to is plural and this plural is retained in the English translation.	1. Look! There are carrots in the fridge.
2. Il y a deux cent ans la distribution d'eau potable était un gros problème dans les villes européennes.	2. This is a translation of *il y a* which is unique; it refers to dates and does not change.	2. Two hundred years ago the distribution of drinking water was a big problem in European towns.
3. Si ça te dit, il y a du pain et du fromage sur la table de la cuisine.	3. *Il y a* refers to two naming words here, but they are both treated as two separate singular entities.	3. If you want, there is bread and cheese on the kitchen table.
4. Il y a cent ans dans un siècle.	4. The naming word which *il y a* refers to is plural and this plural is retained in the English translation.	4. There are a hundred years in a century.
5. On me dit qu'il y a beaucoup de gens qui prévoient de passer leurs vacances dans ce pays.	5. The naming word which *il y a* refers to is plural and this plural is retained in the English translation.	5. I am told that there are many people who envisage spending their holidays in this country.

12.2   How do I translate *lui*?

Translate the following sentences into English, translating *lui* in an appropriate way.

Questions 12.2	Explanations 12.2	Answers 12.2
1. Je ne sais pas si elle est plus intelligente que lui. Il est bien difficile de porter un jugement sur ces choses-là. 2. Pensez-vous qu'elle le lui donnera demain comme prévu (as planned)? 3. Werther a vu comment tous les petits enfants se rassemblaient autour de lui. 4. Excusez-moi, Monsieur, mais je ne peux pas lui permettre de sortir seul. 5. Oui, ma confiance en lui est limitée.	1. *Lui* is part of a comparison here and can only be translated in one way. 2. Here *lui* is used with a doing word which takes *à* (*donner quelque chose à quelqu'un*). 3. *Lui* can only be translated in one way here; it is being used with a positional word: *autour de*. 4. Here *lui* is used with a doing word which takes *à* (*permettre à quelqu'un de faire quelque chose*). 5. *Lui* can only be translated in one way here; it is being used with a positional word *en*.	1. I don't know if she is more intelligent than him. It is very difficult to come to a judgement on this sort of thing. 2. Do you think that she will give it to him/to her tomorrow as planned? 3. Werther saw how all the children gathered around him. 4. I am sorry, Sir, but I cannot allow him to go out alone. 5. Yes, my confidence in him is limited.

12.3   When do I use *leur* (and *leurs*)?

Translate the following sentences into English; you have a choice to translate *leur* (and *leurs*) by 'to them', 'them' and 'their'.

Questions 12.3	Explanations 12.3	Answers 12.3
1. Je leur ai raconté tout ce que j'ai vu. 2. J'hésite à leur dire ce que je pense, puisqu'ils ne tiennent jamais aucun compte de mes conseils. 3. Tous les enfants ont sorti leurs bonbons de leurs poches pour les mettre sur la grande table au milieu de la salle de classe. 4. Avec un soleil aussi éblouissant, il faut leur montrer comment conserver de l'eau. 5. Les joueurs de base-ball ont mis leur casquette.	1. Here *leur* appears with a doing word which takes *à*. You have a choice. 2. *Leur* appears with a doing word which takes *à*. You have a choice. 3. Here both occurrences of *leurs* are translated in the same way. The children have more than one pocket and more than one sweet; that is why *leur* has an 's'. 4. *Leur* appears with a doing word which takes *à*. You have a choice. 5. *Leur* refers to singular naming words and also to things that people only have **one** of (for example: head) and one at any one particular time; 'cap' is an basic example of this type of usage.	1. I told them everything that I saw. 2. I hesitate to tell them what I think, since they never take on board my advice. 3. All the children took out their sweets from their pockets in order to put them on the big table in the centre of the classroom. 4. With the sun as bright as this, you have to show them how to save water. 5. The baseball players put on their caps.

13

There are five ways of saying something in English, where there is only one in French

13.1   How do I translate *on*?

When you translate the sentences below into English, there is not only one correct answer, but two or even three appropriate choices from the following series: 'you', 'one', 'we', 'I' and 'they'.

Questions 13.1	Explanations 13.1	Answers 13.1
1. On pourrait dire que la plupart des Français et des Anglais sont patriotes.	1. This is a general statement and *on* here does not refer to a specific group of people as the speaker. There are three possible translations in this case.	1. We/one/you could say that most of the French and the English are patriotic.
2. Allez Jacques, lève-toi, on va boire un café ensemble, d'ac? (INFORMAL)	2. Here there is a clear reference to a couple which includes the speaker. There is a best translation in this case.	2. Come on Jack, get up, we are going to have a coffee together, ok? (INFORMAL)
3. Dans l'autre association on veut tenir des réunions toutes les semaines.	3. In this sentence you can see that there is a reference to another association and an implicit comparison is being made between that one and perhaps another one to which the speaker belongs.	3. In the other association, they want to hold meetings every week.
4. Il y avait une représentation de Roméo et Juliette au théâtre hier soir et on y est allé avec Marie et Jean.	4. Here *on* could refer to a single person, the speaker, or to an unnamed group. So there are two options in this case.	4. There was a performance of Romeo and Juliet at the theatre last night and we went to it with Marie and Jean.
5. Quand est-ce que tu veux qu'on fasse le bilan de la journée? Qu'est-ce que tu dirais de six heures et demie?	5. Here there appears to be a reference to a group which includes the speaker; so there is a best translation in this case.	5. When do you want us to take stock of the day? What would you say to half past six?

13.2 There is one word in French which means 'nil', 'o', 'zero', 'love' and 'nought'?

Translate the sentences below into English, using 'nil', 'o', 'zero', 'love' and 'nought' as appropriate.

Questions 13.2	Explanations 13.2	Answers 13.2
1. Je te donne le code de la porte d'entrée: 'zéro, x, soixante-huit'. 2. En avril dernier Bayer Leverkusen s'est imposé trois à zéro face à Everton. 3. A Rolland Garros, Fussenegger mène actuellement quinze-zéro contre Denoël. 4. N'oubliez pas que le code se termine par un zéro. 5. Le thermomètre indique zéro degré dans notre jardin ce matin.	1. Here *zéro* comes in a series of numbers (three or more). You could say 'zero' in English too of course, but there is another more frequent way of translating it. 2. This is a way of saying *zéro* which belongs to the specialist vocabulary of football. 3. This is a way of translating *zéro* which belongs to the specialist vocabulary of tennis. 4. This is an older, rarer way of saying *zéro* in English, which is used when *zéro* is the only figure mentioned in the sentence. 5. This is a fixed expression which translates *zéro* in the domain of temperature.	1. Here is the code for the external door: 'o, x, six, eight'. 2. This April Bayer Leverkusen beat Everton three nil. 3. At Rolland Garros, Fussenegger leads Denoël fifteen love. 4. Don't forget that the code ends in a nought. 5. The thermometer shows that it is zero degrees Celsius in our garden this morning.

INDEX AND GRAMMAR
TERMINOLOGY BUSTER

MEMBER OF SCABRINI MEDIA

Quebec, Canada
2004